GLENCOE SCIENCE VOYAGES

Exploring the Life, Earth, and Physical Sciences

ACTIVITY WORKSHEETS

Glencoe McGraw-Hill

New York, New York   Columbus, Ohio   Woodland Hills, California   Peoria, Illinois

Glencoe Science Voyages

Student Edition
Teacher Wraparound Edition
Assessment
    Chapter Review
    Standardized Test Practice
    Performance Assessment
    Assessment—Chapter and Unit Tests
    ExamView Test Bank Software
    Performance Assessment in the Science Classroom
    Alternate Assessment in the Science Classroom
Study Guide for Content Mastery, SE and TE
Chapter Overview Study Guide, SE and TE
Reinforcement
Enrichment
Critical Thinking/Problem Solving
Multicultural Connections
Activity Worksheets

Laboratory Manual, SE and TE
Science Inquiry Activities, SE and TE
Home Involvement
Teaching Transparencies
Section Focus Transparencies
Science Integration Transparencies
Spanish Resources
Lesson Plans
Lab and Safety Skills in the Science Classroom
Cooperative Learning in the Science Classroom
Exploring Environmental Issues
MindJogger Videoquizzes and Teacher Guide
English/Spanish Audiocassettes
Interactive Lesson Planner CD-ROM
Interactive CD-ROM
Internet Site
Using the Internet in the Science Classroom

TO THE TEACHER

Each activity in this booklet is an expanded version of an activity featured in each Student Edition chapter of *Glencoe Science Voyages*. All materials lists, procedures, and questions are repeated so that students will be able to read and complete an activity in most cases without having to have a textbook on the desk or lab table. Activities that require recorded data also have enlarged versions of the Data and Observations table for that activity. All activity Analyze and Conclude and Apply questions are reprinted with rules on which students can write their answers. In addition, for the safety of the students, all appropriate safety symbols and caution statements have been reproduced on these expanded pages. This booklet also contains a worksheet and answer page for each MiniLAB found in each chapter of *Glencoe Science Voyages*.

Glencoe/McGraw-Hill
A Division of The McGraw·Hill Companies

Copyright © by the McGraw-Hill Companies, Inc. All rights reserved. Permission is granted to reproduce the material contained herein on the condition that such materials be reproduced only for classroom use; be provided to students, teachers, and families without charge; and be used solely in conjunction with the *Glencoe Science Voyages* program. Any other reproduction, for sale or other use, is expressly prohibited.

Send all inquiries to:
Glencoe/McGraw-Hill
8787 Orion Place
Columbus, OH 43240

ISBN 0-07-824405-6
Printed in the United States of America.
1 2 3 4 5 6 7 8 9 10 009 05 04 03 02 01 00

TABLE OF CONTENTS

Chapter 1 The Nature of Science
- 1-1 Using Scientific Methods 1
- MiniLAB 1-1 3
- MiniLAB 1-2 4

Chapter 2 The Structure of Organisms
- 2-1 Comparing Light Microscopes 5
- 2-2 Comparing Plant and Animal Cells 7
- MiniLAB 2-1 9
- MiniLAB 2-2 10

Chapter 3 Cell Processes
- 3-1 Observing Osmosis 11
- 3-2 Photosynthesis and Respiration . . 13
- MiniLAB 3-1 15
- MiniLAB 3-2 16

Chapter 4 Cell Reproduction
- 4-1 Mitosis in Plant and Animal Cells 17
- 4-2 Modeling of DNA 19
- MiniLAB 4-1 21
- MiniLAB 4-2 22

Chapter 5 Plant Reproduction
- 5-1 Comparing Mosses, Liverworts, and Ferns 23
- 5-2 Germination Rate of Seeds 25
- MiniLAB 5-1 27
- MiniLAB 5-2 28

Chapter 6 Heredity
- 6-1 Expected and Observed Results 29
- 6-2 Determining Polygenic Inheritance 31
- MiniLAB 6-1 33
- MiniLAB 6-2 34

Chapter 7 Change Through Time
- 7-1 Recognizing Variation in a Population 35
- 7-2 A Model of Natural Selection 37
- MiniLAB 7-1 39
- MiniLAB 7-2 40

Chapter 8 Classifying Living Things
- 8-1 Classifying Seeds 41
- 8-2 Using a Dichotomous Key 43
- MiniLAB 8-1 45
- MiniLAB 8-2 46

Chapter 9 Bacteria
- 9-1 Observing Cyanobacteria 47
- 9-2 Are there bacteria in foods? 49
- MiniLAB 9-1 51
- MiniLAB 9-2 52

Chapter 10 Protists and Fungi
- 10-1 Comparing Algae and Protozoans 53
- 10-2 Comparing Types of Fungi 55
- MiniLAB 10-1 57
- MiniLAB 10-2 58

Chapter 11 Plants
- 11-1 Comparing Seedless Plants 59
- 11-2 Comparing Monocots and Dicots 61
- MiniLAB 11-1 63
- MiniLAB 11-2 64

Chapter 12 Invertebrate Animals
- 12-1 Garbage-eating Worms 65
- 12-2 Observing Complete Metamorphosis 67
- MiniLAB 12-1 69
- MiniLAB 12-2 70

Chapter 13 Vertebrate Animals
- 13-1 Frog Metamorphosis 71
- MiniLAB 13-1 73
- MiniLAB 13-2 74

Chapter 14 Life and the Environment
- 14-1 Soil Composition 75
- 14-2 Identifying a Limiting Factor 77
- MiniLAB 14-1 79
- MiniLAB 14-2 80

Chapter 15 Ecosystems
- 15-2 Studying a Land Environment ... 81
  - MiniLAB 15-1 ... 83
  - MiniLAB 15-2 ... 84

Chapter 16 Bones, Muscles, and Skin
- 16-1 Observing Bones ... 85
- 16-2 Observing Muscle ... 87
  - MiniLAB 16-1 ... 89
  - MiniLAB 16-2 ... 90

Chapter 17 Nutrients and Digestion
- 17-1 Identifying Vitamin C Content ... 91
- 17-2 Protein Digestion ... 93
  - MiniLAB 17-1 ... 95
  - MiniLAB 17-2 ... 96

Chapter 18 The Circulatory System
- 18-1 The Heart as a Pump ... 97
- 18-2 Comparing Blood Cells ... 99
  - MiniLAB 18-1 ... 101
  - MiniLAB 18-2 ... 102

Chapter 19 Respiration and Excretion
- 19-1 The Effects of Exercise on Respiration ... 103
- 19-2 Kidney Structure ... 105
  - MiniLAB 19-1 ... 107
  - MiniLAB 19-2 ... 108

Chapter 20 The Nervous and Endocrine Systems
- 20-1 Reaction Time ... 109
- 20-2 Investigating Skin Sensitivity ... 111
  - MiniLAB 20-1 ... 113
  - MiniLAB 20-2 ... 114

Chapter 21 Reproduction and Growth
- 21-1 Interpreting Diagrams ... 115
- 21-2 Average Growth Rate in Humans ... 117
  - MiniLAB 21-1 ... 119
  - MiniLAB 21-2 ... 120

Chapter 22 Immunity
- 22-1 Microorganisms and Disease ... 121
- 22-2 Microorganism Growth ... 123
  - MiniLAB 22-1 ... 125
  - MiniLAB 22-2 ... 126

Chapter 23 Light, Mirrors, and Lenses
- 23-1 Reflection from a Plane Mirror ... 127
- 23-2 Image Formation by a Convex Lens ... 129
  - MiniLAB 23-1 ... 131
  - MiniLAB 23-2 ... 132

Chapter 24 Forces and Motion
- 24-1 Time Trials ... 133
  - MiniLAB 24-1 ... 135
  - MiniLAB 24-2 ... 136

Chapter 25 Work and Simple Machines
- 25-1 Building the Pyramids ... 137
- 25-2 Pulley Power ... 139
  - MiniLAB 25-1 ... 141
  - MiniLAB 25-2 ... 142

Chapter 26 Electricity
- 26-1 A Model for Voltage and Current ... 143
- 26-2 Current in a Parallel Circuit ... 145
  - MiniLAB 26-1 ... 147
  - MiniLAB 26-2 ... 148

Chapter 27 Rocks
- 27-1 Igneous Rocks ... 149
- 27-2 Sedimentary Rocks ... 151
  - MiniLAB 27-1 ... 153
  - MiniLAB 27-2 ... 154

Chapter 28 Resources and the Environment
- 28-1 Is it biodegradable? ... 155
- 28-2 Modeling the Greenhouse Effect ... 157
  - MiniLAB 28-1 ... 159
  - MiniLAB 28-2 ... 160

Chapter 29 Clues to Earth's Past
- 29-1 Relative Age Dating ... 161
- 29-2 Radioactive Decay ... 163
  - MiniLAB 29-1 ... 165
  - MiniLAB 29-2 ... 166

Chapter 30 Geologic Time
- 30-1 Changing Species ... 167
  - MiniLAB 30-1 ... 169
  - MiniLAB 30-2 ... 170

Answers to Activities and MiniLABs ... 171

NAME _____ DATE _____ CLASS _____

FLEX YOUR BRAIN

1 TOPIC: _____

2 **? What do I already know?**
1. _____
2. _____
3. _____
4. _____

3 Ask a question
Q: _____

4 Guess an answer
A: _____

5

How sure am I? (circle one)				
Not sure				Very sure
1	2	3	4	5

6 **? How can I find out?**
1. _____
2. _____
3. _____
4. _____

7 EXPLORE

8 Do I think differently?   yes / no

9 **? What do I know now?**
_____
_____
_____

10 SHARE
1. _____
2. _____
3. _____

Copyright © Glencoe/McGraw-Hill, a division of The McGraw-Hill Companies, Inc.

Chapter 1
ACTIVITY 1-1

Using Scientific Methods

Design Your Own Experiment

Lab Preview

1. If an organism lives in the ocean, what can you infer about its dependency on salt?

2. What special precaution should you take when working with live organisms?

You are to use scientific methods to determine how salt affects the growth of brine shrimp. Brine shrimp are tiny organisms that live in the ocean. How can you find out why they live where they do?

Recognize the Problem
How can you use scientific methods to determine how salt affects the hatching and growth of brine shrimp?

Form a Hypothesis
Based on your observations, make a hypothesis about how salt affects the hatching and growth of brine shrimp.

Goals
- **Design and carry out an experiment** using scientific methods.
- **Infer** why brine shrimp live in the ocean.

Safety Precautions
Protect clothing and eyes. Be careful when working with live organisms.

Possible Materials
- widemouthed, 0.5-L containers (3)
  *clear plastic cups (3)
- brine shrimp eggs
- wooden splint
- distilled water (500-mL)
- weak salt solution (500-mL)
- strong salt solution (500-mL)
- wax pencil
  *labels (3)
- hand lens
  *alternate materials

Test Your Hypothesis
Plan
1. As a group, agree upon and **write out** the hypothesis statement.

2. **List** the steps that you need to take to test your hypothesis. Be specific. **Describe** exactly what you will do at each step. **List** your materials.

3. How will you know whether brine shrimp hatch and grow?

4. **Decide** what data you need to collect during the experiment. **Design** a data table in your Science Journal to **record** your observations.

5. **Identify** the steps in solving a problem that each of your actions presents. For example, what action have you taken that represents stating the problem or gathering information? Make sure you include all the steps needed to reach a conclusion.

6. **Read** over your entire experiment to make sure that all steps are in logical order.

NAME _____ DATE _____ CLASS _____

Activity (continued)

7. **Identify** any constants, variables, and controls of the experiment.
_____

8. Can you explain what variable you are testing?
_____

9. **Decide** whether you need to run your tests more than once. Can your data be summarized in a graph?
_____

Do
1. Make sure your teacher approves your plan before you proceed.
2. **Carry out** the experiment as planned.
3. While the experiment is going on, **write down** any observations that you make and complete the data table.

Day	Water Environment		
	Distilled water	Weak salt solution	Strong salt solution
0	Brine shrimp	Brine shrimp	Brine shrimp
1			
2	die	live	live
3			

Analyze Your Data
1. **Compare** your results with those of other groups.
_____

2. Was your hypothesis supported by your data? **Explain** your answer.
_____
_____

Draw Conclusions
1. **Describe** how the physical conditions in the container in which the brine shrimp hatched and grew best are similar to those in the ocean.
_____

2. How did you use scientific methods to solve this problem? Give examples from this activity.
_____

Chapter 1
MINILAB 1-1

Inferring from Pictures

Procedure
1. Fill in the table below with your observations.

Observations and Inferences

Picture	Observations	Inferences
1		
2		

2. Study the two pictures on the same page in the textbook as this minilab. Write down all your observations in the table.

3. Make inferences based on your observations. Record your inferences.

4. Share your inferences with others in your class.

Analysis
1. Analyze the inferences that you made. Are there other explanations for what you observed?

2. Why must you be careful when making inferences?

3. Create your own picture and description. Have other students make inferences based on the picture and description.

NAME _____ DATE _____ CLASS _____

Chapter 1
MINILAB 1-2

Comparing Paper Towels

Procedure

1. Record observations in the data table below.
2. Cut a 5-cm by 5-cm square from each of the three brands of paper towel. Lay each piece on a smooth, level, waterproof surface.
3. Add drop of water to each square.
4. Continue to add drops until the piece of paper towel can no longer absorb the water.
5. Record your observations in your data table and graph your results.

Data and Observations

Paper Towel Absorbency (drops of water/sheet)			
Trial	Brand A	Brand B	Brand C
1			
2			
3			
4			

Analysis

1. Did all the squares of paper towels absorb equal amounts of water? _____

2. If one brand of paper towel absorbs more water than the others, can you conclude that it is the towel you should buy? Explain. _____

3. Which scientific methods did you use to answer the question of which paper towel is most absorbent? _____

NAME _____ DATE _____ CLASS _____

Chapter 2
ACTIVITY 2-1

Comparing Light Microscopes

Design Your Own Experiment

Lab Preview

1. Describe a compound light microscope. _____
   _____

2. Describe a stereoscopic light microscope. _____
   _____
   _____

You're a technician in a police forensic laboratory. You use stereoscopic and compound light microscopes in the laboratory. A detective just returned from a crime scene with bags of evidence. You must examine each piece of evidence under a microscope. How do you decide which microscope is the best tool to use?

Recognize the Problem
Microscopes are very useful tools for scientists. Stereoscopic and compound light microscopes are used for many tasks. What things are better viewed with a compound light microscope? What things are better viewed with a stereoscopic microscope?

Form a Hypothesis
Compare the items to be examined under the microscopes. Which microscope will be used for each item?

Goals
- **Learn** how to use a stereoscopic microscope and a compound light microscope.
- **Compare** the uses of the stereoscopic and compound light microscopes.

Possible Materials
- a compound light microscope
- a stereoscopic light microscope
- any eight items from the classroom; include some living or once-living items
- microscope slides and coverslips
- plastic petri dishes
- distilled water
- dropper

Safety Precautions
Thoroughly wash your hands when you have completed this experiment.

Test Your Hypothesis
Plan
1. As a group, **decide** how you will test your hypothesis.
2. **List** the steps that you will need to complete this experiment. Be specific, describing exactly what you will do at each step. Make sure the steps are in a logical order. Remember that you must place an item in the bottom of a plastic petri dish to **examine** it under the stereoscopic microscope. You must **make a wet mount** of any item to be examined under the compound light microscope.
3. If you need a data or observation table, **design** one in your Science Journal.

Copyright © Glencoe/McGraw-Hill, a division of The McGraw-Hill Companies, Inc.

5

| NAME | DATE | CLASS |

Activity (continued)

Do

1. Make sure your teacher approves the objects you'll examine, your plan, and your data table before you proceed.
2. **Carry out** the experiment as planned.
3. While doing the experiment, **record** your observations and **complete** the data table.

Analyze Your Data

1. **Compare** the items you examined with those of your classmates.

2. Based on this experiment, **classify** the eight items you observed.

Draw Conclusions

1. **Infer** which microscope a scientist might use to examine a blood sample, fibers, and live snails.

2. If you examined an item under both microscopes, how would the images differ?

3. **List** five careers that require people to use a stereomicroscope.
    a.
    b.
    c.
    d.
    e.

4. **List** five careers that require people to use a compound light microscope.
    a.
    b.
    c.
    d.
    e.

NAME _____ DATE _____ CLASS _____

Chapter 2
ACTIVITY 2-2

Comparing Plant and Animal Cells

Lab Preview

1. Why do you use the low power objective to locate cells on a slide?
   _____

2. What is a chloroplast?
   _____
   _____

If you were to compare a goldfish with a rose bush, you would find the two to be different. However, when the individual cells of these organisms are compared, will they be as different? Try this activity to see how plant and animal cells compare.

What You'll Investigate
In this exercise, you will observe an animal cell, a human cheek cell, and a plant cell, *Elodea*, under a compound light microscope.

Goals
- **Compare and Contrast** an animal cell and a plant cell.

Safety Precautions

Materials
- microscope
- microscope slide
- coverslip
- forceps
- dropper
- *Elodea* plant
- prepared slide of human cheek cells

Procedure
1. **Copy** the data table in your Science Journal. Check off the cell parts as you observe them.

2. Follow the directions in your textbook for using low and high power objectives on your microscope and for making a wet-mount slide.

3. Using forceps, **make** a wet-mount slide of a young leaf from the tip of an *Elodea* plant.

4. **Observe** the leaf on low power. Focus on the top layer of cells. Carefully focus down through the top layer of cells to observe other layers of cells.

5. Switch to high power and focus on one cell. Does the center of the cell appear empty? This is the central vacuole that contains water and stores cell products. **Observe** the chloroplasts in the cytoplasm, the green disk-shaped objects moving around the central vacuole. Try to find the cell nucleus. It looks like a clear ball.

6. Make a drawing of the *Elodea* cell. **Label** the cell wall, cytoplasm, chloroplasts, central vacuole, and nucleus. Return to low power and remove the slide.

7. Place a prepared slide of cheek cells on the microscope stage. Locate the cells under low power.

8. Switch to high power and **observe** the cell nucleus. **Draw** and **label** the cell membrane, cytoplasm, and nucleus.

NAME _____ DATE _____ CLASS _____

Activity (continued)

Data and Observations

Cell part	Elodea	Cheek
cytoplasm		
nucleus		
chloroplasts		
cell wall		
cell membrane		

Diagrams of cells:

Conclude and Apply

1. How many cell layers could you see in the *Elodea* leaf?

2. **Compare and contrast** the shape of the cheek cell and the *Elodea* cell.

3. What can you conclude about the differences between plant and animal cells?

NAME _____ DATE _____ CLASS _____

Chapter 2
MINILAB 2-1

Observing Magnified Objects

Procedure
1. Look at a newspaper through both the curved side and the flat bottom of an empty, clear glass.
2. Look at the newspaper through a clear glass bowl filled with water and then look at the newspaper with a magnifying glass.

Data and Observations

Tools	Observations
flat bottom of glass	
curved side of glass	
bowl filled with water	
magnifying glass	

Analysis
1. In your Science Journal, compare how well you can see the newspaper through each of the objects.

   _____
   _____

2. What did early scientists learn by using such tools?

   _____
   _____
   _____

Copyright © Glencoe/McGraw-Hill, a division of The McGraw-Hill Companies, Inc.

Chapter 2
MINILAB 2-2

Modeling Cytoplasm

Procedure
1. Fill a beaker with 100 mL water.
2. Add unflavored gelatin and stir.
3. Shine a flashlight through the beaker.

Analysis
1. Describe what you see.

2. How does a model help you understand what a real thing looks like?

Chapter 3
ACTIVITY 3–1

• Observing Osmosis

Lab Preview

1. What safety symbols are associated with this activity? _____
   _____
2. What is osmosis? _____
   _____

It is difficult to see osmosis occurring in cells because most cells are so small. However, a few cells can be seen without the aid of a microscope. Try this activity to see how osmosis occurs in a large cell.

What You'll Investigate
How does osmosis occur in an egg cell?

Goals
- **Observe** osmosis in an egg cell.
- **Determine** what affects osmosis.

Materials
- egg
- containers (500-mL) with covers (2)
- white vinegar (250 mL)
- light corn syrup (250 mL)
- graduated cylinder (100-mL)
- labels (A and B)
- small bowl
- spoon

Procedure
1. **Copy** the tables below and use them to record your data and observations.
2. **Place** label A on one of the 500-mL containers and label B on the other. **Pour** the vinegar into container A and the syrup into container B. **Record** data on the table. **Cover** container B.
3. **Place** the egg in container A and **cover** the container.
4. **Observe** the egg after 30 minutes, then again in two days. After each observation, **record** the egg's appearance on the table.

Volume Data

	Beginning volume	Ending volume
Vinegar		
Syrup		

Egg Observations

After 30 minutes	
After 2 days	
After 3 days	

Copyright © Glencoe/McGraw-Hill, a division of The McGraw-Hill Companies, Inc.

11

NAME _____ DATE _____ CLASS _____

Activity (continued)

5. After the second observation, **remove** container A's cover. Carefully **remove** the egg from the liquid with a spoon, and gently rinse the egg in a slow stream of cool tap water.

6. **Remove** the cover from container B. Carefully **place** the egg in the syrup and replace the cover.

7. **Measure** the volume of liquid in container A and **record** on the table.

8. **Observe** the egg the next day and **record** its appearance on the table.

9. **Remove** container B's cover. Gently remove the egg and allow the syrup to drain back into container B. Then, place the egg in the small bowl. **Measure** the volume of syrup and **record** on the table.

Conclude and Apply

1. What caused the change in volume of container A and container B?

_____
_____
_____
_____

2. Calculate the amount of water that moved into and out of the egg.

_____
_____
_____

3. **Infer** what part of the egg controlled what moved into and out of the cell.

_____
_____
_____
_____

Chapter 3
ACTIVITY 3-2

Photosynthesis and Respiration

Lab Preview

1. What safety symbols are associated with this activity?
   _____
2. What is photosynthesis? _____
   _____

Every living cell carries on many chemical processes. Two important chemical processes are respiration and photosynthesis. Every cell, including the ones in your body, carries on respiration. But, some plant cells, unlike your cells, carry on both. In this experiment, you will investigate when these processes occur in plant cells.

What You'll Investigate
When do plants carry on photosynthesis and respiration?

Goals
- **Observe** green water plants in the light and dark.
- **Determine** if green plants carry on both photosynthesis and respiration.

Safety Precautions
Protect clothing and eyes and be careful using chemicals. Do not get chemicals on your skin.

Materials
- test tubes, 16-mm × 150-mm with stoppers (4)
  small, clear-glass baby food jars with lids (4)
- test-tube rack
- stirring rod
- balance scale
- scissors
- sodium hydrogen carbonate
- bromothymol blue solution in dropping bottle
- aged tap water
  distilled water
- pieces of *Elodea* (2)
  other water plants alternate materials

Procedure
1. **Label** each test tube using the numbers 1, 2, 3, and 4. Pour 5 mL aged tap water into each test tube.
2. **Add** 10 drops of carbonated water to test tubes 1 and 2.
3. **Add** 10 drops of bromothymol blue to each test tube. Bromothymol blue turns green to yellow in the presence of an acid.
4. **Cut** two 10-cm pieces of *Elodea*. **Place** one piece of *Elodea* in the liquid in test tube 1 and one piece in the liquid in test tube 3. Stopper the test tubes.
5. Copy the Test Tube Data Table on the next page in your Science Journal. **Record** the color of the solution in each of the four test tubes in your Science Journal.
6. **Place** test tubes 1 and 2 in bright light. Place tubes 3 and 4 in the dark. Observe the test tubes at the end of 30 minutes or until there is a color change. Record the colors.

NAME _____ DATE _____ CLASS _____

Activity (continued)

Data and Observations

Test tube	Color at start	Color after 30 minutes
1		
2		
3		
4		

Conclude and Apply

1. What is indicated by the color of the water in all four test tubes at the start of the activity?
   _____
   _____

2. **Infer** what happened in the test tube or tubes that changed color after 30 minutes.
   _____
   _____

3. What can you **conclude** about the test tube or tubes that didn't change color after 30 minutes?
   _____
   _____

4. **Describe** the purpose of test tubes 2 and 4.
   _____
   _____

5. Does this experiment show that both photosynthesis and respiration occur in plants? Explain.
   _____
   _____

Chapter 3

MINILAB 3-1

Determining How Enzymes Work

Procedure
1. Make a mark on one of two clean test tubes. Place them in a test-tube rack, then fill each halfway with milk.
2. Place a tablet of rennin, an enzyme, in a small plastic bowl. Crush the tablet using the back of a metal spoon. Add the crushed tablet to the marked test tube.
3. Let both test tubes stand undisturbed during your class period.
4. Observe what happens to the milk.

Analysis
1. What effect did the rennin have on the milk?

2. Predict what would eventually happen to the milk without rennin.

3. Infer how rennin's effect on milk might be useful to the dairy industry.

NAME _____ DATE _____ CLASS _____

Chapter 3
MINILAB 3-2

Observing the Rate of Diffusion

Procedure
1. Use two beakers of equal size. Label one "hot," then fill it halfway with hot water. Label the other "cold," then fill it halfway with cold water. **CAUTION:** *Do not spill hot water on your skin.*
2. Add one drop of food coloring to each beaker. Carefully release the drop just above the water's surface to avoid splashing and disturbing the water.
3. Observe the beakers and record your observations. Repeat your observations after 10 minutes and record them again.

Data and Observations

Beaker	Initial Observations	After 10 minutes
cold water		
hot water		

Analysis
1. Describe what happens when food coloring is added to each beaker.
   _____
   _____

2. How does temperature affect the rate of diffusion?
   _____
   _____

Chapter 4
ACTIVITY 4–1
Mitosis in Plant and Animal Cells

Lab Preview
1. What is mitosis? _____
   _____
   _____

2. Why is mitosis necessary? _____
   _____

Reproduction of cells in plants and animals is accomplished by mitosis. In this activity, you will study prepared slides of onion root-tip cells and whitefish embryo cells. These slides are used because they show cells in the various stages of mitosis.

What You'll Investigate
How mitosis in a plant cell is different from mitosis in an animal cell.

Materials
- Prepared slide of an onion root tip
- Prepared slide of a whitefish embryo
- Microscope

Goals
- **Compare** the sizes of the whitefish embryo cells and the onion root-tip cells.
- **Observe** the chromosomes of the whitefish embryo and onion root tip.

Procedure
1. **Obtain** prepared slides of onion root-tip cells and whitefish embryo cells.
2. Set your microscope on low power and **examine** the onion root tip. Move the slide until you can see the area just behind the root tip. Turn the nosepiece to high power.
3. Use the figure to help you find a cell in prophase. **Draw** and **label** the parts of the cell you observe.
4. Repeat step 3 for metaphase, anaphase, and telophase.
5. Turn the microscope back to low power. Remove the onion root-tip slide.
6. Place the whitefish embryo slide on the microscope stage under low power. Focus and find a region of dividing cells. Switch to high power.
7. Repeat steps 3 and 4 using the whitefish embryo slide.
8. Return the nosepiece to low power. Remove the whitefish embryo slide from the microscope stage.

Whitefish embryo cells

Onion root-tip cells

NAME   **DATE**   **CLASS**

Activity (continued)

Conclude and Apply

1. **Compare** the cells in the region behind the onion root tip to those in the root tip.

2. **Describe** the shapes of the cells in the onion root tip and the whitefish embryo.

3. **Infer** why embryo cells and root-tip cells are used to study mitosis.

4. Copy the following statements in your Science Journal, then fill in each blank with the name of the correct phase of mitosis.

   _____ Nuclear membrane re-forms.

   _____ Chromosomes move to the center of the cell.

   _____ Spindle fibers appear.

   _____ Chromosomes move in opposite directions.

Chapter 4
ACTIVITY 4-2

Modeling of DNA

Lab Preview

1. What safety symbols are associated with this activity?
   _____
2. What are the parts of a DNA molecule?
   _____
   _____

Bits of metal, pieces of wire, and cardboard cutouts are not usually considered scientific equipment. But, that's what Nobel prize winners James Watson and Francis Crick used to construct their model of DNA. In this lab you will use colored construction paper to make a model of DNA.

What You'll Investigate
You will examine the structure of a DNA molecule.

Goals
- **Design and construct** a model of DNA that is four base pairs long.

Safety Precautions
Use scissors carefully.

Materials
- 6 colors of construction paper (8" × 11") (2 of each color)
- scissors
- 2 cardboard patterns, a circle and a pentagon
- tape

Procedure
1. **Plan** your DNA molecule. Write down the four base pairs and enter them in your Science Journal.

2. **Assign** one color of paper to represent each of the following: phosphate groups, sugar molecules, guanines, adenines, thymines, and cytosines.

3. Using the circle pattern for each phosphate group and the pentagon pattern for each sugar molecule, **trace** and **cut out** enough figures to make the sugar-phosphate sides of your DNA molecule.

4. **Tape** a circle to each pentagon, as seen in illustration A.

5. Use the pentagon pattern to make the nitrogen bases. For each adenine and guanine, **trace** and **cut out** two pentagons of the same color and tape them together, as seen in illustration B. Trace and cut out just one pentagon for each thymine and each cytosine.

6. **Tape** a nitrogen base to each sugar-phosphate unit.

7. **Construct** the DNA molecule that you planned in step 1 by taping the correct nitrogen bases together.

Activity (continued)

Conclude and Apply

1. **Compare** your models with those of other groups. Were the molecules your group created the same as those of other groups?
   _____
   _____

2. Compile a list of all the DNA sequences made and enter them in your Science Journal.

3. Based on your observations of the DNA molecule model, **infer** why a DNA molecule seldom copies itself incorrectly.
   _____
   _____

4. **Explain** why models are useful to scientists.
   _____
   _____
   _____

A.

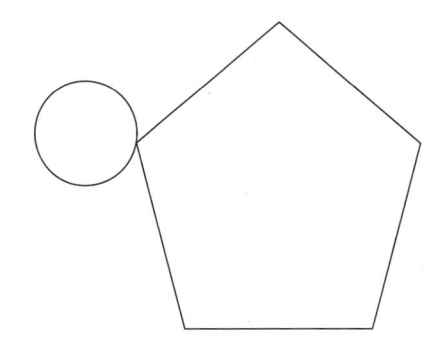

B.

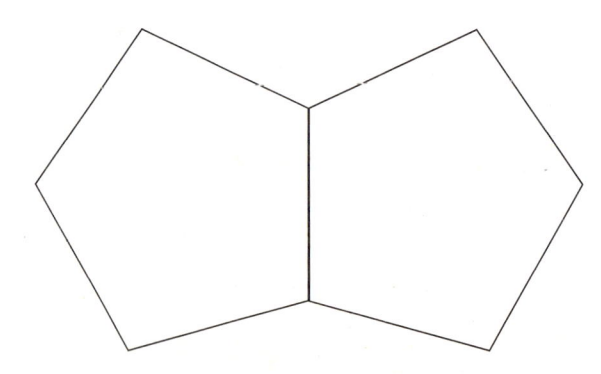

Chapter 4
MINILAB 4-1

Modeling Mitosis

Procedure
1. Make models of cell division using materials supplied by your teacher.
2. Use four chromosomes in your model.
3. When finished, arrange the models in the order in which mitosis occurs.

Analysis
1. In which steps is the nucleus visible?

2. How many cells does a dividing cell form?

Chapter 4
MINILAB 4-2

Comparing DNA Sequences

Procedure

1. Suppose you have a segment of DNA that is six nitrogen base pairs in length. In the space below, using the letters A, T, C, and G, write down a combination of six pairs remembering that A and T are always a pair and C and G are always a pair.

2. Now replicate your segment of DNA. On paper, diagram how this happens and show the new DNA segments.

Analysis
Compare the order of bases of the original DNA to the new DNA molecules.

_____
_____
_____
_____

Chapter 5
ACTIVITY 5-1

Comparing Mosses, Liverworts, and Ferns

Lab Preview

1. Why is it important to be careful when using coverslips? _____
_____

2. What do mosses and liverworts have in common? _____
_____

Mosses and liverworts make up the division of plants called bryophytes. Ferns make up the division Pterophyta and are called pteridophytes (tuh RIH duh fites). Try this activity to observe the similarities and differences in these groups of plants.

What You'll Investigate
How are the gametophyte and sporophyte stages of liverworts, mosses, and ferns similar and different?

Goals
- **Describe** the sporophyte and gametophyte forms of liverworts, mosses, and ferns.
- **Identify** the spore-producing structures of liverworts, mosses, and ferns.

Materials
- live mosses, liverworts, and ferns with gametophytes and sporophytes
- hand lens
- forceps
- dropper
- microscope slide and coverslip
- microscope
- dissecting needle
- pencil with eraser

Procedure
1. Obtain a gametophyte of each plant. With a hand lens, **observe** the rhizoids, leafy parts, and stemlike parts, if any are present.

2. Obtain a sporophyte of each plant, and use a hand lens to **observe** it.

3. Locate the spore structure on the moss plant. **Remove** it and place it in a drop of water on the slide. Place a coverslip over it. Use the eraser of a pencil to gently push on the coverslip to release the spores. **CAUTION:** *Do not break the coverslip.* **Observe** the spores under low and high power.

4. Make labeled drawings of all observations on the next page.

Activity (continued)
Data and Observations

Conclude and Apply

1. For each plant, **compare** the gametophyte's appearance to the sporophyte's appearance.

2. List the structure(s) common to all three plants.

3. **Form a hypothesis** about why each plant produces a large number of spores.

NAME _____ DATE _____ CLASS _____

Chapter 5
ACTIVITY 5-2

Germination Rate of Seeds
Design Your Own Experiment

Lab Preview
1. What happens to a seed during germination?
   _____
2. What safety symbols are associated with this activity?
   _____
   _____

Many environmental factors affect the germination rate of seeds. Among these are soil temperature, air temperature, moisture content of soil, and salt content of soil. What happens to the germination rate when one of these variables is changed? Can you determine a way to predict the best conditions for seed germination?

Recognize the Problem
How does an environmental factor affect seed germination?

Form a Hypothesis
Based on your knowledge of seed germination, state a hypothesis about how environmental factors affect germination rates.

Goals
- **Design an experiment** to test the effect of an environmental factor on seed germination rate.
- **Compare** germination rates under different conditions.

Safety Precautions
Some kinds of seeds are poisonous. Do not place any seeds in your mouth. Be careful when using any electrical equipment to avoid shock hazards.

Possible Materials
- seeds
- water
- salt
- potting soil
- plant trays or plastic cups
  *seedling warming cables
- thermometer
- graduated cylinder
- beakers
  *alternate materials

Test Your Hypothesis
Plan
1. As a group, agree upon and **write** out the hypothesis statement.
2. As a group, list the steps that you need to take to test your hypothesis. Be specific, and **describe** exactly what you will do at each step. **List** your materials.
3. **Identify** any constants, variables, and controls of the experiment.
4. What measurements will you take? What data will you collect? How often will you collect data? If you need a data table, **design** one in your Science Journal so that it is ready to use as your group collects data. Will the data be summarized in a graph?
5. **Read** over your entire experiment to make sure that all steps are in logical order. How many tests will you run?

Copyright © Glencoe/McGraw-Hill, a division of The McGraw-Hill Companies, Inc.

Activity (continued)

Do
1. Make sure your teacher approves your plan before you proceed.
2. Carry out the experiment as planned.
3. While the experiment is going on, **record** any observations that you make and complete the data table in your Science Journal.

Analyze Your Data
1. **Compare** your results with those of other groups. Explain.

2. Did changing the variable affect germination rates? Explain.

3. In the space below, **graph** your results using a bar graph, placing germination rate on the y-axis and the environmental variables on the x-axis.

Draw Conclusions
1. **Interpret** your graph to estimate the conditions that give the best germination rate.

2. What things affect the germination rate?

Chapter 5
MINILAB 5-1

Observing Gymnosperm Cones

Procedure
1. Using a hand lens, look at the parts of a gymnosperm cone.
2. On a large paper towel, open the cone and note where the seeds are located.

Analysis
1. Make a drawing of the cone and seeds in the space below.

2. Where are the seeds located?

3. Predict how this location is an advantage for the tree species.

Chapter 5
MINILAB 5-2

Identifying How Seeds Disperse

Procedure
1. Make a list of ten different seeds, including some mentioned in the textbook.
2. Research each of the ten seeds to determine how they are dispersed.

Data and Observations

Type of seed	Dispersal method
1.	
2.	
3.	
4.	
5.	
6.	
7.	
8.	
9.	
10.	

Analysis
1. How are the seeds of each plant on your list dispersed—by wind, water, insects, birds, or mammals?

   _____
   _____
   _____

2. Identify features that tell you how each kind of seed is dispersed.

   _____
   _____
   _____

Chapter 6
ACTIVITY 6–1

Expected and Observed Results

Lab Preview

1. What are alleles? _____
   _____

2. What is probability? _____
   _____

Could you predict how many white flowers would result from crossing two heterozygous red flowers if you knew that white color was a recessive trait? Try this experiment to find out.

What You'll Investigate
How does chance affect combinations of genes?

Goals
- **Model** chance events in heredity.
- **Compare and contrast** predicted and actual results.

Materials
- paper bags (2)
- red beans (100)
- white beans (100)

Safety Precautions
CAUTION: Do not taste, eat, or drink any materials used in lab.

Procedure
1. Place 50 red beans and 50 white beans into a paper bag. Place 50 red beans and 50 white beans into a second bag. Each bean represents an allele for flower color.
2. **Label** one of the bags "female" for the female parent. **Label** the other bag "male" for the male parent.
3. Without looking, remove one bean from each bag. The two beans represent the alleles that combine when sperm and egg join.
4. Use a Punnett square to **predict** how many red/red, red/white, white/white combinations are possible.
5. **Use** a data table to **record** the combination of the beans each time you remove two beans. Your table will need to accommodate 100 picks. After recording, return the beans to their original bags.
6. **Count and record** the total numbers of combinations in your data table.
7. **Compile and record** the class totals.

Gene Combinations

Beans	Red/Red	Red/White	White/White
Your total			
Class total			

Activity (continued)

Predicted outcome: Female Parent

Male
Parent

R/R _____ %

R/W _____ %

W/W _____ %

Conclude and Apply

1. **Which** combination occurred most often?

2. **Calculate** the ratio of red/red to red/white to white/white.

3. **Compare** your predicted (expected) results with your observed (actual) results.

4. Does chance affect allele combination? Explain.

5. How do the results of a small sample compare with the results of a large sample?

6. **Hypothesize** how you could get predicted results to be closer to actual results.

Chapter 6
ACTIVITY 6-2

Determining Polygenic Inheritance

Lab Preview

1. What is polygenic inheritance?

   _____

2. What are some traits polygenic inheritance controls?

   _____

When several genes at different locations on chromosomes act together to produce a single trait, a wide range of phenotypes for the trait can result. By measuring the range of phenotypes and graphing them, you can determine if a trait is produced by polygenic inheritance. How would graphs differ if traits were inherited in a simple dominant or recessive pattern?

What You'll Investigate
How can the effect of polygenic inheritance be determined?

Goals
- **Measure** the heights of students to the nearest centimeter.
- **Create** a bar graph of phenotypes for a polygenic trait.

Safety Precautions
Always obtain the permission of any person included in an experiment on human traits.

Materials
- meterstick
- graph paper
- pencil

Procedure
1. **Form a hypothesis** about what a bar graph that shows the heights of the students in your class will look like.

2. **Measure** and **record** the height of every student in the class to the nearest centimeter.

3. **Design** a table on the next page like the one shown. Count the number of students for each interval and complete the table.

Height in cm	Number of students
A 101 – 110	1
B 111 – 120	2
C 121 – 130	5
D 131 – 140	6
E 141 – 150	6
F 151 – 160	2
G 161 – 170	2
H 171 – 180	1

4. **Plot** the results from the table on a bar graph in the space on the next page. The height should be graphed on the horizontal axis and the number of students of each height along the vertical axis. If you need help, refer to Making and Using Graphs in the **Skill Handbook**.

5. The *range* of a set of data is the difference between the greatest measurement and the smallest measurement. The *median* is the middle number when the data are placed in order. The *mean* is the sum of all the data divided by the sample size. The *mode* is the number that appears most often in the measurements. Calculate each of these numbers and record them on the next page.

Copyright © Glencoe/McGraw-Hill, a division of The McGraw-Hill Companies, Inc.

31

Activity (continued)

Data and Observations

Conclude and Apply

1. How does the bar graph differ from one that would be produced for a trait controlled by a single gene?

2. How can you tell if a trait is controlled by more than one gene?

3. Can you **infer** from your data that height is controlled by more than two genes? Explain why or why not.

Chapter 6
MINILAB 6-1

Comparing Common Traits

Procedure
1. Always obtain the permission of any person included in an experiment on human traits.
2. Survey ten students in your class or school for the presence of freckles, dimples, cleft or smooth chins, and attached or detached earlobes.
3. A data table below lists each of the traits.
4. Fill in the table.

Data and Observations

Trait	Number of students
Freckles	
Dimples	
Cleft Chin	
Attached Earlobes	

Analysis
1. Compare the number of people who have one form of a trait with those who have the other form. How do those two groups compare?

_____
_____
_____

2. What can you conclude about the number of variations you noticed?

_____
_____

Copyright © Glencoe/McGraw-Hill, a division of The McGraw-Hill Companies, Inc.

Chapter 6

MINILAB 6-2

Interpreting Fingerprints

Procedure
1. Look at the figure on the same page in the textbook as the minilab.
2. With a pencil lead, rub a spot large enough for your finger onto a piece of paper.
3. Rub your finger in the pencil markings.
4. Stick clear tape to your finger.
5. Remove the tape and stick it to the paper. **CAUTION:** *Wash hands after taking fingerprints.*
6. Using a magnifying lens, observe your fingerprints to see if you can find a whorl, arch, or loop pattern.

Analysis
1. What patterns did you find?

_____

_____

2. Are fingerprints inherited as a simple Mendelian pattern or as a more complex pattern?

_____

_____

NAME _____ DATE _____ CLASS _____

Chapter 7
ACTIVITY 7-1

Recognizing Variation in a Population

Design Your Own Experiment

Lab Preview
1. What is a species? _____
_____
_____

2. Name some variations found in seeds. _____
_____

When you first see a group of plants or animals of one species, they may all look alike. However, when you look closer, you will notice minor differences in each characteristic. Variations must exist in a population for evolution to occur. What kinds of variations have you noticed among species of plants or animals?

Recognize the Problem
How can you measure variation in a plant or animal population?

Form a Hypothesis
Make a hypothesis about the amount of variation in seeds, leaves, or flowers of one species of plant.

Goals
- **Design an experiment** that will allow you to collect data about variation in a population.
- **Observe, measure,** and **analyze** variations in a population.

Possible Materials
- leaves, flowers, and seeds from one species of plant
- metric ruler
- magnifying glass
- graph paper

Safety Precautions
Do not put any seeds, flowers, or plant parts in your mouth. Wash your hands after handling plant parts.

Copyright © Glencoe/McGraw-Hill, a division of The McGraw-Hill Companies, Inc.

35

Activity (continued)

Test Your Hypothesis
Plan
1. As a group, agree upon and write out the hypothesis statement.
2. List the steps you need to take to **test your hypothesis**. Be specific. Describe exactly what you will do at each step. List your materials.
3. Decide what characteristic of seeds, leaves, or flowers you will study. For example, you could **measure** the length of seeds, the width of leaves, or the number of petals on the flowers of plants.
4. **Design a data table** in your Science Journal to collect data about one variation. Use the table to record the data your group collects as you complete the experiment.
5. **Identify** any constants, variables, and controls of the experiment.
6. How many seeds, leaves, or flowers will you examine? Will your data be more accurate if you examine larger numbers?
7. **Summarize** the data in a graph or chart.

Do
1. Make sure your teacher approves your plan before you proceed.
2. Carry out the experiment as planned.
3. While the experiment is going on, write down any observations that you make and complete the data table in your Science Journal.

Analyze Your Data
1. **Compare** your results with those of other groups.
   _____
   _____

2. How did you determine the amount of variation present?
   _____
   _____

Draw Conclusions
1. **Graph** your results, placing the *range* of variation on the *x*-axis and the number of organisms that had that measurement on the *y*-axis.
   _____
   _____

2. **Calculate** the *mean* and *range* of variation in your experiment.
   _____
   _____
   _____

Chapter 7
ACTIVITY 7-2
A Model of Natural Selection

Lab Preview

1. What is a fossil?

2. Why do scientists study fossils?

Natural selection has been observed in a variety of organisms in nature. Studying natural selection takes a long time because natural selection occurs in populations that may take years to produce a new generation. However, the process occurs in a way that can be explained by a simple model.

What You'll Investigate
What is the result of natural selection?

Safety Precautions
Caution: *Do not taste or eat any material used in the lab.*

Materials
- red beans and white beans
- paper bags
- pencils and paper

Procedure

Part A

1. Take a paper bag and write "Rabbit Gene Pool" on it.

2. Place 10 red beans and 10 white beans in the bag.

3. Make a table that you can use to record the genetics in the population. Assume that pairs of beans are rabbits. A pair of red beans makes a brown rabbit. A red bean and a white bean make a gray rabbit, and a pair of white beans makes a white rabbit.

4. Without looking into the bag, take out two beans to represent an offspring. Do not return the beans to the bag. Write the colors of the beans on the chart.

5. Continue taking the beans out of the bag two at a time until all beans are removed. Write the results on the chart.

Part B

1. To model selection, assume that predators eat all of the white rabbits and one half of the gray rabbits.

2. For each brown rabbit from Part A, put 14 red beans (two beans for the brown rabbit and 12 beans representing six baby brown rabbits) into the bag.

3. For each remaining gray rabbit from Part A, put 7 red beans and 7 white beans (one of each color for the remaining gray rabbit and six of each color for six baby gray rabbits) into the bag.

4. Repeat steps 3–5 of Part A.

Activity (continued)

Data and Observations

Rabbit Offspring		
Rabbit #	Bean colors	Rabbit color
1		
2		
3		
4		
5		
6		
7		
8		
9		
10		

Analysis

1. How did the rabbit gene pool change during the activity?

2. What eventually happens to the white rabbits?

3. Describe how this model is similar to the way natural selection occurs in nature.

4. How is this model unlike the way natural selection occurs in nature?

Chapter 7
MINILAB 7-1

Relating Evolution to Species

Procedure
1. On a piece of paper, print the alphabet in lowercase letters.
2. Order the letters into three groups. Put all of the vowels in the first group. Place all of the consonants that do not drop below the line into the second group and all of the consonants that do drop below the line in the third group.

Analysis
1. How are the three groups of letters similar to each other?

   _____

   _____

   _____

2. If the letters were organisms, how would scientists know how closely related the letters were to each other? _____

   _____

   _____

   _____

Chapter 7

MINILAB 7-2

Living Without Thumbs

Procedure

1. Tape your thumb securely to your hand. Do this for both hands.

2. Leave your thumbs taped down for at least two hours. During this time, do the following activities: eat a meal, change clothes, and brush your teeth. Be careful not to try anything that could be dangerous.

3. Write about your experience in the space below.

Data and Observations

Analysis

1. Did not having usable thumbs significantly affect the way you did things? Explain.

2. Infer how having opposable thumbs may have influenced primate evolution.

Chapter 8
ACTIVITY 8-1
• Classifying Seeds

Design Your Own Experiment

Lab Preview
1. What is a seed?
   _____
   _____

2. Name a seed plant.
   _____
   _____
   _____

Scientists have developed classification systems to show how organisms are related. How do they determine what features they will use to classify organisms? Can you learn to use the same methods?

Recognize the Problem
You are given several kinds of seeds and are asked to classify them into groups of similar seeds. How would you begin?

Form a Hypothesis
Make a hypothesis about the traits or physical features that may be used to help classify various kinds of seeds.

Goals
- **Observe** the seeds provided and notice their distinctive features.
- **Classify** seeds using your model.

Possible Materials
- packets of seeds (10 different kinds)
- hand lens
- metric ruler
- sheets of paper (2)

Safety Precautions
Do not eat any seeds or put them in your mouth. Some may have been treated with chemicals.

41

| NAME | DATE | CLASS |

Test Your Hypothesis

Plan

1. As a group, list the steps that you need to take to classify seeds. Be specific, and describe exactly what you will do at each step. List your materials.
2. **Classify** your seeds by making a model.
3. Make a key to identify your seeds.
4. Read over your entire experiment to make sure that all steps are in logical order.

Do

1. Make sure your teacher approves your model before you proceed.
2. Carry out the experiment as planned.
3. While you are working, write down any observations that you make that would cause you to change your model.
4. **Complete** the plan.

Analyze Your Data

1. **Compare** your key and branching model with those made by other groups.

2. Check your key by having another group use it.

Draw Conclusions

1. In what ways can groups of different types of seeds be classified?

2. Why is it an advantage for scientists to use a standardized system to classify organisms? What observations did you make to support your answer?

NAME _____ DATE _____ CLASS _____

Chapter 8
ACTIVITY 8-2 • Using a Dichotomous Key

Lab Preview
1. What is binomial nomenclature?
   _____

2. Who introduced binomial nomenclature?
   _____

Scientists who classify organisms have made many keys that allow you to identify unknown organisms. Try this activity to see how it is done.

What You'll Investigate
How a dichotomous key can be used to identify native cats in the United States.

Goals
- **Learn** to use a dichotomous key.
- **Identify** two native cats of North America.

Materials
- paper and pencil

Procedure
1. **Observe** the cats pictured below.
2. Begin with 1 of the key to the right. **Identify** the cat labeled A.
3. On your paper, write the common and scientific name for the cat and list all of its traits given in the key.
4. Use the same procedure to **identify** the species of the cat labeled B.

Key to Native Cats of North America

1. Tail length
   a. short, go to 2
   b. long, go to 3

2. Cheek ruff
   a. no cheek ruff; long ear tuffs tipped with black; coat distinctly mottled; lynx, *Lynx canadensis*
   b. broad cheek ruffs; ear tuffs short; coat with indistinct spots; bobcat, *Lynx rufus*

3. Coat
   a. plain colored, go to 4
   b. patterned, go to 5

4. Coat color
   a. yellowish to tan above with white to buff below; mountain lion, *Felis concolor*
   b. all brown or black; jaguarundi, *Felis yagouaroundi*

5. Coat pattern
   a. lines of black-bordered brown spots; ocelot, *Felis pardalis*
   b. irregular tan and black, go to 6

6. Animal size
   a. large cat; rows of black rosettes or rings unevenly distributed; jaguar, *Panthera onca*
   b. small cat; four dark-brown stripes on the back and one on the neck; some irregularly shaped spots; margay, *Felis wiedii*

Copyright © Glencoe/McGraw-Hill, a division of The McGraw-Hill Companies, Inc.

43

Activity (continued)

Conclude and Apply

1. According to the key, how many species of native cats reside in North America?

2. How do you know that this key doesn't contain all the species of native cats in the world?

3. **Infer** why you couldn't identify a lion using this key.

4. **Explain** why it wouldn't be a good idea to begin in the middle of a key instead of with the first step.

Chapter 8
MINILAB 8-1

Using Binomial Nomenclature

Procedure
1. Make a model of a fictitious organism.
2. Give your organism a scientific name.
3. Make sure that your name is Latinized and supplies information about the species.

Analysis
1. Present your organism to the class. Ask them to guess its name.
   _____
   _____

2. Why do scientists use Latin when they name organisms?
   _____
   _____

Chapter 8
MINILAB 8-2

Communicating Ideas

Procedure
1. Find a picture in a magazine of a piece of furniture that you could both sit or lie down on.
2. Show the picture to ten people and ask them to tell you what they call the piece of furniture.
3. Keep a record of the answers in the space below.

Data and Observations

People Surveyed	Response to Question
1	
2	
3	
4	
5	
6	
7	
8	
9	
10	

Analysis
1. Infer how using common names can be confusing when communicating with others.
   _____
   _____
   _____

2. How does using scientific names make communication between scientists easier?
   _____
   _____

Chapter 9
ACTIVITY 9-1
Observing Cyanobacteria

Lab Preview
1. What safety symbols are associated with this activity? _____
   _____
2. What is the common name for cyanobacteria? _____
   _____

You can obtain many species of cyanobacteria from ponds. When you look at these organisms under a microscope, you will find that they have many similarities but that they are also different from each other in important ways. In this activity, you will compare and contrast species of cyanobacteria.

What You'll Investigate
What do cyanobacteria look like?

Materials
- micrograph photos
  *microscope
  *prepared slides of Gloeocapsa and Anabaena
  *alternate materials

Goals
- **Observe** several species of cyanobacteria.
- **Describe** the structure and function of cyanobacteria.

Procedure
1. Indicate whether each cyanobacterium sample is in colony form or filament form. Write a *yes* or *no* in the data table for the presence or absence of each characteristic in each type of cyanobacterium.

2. **Observe** photos or prepared slides, if available, of *Gloeocapsa* and *Anabaena*. If using slides, observe under the low and high power of the microscope. Notice the difference in the arrangement of the cells. Draw and label a few cells of each species of cyanobacterium.

3. **Observe** photos of *Nostoc* and *Oscillatoria*. In your Science Journal, draw and label a few cells of each.

| NAME | DATE | CLASS |

Activity (continued)

Cyanobacteria Observations

Structure	Anabaena	Gloeocapsa	Nostoc	Oscillatoria
Filament or colony				
Nucleus				
Chlorophyll				
Gel-like layer				

Conclude and Apply

1. How does the color of cyanobacteria compare with the color of leaves on trees? What can you infer from this?

2. How can you tell by **observing** them that cyanobacteria belong to Kingdom Eubacteria?

3. **Describe** the general appearance of cyanobacteria.

NAME _____ DATE _____ CLASS _____

Chapter 9
ACTIVITY 9-2

• Are there bacteria in foods?

Lab Preview

1. What is an indicator?
   _____
   _____

2. Why are separate droppers and craft sticks used in this activity?
   _____
   _____

You've learned that bacteria are too small to be seen without a microscope, but is there some way that you can tell if they are present in foods? Because bacteria respire by producing carbon dioxide like other living things, a chemical test that indicates the respiration of bacteria can be used to tell if bacteria are growing in foods you eat.

What You'll Investigate
Is there bacteria in the food you eat?

Goals
- **Observe** color changes in test tubes containing food.
- **Determine** which foods contain the most bacteria

Safety Precautions

Materials
- 6 test tubes
- 6 stoppers
- test-tube rack
- felt-tip marker
- 3 droppers
- 3 craft sticks
- milk, buttermilk, cottage cheese, yogurt, sour cream, water
- bromothymol blue solution (150 mL)

Procedure

1. Use the marker to label the test tubes 1 through 6 and place them in the test-tube rack.

2. Add 25 mL of bromothymol blue–indicator solution to each test tube.

3. Using a different dropper each time, add four drops of water to tube 1, four drops of milk to tube 2, and four drops of buttermilk to tube 3. Be careful not to let the drops go down the sides of the tubes.

4. Using a different craft stick each time, add an amount of yogurt about the size of a green pea to tube 4, the same amount of cottage cheese to tube 5, and the same amount of sour cream to tube 6.

5. Loosely place a stopper in each tube and record the color of the contents of each tube in the data table below.

6. Leave the tubes undisturbed until the end of the class period. Record the color of the contents of the tubes in the data table below.

7. The next time you arrive in class, record the color of the contents of the tubes again.

Copyright © Glencoe/McGraw-Hill, a division of The McGraw-Hill Companies, Inc.

NAME _____ DATE _____ CLASS _____

Activity (continued)

Data and Observations

Tube	Contents	Color at Start	Color at End of Class	Color One Day Later	Test + or −	Bacteria Present?
1	Water					
2	Milk					
3	Buttermilk					
4	Yogurt					
5	Cottage cheese					
6	Sour cream					

Data Table for Test of Bacteria in Food

Conclude and Apply

1. Why was water added to tube 1?

   _____
   _____
   _____

2. What color does bromothymol turn if carbon dioxide is present?

   _____
   _____
   _____

3. Using strength of the color change as a guide, judge which tubes contain the most bacteria.

   _____
   _____
   _____

Chapter 9
MINILAB 9-1

Observing Bacterial Growth

Procedure
1. Obtain two or three dried beans.
2. Break them into halves and place the halves into 10 mL of distilled water in a glass beaker.
3. Observe how many days it takes for the water to become cloudy and develop an unpleasant odor.
4. Use methylene blue to dye a drop of water from the beaker and observe it under the microscope.

Analysis
1. How long did it take for the water to become cloudy?

2. What did you observe on the slide that would make the water cloudy?

3. What do you think the bacteria were feeding on?

Chapter 9
MINILAB 9-2

Making Yogurt

Procedure

1. Bring a liter of milk almost to a boil in a saucepan. **CAUTION:** *Always be careful when using a stove or hot plate. Do not eat food used in a classroom activity.*

2. Remove the pan from the burner and allow it to cool until it is lukewarm.

3. Add one or two heaping tablespoons of yogurt starter with live cultures and stir.

4. Pour the mixture into a clean thermos and put on the lid.

5. Let stand for six hours and then refrigerate overnight.

Analysis

1. What do you think was in the yogurt starter?

2. Infer why you let the milk cool before adding the starter.

NAME _____ DATE _____ CLASS _____

Chapter 10
ACTIVITY 10-1
Comparing Algae and Protozoans

Lab Preview
1. How do plant cells that, like algae, contain chloroplasts differ from animal cells? _____
   _____
2. How many cells do protozoans have? _____

Algae and protozoan cells have characteristics that are similar enough to place them within the same kingdom. However, the variety of forms within Kingdom Protista is great. In this activity, you can observe many of the differences that make organisms in Kingdom Protista so diverse.

What You'll Investigate
What are the differences between algae and protozoans?

Goals
- **Draw and label** the organisms you examine.
- **Observe** the differences between algae and protozoans.

Safety Precautions
Make sure to wash your hands after handling algae and protozoans.

Materials
- cultures of *Paramecium, Amoeba, Euglena,* and *Spirogyra*
  *prepared slides of above organisms
- prepared slide of slime mold
- coverslips (5)
- microscope
  *stereomicroscope
- dropper
- microscope slides (5)
  *alternate materials

Procedure
1. Record your drawings and observations in the table on the next page.
2. **Make** a wet mount of the *Paramecium* culture. If you need help doing this, refer to Appendix D.
3. **Observe** the wet mount first under low and then under high power. Draw and label the organism.
4. Repeat steps 2 and 3 with the other cultures. Return all preparations to your teacher and wash your hands.
5. **Observe** the slide of slime mold under low and high power. Record your observations.

Copyright © Glencoe/McGraw-Hill, a division of The McGraw-Hill Companies, Inc.

53

| NAME | DATE | CLASS |

Activity (continued)

Protist Observations

	Paramecium	Amoeba	Euglena	Spirogyra
Drawing				

Conclude and Apply

1. For each organism that could move, **label** the structure that enabled the movement.

2. Which protists make their own food? **Explain** how you know that they make their own food.

3. **Identify** those protists with animal characteristics.

Chapter 10
ACTIVITY 10-2
Comparing Types of Fungi

Lab Preview
1. What safety symbol is associated with this activity?
   _____

2. Name three ways in which fungi benefit people.
   _____
   _____

Fungi differ mainly in their reproductive structures. The diversity of these structures allows scientists to classify fungi as zygote fungi, club fungi, sac fungi, or imperfect fungi. In this activity, you will compare the reproductive structures in cultures of fungi.

What You'll Investigate
How do reproductive structures of fungi compare?

Goals
- **Observe** the appearance of fungi colonies.
- **Compare** the reproductive structures of fungi cultures.
- **Draw, label,** and **identify** different types of fungi.

Safety Precautions
Make sure to wash your hands after handling fungi.

Materials
- cultures of fungi (bread mold, mushrooms, yeasts, lichens, or *Penicillium*)
- cellophane tape
- microscope
- microscope slides
- coverslips
- magnifying lens

Procedure
1. **Design** a data table in your Science Journal with columns labeled *Fungus, Colony Appearance, Reproductive Structures,* and *Fungi Division.*

2. **Compare** and **contrast** the cultures of fungi in drawings that you labeled.

3. Your teacher will demonstrate how to collect the reproductive structures of fungi with cellophane tape by gently touching the tape to your samples.

4. Place the tape, adhesive side up, on a microscope slide, and cover it with a coverslip.

5. Draw and label the reproductive structures.

6. Repeat this procedure for each culture of fungus.

55

| NAME | DATE | CLASS |

Activity (continued)

Conclude and Apply

1. Write a description of the reproductive structures you observed. Include relative numbers, shape of cells, and size.

   _____

   _____

   _____

2. From your descriptions, explain why fungi are classified based on their reproductive structures.

   _____

   _____

   _____

3. List the four divisions of fungi, and give an example of each division.

   _____

   _____

   _____

   _____

Data and Observations

Fungi Observations			
Fungus	Colony appearance	Reproductive structures	Fungi division
mushroom			
bread mold			
Penicillium			

Chapter 10
MINILAB 10-1

Observing Slime Molds

Procedure
1. Obtain live specimens of the slime mold *Physarum polycephaalum* from your teacher.
2. Observe the mold for four days.

Analysis
1. Make daily drawings and observations of the mold as it grows. Use a magnifying glass.
2. Predict the conditions under which the slime mold will change from the amoeboid form to the spore-producing form.

_____
_____

Data and Observations

Day	Drawings	Observation
1		
2		
3		
4		

Chapter 10
MINILAB 10-2

Interpreting Spore Prints

Procedure
1. Obtain several mushrooms from the grocery store and let them age until the undersides look brown.
2. Remove the stems and arrange the mushroom caps with the gills down on a piece of unlined white paper.
3. Let the mushroom caps sit undisturbed overnight and remove them from the paper the next day.

Analysis
1. Draw and label a sketch of the results in the space below.

2. Describe the marks on the page and what made them.
_____
_____

3. How could you estimate the number of new mushrooms that could be produced from one mushroom cap?
_____
_____
_____

Chapter 11

ACTIVITY 11-1

Comparing Seedless Plants

Lab Preview

1. What are the two categories of seedless plants?

2. What is the name of the threadlike roots that hold mosses and liverworts in place?

Liverworts, mosses, ferns, horsetails, and club mosses have at least one common characteristic—they reproduce by spores. But, do they have other things in common? In this activity, discover their similarities and differences.

What You'll Investigate
How are seedless plants alike and how are they different?

Goals
- **Observe** types of seedless plants.
- **Compare and contrast** seedless plants.

Materials
One living example of each of these plants:
- moss
- liverwort
- club moss
- horsetail
- fern
  *detailed photographs of the above plant types
  *alternate material

Procedure

1. Review the Plant Observations table on the next page.

2. Examine each plant and fill in the table using the following guidelines:
   Color—green or not green
   Growth—mostly flat and low or mostly upright
   Root Type—small and fiberlike or rootlike
   Leaf Form—needlelike, scalelike, or leaflike

59

Activity (continued)

Plant Observations

Plant	Color	Growth	Root Type	Leaf Form
Moss				
Liverwort				
Club moss				
Horsetail				
Fern				

Conclude and Apply

1. **Observe and infer** what characteristics seedless plants have in common.

2. **Hypothesize** about the differences in growth.

3. **Compare and contrast** the seedless plants.

Chapter 11
ACTIVITY 11-2
Comparing Monocots and Dicots

Lab Preview

1. What safety symbols are associated with this activity?
   _____

2. What is a seed?
   _____
   _____

You have read that monocots and dicots are similar because they are both groups of flowering plants. However, you have also learned that these two groups are different. Try this activity to compare and contrast monocots and dicots.

What You'll Investigate
How do the characteristics of monocots and dicots compare?

Goals
- **Observe** similarities and differences between monocots and dicots.
- **Classify** plants as monocots or dicots based on flower characteristics.
- **Infer** what type of food is stored in seeds.

Safety Precautions

Materials
- monocot and dicot flowers
- monocot and dicot seeds
- scalpel
- forceps
- iodine solution

Procedure

1. Use the Data and Observations table on page 76 to record your observations.

2. **Observe** the leaves on the stem of each flower. In your Science Journal, describe the monocot and the dicot leaf.

3. **Examine** the monocot and the dicot flower. For each flower, remove and count the outer row of sepals. Enter this number on your table. Do the same with the petals.

4. Locate, remove, and **observe** the structures inside each flower. Notice that there are two different types of structures. How many of each kind are there? Enter these numbers in the "Other Observations" column.

5. Examine the two seeds. **Cut** the seeds lengthwise and **observe** the two halves. Try to **identify** the embryo and cotyledon(s).

6. Test the seeds for starch by placing a drop of iodine on different parts of the seed. A blue-black color indicates the presence of starch. **CAUTION:** *Iodine is poisonous and may stain or burn the skin.*

61

NAME _____ DATE _____ CLASS _____

Activity (continued)

Data and Observations

	Number of sepals	Number of petals	Number of cotyledons	Other observations
Monocot				
Dicot				

Conclude and Apply

1. **Compare** the numbers of sepals and petals of monocot and dicot flowers.

   _____
   _____
   _____

2. What characteristics are the same for monocot and dicot flowers?

   _____
   _____
   _____

3. Distinguish between a monocot and a dicot seed.

   _____
   _____

4. What type of food stored in monocot and in dicot seeds?

   _____
   _____

Chapter 11
MINILAB 11-1

Measuring Water Absorption by a Moss

Procedure
1. Place a few teaspoons of *Sphagnum* moss on a piece of cheesecloth. Twist the cheesecloth to form a ball and tie it securely.
2. Weigh the ball.
3. Put 200 mL of water in a container and add the ball.
4. Predict how much water the ball will absorb.
5. Wait 15 minutes. Remove the ball and drain the excess water back into the container.

Analysis
1. Weigh the ball and measure the amount of water left in the container.

2. In your Science Journal, calculate how much water the *Sphagnum* moss absorbed.

Chapter 11

MINILAB 11-2

Observing Water Moving in a Plant

Procedure
1. Into a clear container, about 10 cm tall and 4 cm in diameter, pour water to a depth of 1.5 cm. Add 15 drops of red food coloring to the water.
2. Put the root end of a whole green onion in the colored water in the container. Do not cut the onion in any way.
3. Let the onion stand overnight.
4. The next day, examine the outside of the onion. Peel off the layers of leaves and examine them.

Analysis
1. Compare the appearance of the onion before and after it was in the colored water.

2. Describe the location of red color inside the onion.

3. Infer how the red color inside the onion might be related to vascular tissue.

Chapter 12

ACTIVITY 12-1

Garbage-eating Worms

Design Your Own Experiment

Lab Preview

1. What safety symbols are associated with this activity?
   _____
2. How do earthworms use the soil they live in? _____
   _____
   _____

You know that soil conditions can influence the growth of plants. You are trying to decide what factors might improve the soil in your backyard garden. A friend suggests that earthworms improve the quality of the soil. Does the presence of earthworms have any value in improving soil conditions?

Recognize the Problem
How does the presence of earthworms change the condition of the soil?

Form a Hypothesis
Based on your reading and observations, state a hypothesis about how earthworms might improve the conditions of soil.

Goals
- **Design an experiment** that compares the condition of soil in two environments, one with earthworms and one without.
- **Observe** the change in soil conditions for two weeks.

Possible Materials
- worms (red wigglers)
- plastic containers with drainage holes (4-L) (2)
- soil (7 L)
- chopped food scraps including fruit and vegetable peels, pulverized eggshells, tea bags, and coffee grounds
- shredded newspaper
- spray bottle

Safety Precautions
Be careful when working with live animals. Always keep your hand wet when handling earthworms. Dry hands will remove the mucus from the earthworms.

Test Your Hypothesis
Plan
1. As a group, agree upon the hypothesis and **decide** how you will test it. **Identify** what results will confirm the hypothesis.
2. **List** the steps you will need to take to test your hypothesis. Be specific. **Describe** exactly what you will do in each step. **List** your materials.
3. Prepare a data table in your Science Journal to **record** your observations.
4. **Read** over the entire experiment to make sure all steps are in logical order.
5. **Identify** all constants, variables, and controls of the experiment.

Do
1. Make sure your teacher approves your plan and your data table before you proceed.
2. Carry out the experiment as planned.
3. While doing the experiment, **record** your observations and complete the data table in your Science Journal.

Copyright © Glencoe/McGraw-Hill, a division of The McGraw-Hill Companies, Inc.

Activity (continued)

Analyze Your Data

1. **Compare** the changes in the two sets of soil samples.

2. **Compare** your results with those of other groups.

3. What was your control in this experiment?

4. What were your variables?

Draw Conclusions

1. Did the result support your hypothesis? **Explain.**

2. **Describe** what effect you think rain would have on the soil and worms.

Chapter 12
ACTIVITY 12-2
Observing Complete Metamorphosis

Lab Preview

1. What safety symbols are associated with this activity?
   _____

2. Do you expect to see a nymph stage during this activity? Why or why not?
   _____

Many insects go through the four stages of complete metamorphosis during their life cycles. Chemicals that are secreted by the body of the animal control the changes. How different do the body forms look between the stages of metamorphosis?

What You'll Investigate
What do the stages of metamorphosis look like for a darkling beetle?

Goals
- **Observe** the stages of metamorphosis of mealworms to adult darkling beetles.
- **Compare** the physical appearance of the beetles as they go through two stages of metamorphosis.

Safety Precautions

Materials
- large-mouth jar or old fishbowl
- bran or oatmeal
- dried bread or cookie crumbs mixed with flour
- slice of apple or carrot
- paper towel
- cheesecloth
- mealworms
- rubber band

Procedure
1. **Set up** a habitat for the mealworms by placing a 1-cm layer of bran or oatmeal on the bottom of the jar. Add a 1-cm layer of dried bread or cookie crumbs mixed with flour. Then, add another layer of bran or oatmeal.

2. **Add** a slice of apple or carrot as a source of moisture. Replace the apple or carrot daily.

3. **Place** 20 to 30 mealworms in the jar. Add a piece of crumpled paper towel.

4. **Cover** the jar with a piece of cheesecloth. Use the rubber band to secure the cloth to the jar.

5. **Observe** the mealworms daily for two to three weeks. **Record** daily observations in your Science Journal.

| NAME | DATE | CLASS |

Activity (continued)

Conclude and Apply

1. In your Science Journal, **draw** and **describe** the mealworms' metamorphoses to adults.

2. **Identify** the stages of metamorphosis that mealworms go through to become adult darkling beetles.

3. Which of these stages did you not see during this investigation?

4. What are some of the advantages of an insect's young being different from the adult form?

5. Based on the food you placed in the habitat, **infer** where you might find mealworms or adult darkling beetles in your house.

6. Why do you think pet stores would stock and sell mealworms?

Chapter 12
MINILAB 12-1

Observing Sponge Spicules

Procedure
1. Add a few drops of bleach to a microscope slide. **CAUTION:** *Do not inhale the bleach or spill it on your hands or clothing or on the microscope.*
2. Put a small piece of the sponge into the bleach. Add a coverslip. Observe the cells of the sponge.

Analysis
1. Are spicules made of the same materials as the rest of the sponge? Explain.

2. What is the function of a spicule?

Chapter 12
MINILAB 12-2

Modeling Sea Stars

Procedure
1. Hold your arm straight out, palm up.
2. Place a heavy book on your hand.
3. Have another person time how long you can hold your arm up with the book on it.

Analysis
1. Describe how your arm feels after a few minutes.
   _____
   _____

2. If the book models the sea star and your arm models the oyster, infer how a sea star successfully overcomes the oyster to obtain food.
   _____
   _____
   _____

Chapter 13

ACTIVITY 13-1

Frog Metamorphosis

Lab Preview

1. What safety symbols are associated with this activity?

2. What factors affect the rate of amphibian metamorphosis?

Frogs and other amphibians use external fertilization to reproduce. Female frogs lay hundreds of jellylike eggs in water. Male frogs then fertilize these eggs. Once larvae hatch, the process of metamorphosis begins. Over a period of time, young tadpoles develop into adult frogs.

What You'll Investigate
What changes occur as a tadpole goes through metamorphosis?

Goals
- **Observe** how body structures change as a tadpole develops into an adult frog.
- **Determine** how long metamorphosis takes to be completed.

Materials
- aquarium or jar (4-L)
- frog egg mass
- lake or pond water
- stereoscopic microscope
- watch glass
- small fishnet
- aquatic plants
- washed gravel
- lettuce (previously boiled)
- large rock

Procedure

1. Review the data table on the next page.

2. As a class, use the aquarium, pond water, gravel, rock, and plants to prepare a water habitat for the frog eggs.

3. **Place** the egg mass in the water of the aquarium. Use the fishnet to separate a few eggs from the mass. **Place** these eggs in the watch glass. The eggs should have the dark side up. **CAUTION:** *Handle the eggs with care.*

4. **Observe** the eggs. **Record** your observations in the data table.

5. **Observe** the eggs twice a week. **Record** any changes that occur.

6. Continue observing the tadpoles twice a week after they hatch. **Identify** the mouth, eyes, gill cover, gills, nostrils, fin on the back, hind legs, and front legs. **Observe** how tadpoles eat boiled lettuce that has been cooled.

Copyright © Glencoe/McGraw-Hill, a division of The McGraw-Hill Companies, Inc.

71

NAME	DATE	CLASS

Activity (continued)

Frog Metamorphosis

Date	Observations

Conclude and Apply

1. How long does it take for the eggs to hatch and the tadpoles to develop legs?

2. Which pair of legs appears first?

3. **Explain** why the jellylike coating around the eggs is important.

4. **Compare** the eyes of young tadpoles with the eyes of older tadpoles.

5. **Calculate** how long it takes for a tadpole to change into a frog.

NAME _____ DATE _____ CLASS _____

Chapter 13
MINILAB 13-1

Observing Bird Feathers

Procedure
1. Use a hand lens to examine a contour feather.
2. Hold the shaft end while carefully bending the opposite end. Observe what happens when you release the bent end.
3. Examine a down feather with a hand lens.
4. Hold each feather separately. Blow on it. Note any differences in the way each reacts to the stream of air.

Analysis
1. What happens when you release the bent end of the contour feather?

_____
_____

2. Which of the two feathers would you find on a bird's wing?

_____
_____

3. Which type of feather would you find in a pillow? Why?

_____
_____

NAME _____ DATE _____ CLASS _____

Chapter 13
MINILAB 13-2

Observing Hair

Procedure

1. Brush or comb your hair to remove a few loose hairs.
2. Take two hairs from your brush that look like they still have the root attached.
3. Make a wet mount slide of the two hairs, being sure to include the root.
4. Focus on the hairs with the low-power objective. Draw what you see.
5. Switch to the high-power objective and focus on the hairs. Draw what you see.

Data and Observations

Analysis

1. Describe the characteristics of hair and root.
   _____
   _____

2. Infer how hair keeps an organism warm.
   _____
   _____

NAME _____ DATE _____ CLASS _____

Chapter 14
ACTIVITY 14-1

Soil Composition

Lab Preview

1. What are abiotic factors? _____

2. Name at least three abiotic factors. _____
   _____

Soil is more than minerals mixed with the decaying bodies of dead organisms. It contains other biotic and abiotic factors.

What You'll Investigate
What are the components of soil?

Goals
- **Determine** what factors are present in soil.

Materials
- 3 small paper cups containing freshly dug soil
- newspaper
- hand lens
- scale
- beaker of water
- jar with lid

Procedure

1. **Obtain** 3 cups of soil sample from your teacher. **Record** the source of your sample in your Science Journal.

2. **Pour** one of your samples onto the newspaper. **Sort** through the objects in the soil and separate abiotic and biotic items. Use a hand lens to help identify the items. **Describe** your observations in the data table below.

3. Carefully place the second sample in the jar, disturbing it as little as possible. Quickly fill the jar with water and screw the lid on tightly. Without moving the jar, **observe** its contents for several minutes. **Record** your observations in the data table.

4. **Weigh** the third sample. **Record** the weight in the data table. Leave the sample undisturbed for several days, then weigh it again. **Record** the second weight in the data table.

Data and Observations

Cup	Items in soil		Weight	
	Abiotic	Biotic	1st weight	2nd weight
1				
2				
3				

Copyright © Glencoe/McGraw-Hill, a division of The McGraw-Hill Companies, Inc.

75

Activity (continued)

Conclude and Apply

1. Can you **infer** the presence of any organisms?
   _____
   _____

2. **Describe** the abiotic factors in your sample. What biotic factors did you **observe**?
   _____
   _____
   _____

3. Did you **record** any change in the soil weight over time? If so, why?
   _____
   _____

Chapter 14

ACTIVITY 14-2

Identifying a Limiting Factor

Design Your Own Experiment

Lab Preview
1. What is a limiting factor?
   _____
2. What is an abiotic factor?
   _____

Organisms depend on many biotic and abiotic factors in their environment to survive. When these factors are limited or are not available, it can affect an organism's survival. By experimenting with some of these limiting factors, you will see how organisms depend on all parts of their environment.

Recognize the Problem
How do abiotic factors such as light, water, and temperature affect the germination of seeds?

Form a Hypothesis
Based on what you have learned about limiting factors, make a hypothesis about how one specific abiotic factor may affect the germination of a bean seed. Be sure to consider factors that you can change easily.

Goals
- **Observe** the effects of an abiotic factor on the germination and growth of bean seedlings.
- **Design** an experiment that demonstrates whether or not a specific abiotic factor limits the germination of bean seeds.

Safety Precautions
Wash hands after handling soil and seeds.

Possible Materials
- bean seeds
- small planting containers
- soil
- water
- labels
- trowel or spoon
- aluminum foil
- sunny window or other light source
- refrigerator or oven

Test Your Hypothesis
Plan
1. As a group, agree upon and write out a hypothesis statement.
2. Decide on a way to test your group's hypothesis. Keep available materials in mind as you plan your procedure. **List** your materials.
3. **Prepare** a data table on the following page.
4. Remember to **test** only one variable at a time and use suitable controls.
5. **Read** over your entire experiment to make sure that all steps are in logical order.
6. **Identify** any constants, variables, and controls in your experiment.
7. Be sure the factor you test is measurable.

Do
1. Make sure your teacher has approved your plan before you proceed.
2. Carry out the experiment as planned.
3. While the experiment is going on, write down any observations that you make and complete the data table on the following page.

Copyright © Glencoe/McGraw-Hill, a division of The McGraw-Hill Companies, Inc.

***Activity** (continued)*

Analyze Your Data
1. **Compare** your results with those of other groups.
   _____
   _____

2. **Infer** how the abiotic factor you tested affected the germination of bean seeds.
   _____
   _____

3. **Graph** your results using a bar graph that compares the number of bean seeds that germinated in the experimental container with the number of seeds that germinated in the control container.
   _____

Draw Conclusions
1. **Identify** which factor had the greatest effect on the seeds.
   _____
   _____

2. **Determine** whether you could substitute one factor for another and still grow the seeds.
   _____
   _____

Chapter 14
MINILAB 14-1

Observing Symbiosis

Procedure
1. Carefully wash, then examine the roots of a legume plant and a nonlegume plant.
2. Examine a prepared microscope slide of the bacteria that live in the roots of legumes.

Analysis
1. What differences do you observe in the roots of the two plants?
   _____
   _____

2. The bacteria help legumes to thrive in poor soil. What type of symbiotic relationship is this? Explain.
   _____
   _____

Chapter 14

MINILAB 14-2

Modeling the Water Cycle

Procedure
1. With a marker, make a line halfway up on a plastic cup. Fill the cup to the mark with water.
2. Cover the top with plastic wrap and secure it with a rubber band or tape.
3. Put the cup in direct sunlight. Observe the cup for three days. Record your observations.
4. Remove the plastic wrap and observe the cup for a week.

Analysis
1. What parts of the water cycle did you observe in this activity?

   _____
   _____

2. What happened to the water level in the cup when the plastic wrap was removed?

   _____
   _____

Chapter 15
ACTIVITY 15-2

Studying a Land Environment

Lab Preview
1. What is an ecosystem? _____
   _____
2. What is a population? _____
   _____

An ecological study includes observation and analysis of living organisms and the physical features of the environment.

What You'll Investigate
How do you study an ecosystem?

Goals
- Observe biotic and abiotic factors of an ecosystem.
- Analyze the relationships among organisms and their environment.

Materials
- graph paper
- thermometer
- tape measure
- hand lens
- notebook
- binoculars
- pencil
- field guides

Procedure
1. **Choose** a portion of an ecosystem near your school or home as your area of study. You might choose to study a pond, a forest area in a park, a garden, or another area.
2. **Decide** the boundaries of your study area.
3. Using a tape measure and graph paper, **make a map** of your study area.
4. Using a thermometer, **measure and record** the air temperature in your study area.
5. **Observe** the organisms in your study area. Use field guides to identify them. Use a hand lens to study small organisms. Use binoculars to study animals you cannot get near. Also, look for evidence (such as tracks or feathers) of organisms you do not see.
6. **Record** your observations in a table like the one shown. Make drawings to help you remember what you see.
7. **Visit** your study area as many times as you can and at different times of the day for four weeks. At each visit, be sure to make the same measurements and record all observations. Note how biotic and abiotic factors interact.

Environmental Data

Date	Time of day	Temperature	Organisms observed	Observations and comments

Activity (continued)

Conclude and Apply

1. **Identify** relationships among the organisms in your study area, such as predator-prey or symbiosis.
___
___
___

2. **Diagram** a food chain or food web for your ecosystem.
___
___
___

3. **Predict** what might happen if one or more abiotic factors were changed suddenly.
___
___
___

4. **Predict** what might happen if one or more populations were removed from the area.
___

NAME _____ DATE _____ CLASS _____

Chapter 15
MINILAB 15-1

Comparing Tundra and Taiga

Procedure
1. Compare the latitudes where tundra is found in the northern hemisphere with the same latitudes in South America.
2. Compare the latitudes where taiga is found in the northern hemisphere with the same latitudes in South America.

Analysis
Are either of these biomes found in South America? Explain why or why not.

_____

_____

_____

NAME _____ DATE _____ CLASS _____

Chapter 15
MINILAB 15-2

Modeling Freshwater Environments

Procedure
1. Cover the bottom of a self-sealing freezer bag with about 2 cm of gravel, muck, and other debris from the bottom of a pond. If plants are present, add one or two to the bag. Use a dip net to capture small fish, insects, or tadpoles.
2. Carefully pour pond water into the bag until it is about two-thirds full. Seal the bag.
3. Keep the bag indoors at room temperature and out of direct sunlight.

Analysis
1. Using a hand lens, observe as many organisms as possible. Record your observations. After two or three days, return your sample to the original habitat.

   _____
   _____
   _____
   _____

2. Write a short paper describing the organisms in your sample ecosystem and explaining their interactions.

   _____
   _____
   _____
   _____
   _____
   _____
   _____
   _____
   _____
   _____
   _____

Copyright © Glencoe/McGraw-Hill, a division of The McGraw-Hill Companies, Inc.

Chapter 16
ACTIVITY 16-1

Observing Bones

A Traditional Experiment

Lab Preview

1. Other than movement, name three functions of bones. _____
   _____
   _____

2. Why is the sharp object safety symbol necessary? _____
   _____

To move, animals must overcome the force of gravity. A skeleton aids in this movement. Land animals need skeletons that provide support against gravity. A flying animal needs a skeleton that provides support yet also allows it to overcome the pull of gravity and fly. Bones are adapted to the functions they perform. Find out if there is a difference between the bones of a land animal and those of a flying animal.

What You'll Investigate
What are the differences in the bone structures of land animals and flying animals?

Goals
- Learn the parts of a bone.
- Observe the differences between the bones of land animals and those of flying animals.

Materials
- beef bones (cut in half lengthwise)
- chicken leg bones (cut in half lengthwise)
- hand lens
- paper towels

Procedure
1. Copy the data table and use it to record your observations.
2. **Obtain** a beef bone and a chicken leg bone that have been cut in half along the length from your teacher.
3. **Observe** the bones with a hand lens.
4. **Identify** the periosteum, compact bone, spongy bone, and the remains of any marrow that may be present.
5. **Draw** a diagram of the bones and label their parts on the next page.
6. In the data table, **write** down any observations that you make.
7. Try to bend the bones to determine their flexibility.

85

Activity (continued)
Data and Observations
Bone Features

Part	Description of beef bone	Description of chicken bone
Periosteum		
Compact bone		
Spongy bone		
Marrow		

Diagrams of bones:

Conclude and Apply

1. Do your data indicate any adaptations for flight in the bones?

2. **Infer** which type of bone would require more force to move. Explain why.

3. How do the structures of the two types of bone tissue aid their function?

4. Which type of bone tissue was more flexible?

Chapter 16

ACTIVITY 16-2

Observing Muscle

Lab Preview

1. What safety symbols are associated with this activity?

   _____

2. Name the three types of muscles.

   _____

Muscles can be identified by their appearance. In this activity, you will make observations to distinguish among the three types of muscle tissue.

What You'll Investigate

You will distinguish between the three types of muscle tissue. What do different types of muscles look like.

Goal

- **Examine** three types of muscle tissue.
- **Examine** muscle fibers.

Safety Precautions

Materials

- prepared slides of smooth, skeletal, and cardiac muscles
  *detailed posters of the three types of muscle
- microscope
- cooked turkey leg or chicken leg
- dissecting pan or cutting board
- dissecting probes (2)
- hand lens
  *alternate materials

Procedure

1. **Record** your observations in the table on the next page.

2. Using the microscope, first on low power and then on high power, **observe** prepared slides of three different types of muscle.

3. On the data table, **draw** each type of muscle that you **observe.**

4. **Obtain** a piece of cooked turkey leg from your teacher. Muscle tissue is made up of groups of cells held together in fibers, usually by a transparent covering called connective tissue.

5. **Place** the turkey leg in the dissecting pan. Use the forceps to remove the skin. **Locate** and tease apart the muscle fibers.

6. **Use** a hand lens to examine the muscle fibers and any connective tissue you see in the turkey leg.

7. **Draw** and **measure** five turkey leg fibers and **describe** the shape of these muscle fibers.

87

NAME _____ DATE _____ CLASS _____

Activity (continued)

Data and Observations

Types of muscle	Diagram of muscle	Length of fibers	Description of fibers
Skeletal			
Cardiac			
Smooth			

Diagrams of turkey leg fibers:

Lengths of turkey leg fibers _____

Shape of turkey leg fibers _____

Conclude and Apply

1. How are muscle fibers arranged in the prepared slides?
   _____
   _____

2. **Predict** how the shape of a muscle fiber relates to its function.
   _____
   _____

3. Can you **conclude** that striations have anything to do with whether a muscle is voluntary or involuntary? **Explain.**
   _____
   _____

Chapter 16
MINILAB 16-1

Observing Muscle Pairs at Work

Procedure
1. Find out which muscles are used to move your arm.
2. Stretch your arm out straight. Bring your hand to your shoulder, then down again.
3. Use the muscles shown in the figure on the same page as the minilab to determine which skeletal muscles in your upper arm enable you to perform this action.

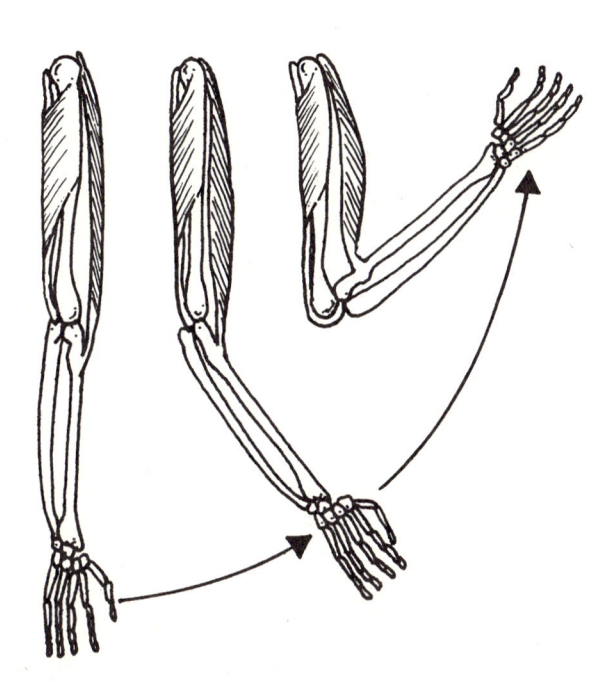

Analysis
1. How many muscles were involved in this action?

_____

2. Which muscle contracted to bring the forearm closer to the shoulder?

_____

Chapter 16
MINILAB 16-2

Recognizing Why You Sweat

Procedure
1. Examine the epidermis and the pores of your skin using a hand lens.
2. Put your hand in a clear plastic bag and taped it closed.
3. Sit quietly for 10 minutes. Observe what happens in the bag.
4. Observe what happened to your hand while it was in the bag.

Analysis
1. Identify what formed inside the bag. Where did this substance come from?

2. Why is it necessary for this substance to form, even when you are inactive?

Chapter 17
ACTIVITY 17-1

Identifying Vitamin C Content

Lab Preview

1. What are vitamins? _____
   _____
2. Why is vitamin C necessary? _____
   _____

Vitamin C is found in a variety of fruits and vegetables. In some plants, the concentration is high; in others, it is low. Try this activity to test various juices and find out which contains the most vitamin C.

What You'll Investigate
Which juices contain vitamin C?

Goals
- Observe differences in the vitamin C content of juices.

Materials
- indophenol solution
- graduated cylinder (10-mL)
  *graduated container
- glass-marking pencil
  *tape
- test tubes (10)
- test-tube rack
  *paper cups
- dropper
- dropping bottles (10)
- test substances: water, orange juice, pineapple juice, apple juice, lemon juice, tomato juice, cranberry juice, carrot juice, lime juice, mixed vegetable juice
  *alternate materials

Procedure
1. **Make** a data table like the example shown to **record** your observations.
2. **Label** the test tubes 1 through 10.
3. **Predict** which juices contain vitamin C. **Record** your predictions in your table.
4. **Measure** 5 mL of indophenol into each of the ten test tubes. **CAUTION:** *Wear your goggles and apron. Do not taste any of the juices.* Indophenol is a blue liquid that turns colorless when vitamin C is present. The more vitamin C in a juice, the less juice it takes to turn indophenol colorless.
5. **Add** 20 drops of water to test tube 1. **Record** your observations.
6. **Begin** adding orange juice, one drop at a time, to test tube 2.
7. **Record** the number of drops needed to turn indophenol colorless.
8. **Repeat** steps 6 and 7 to test the other juices.

Copyright © Glencoe/McGraw-Hill, a division of The McGraw-Hill Companies, Inc.

Activity (continued)

Test Results for Vitamin C

Test Tube	Juice	Prediction (yes or no)	Number of drops
1	water		
2	orange		
3	pineapple		
4	apple		
5	lemon		
6	tomato		
7	cranberry		
8	carrot		
9	lime		
10	vegetable		

Conclude and Apply

1. What is the purpose of testing water for the presence of vitamin C?

2. Does the amount of vitamin C vary in fruit juices?

3. Which juice did not contain vitamin C?

Chapter 17
ACTIVITY 17-2
Protein Digestion
Design Your Own Experiment

Lab Preview
1. What safety symbols are associated with this activity?
   _____
2. Where does chemical digestion take place?
   _____

You learned that proteins are large, complex, organic compounds necessary for living things to carry out their life processes. To be useful for cell functions, proteins must be broken down into their individual amino acids. The process of chemically breaking apart protein molecules involves several different factors, one of which is the presence of the enzyme pepsin in your stomach.

Recognize the Problem
Under what conditions will the enzyme pepsin begin the digestion of protein?

Form a Hypothesis
Formulate a hypothesis about what conditions are necessary for protein digestion to occur. When making your hypothesis, consider the various contents of the digestive juices that are found in your stomach.

Goals
- **Design** an experiment that tests the effect of a variable, such as the presence or absence of acid, on the activity of the enzyme, pepsin.
- **Observe** the effects of pepsin on gelatin.

Possible Materials
- test tubes with gelled, unflavored gelatin (3)
- dropper
- test-tube rack
- pepsin powder
- glass marking pen
- cold water
- dilute hydrochloric acid
- beaker
- watch or clock

Safety Precautions
Always use care when working with acid. Wear goggles and an apron. Avoid contact with skin and eyes. Wash your hands thoroughly after pouring the acid.

93

Activity (continued)

Test Your Hypothesis
Plan
1. **Decide** how your group will test your hypothesis.
2. Your teacher will supply you with three test tubes containing gelled, unflavored gelatin. Pepsin powder will liquify the gelatin if the enzyme is active.
3. As a group, **list** the steps you will need to take to test your hypothesis. Consider the following factors as you plan your experiment. Based on information provided by your teacher, how will you use the pepsin and the acid? How will the gelatin be prepared? How often will you make observations? Be specific and describe exactly what you will do at each step.
4. **List** your materials.
5. **Prepare** a data table and **record** it in your Science Journal so that it is ready to use as your group collects data.
6. **Read** over the entire experiment to make sure that all steps are in logical order.
7. **Identify** any constants, variables, and controls of the experiment.

Do
1. Make sure your teacher approves your plan before you proceed.
2. **Carry** out the experiment as planned.
3. While the experiment is going on, **write** down any observations that you make and complete the data table in your Science Journal.

Analyze Your Data
1. **Compare** your results with those of other groups.

2. Did you **observe** a difference in the test tubes?

3. **Identify** the constants in this experiment.

Draw Conclusions
1. Did the acid have any effect on the activity of the pepsin? How does this relate to the activity of this enzyme in the stomach?

2. **Predict** the effects of the pepsin on the gelatin if you increased or decreased the concentration of the acid.

3. Is time a factor in the effectiveness of the pepsin on the gelatin? **Explain.**

Chapter 17
MINILAB 17-1

Measuring the Water Content of Food

Procedure
1. Use a pan balance to find the mass of an empty 250-mL beaker.
2. Fill the beaker with sliced celery and find the mass of the filled beaker.
3. Estimate the amount of water you think is in the celery.
4. Put the celery on a flat tray. Leave the celery out to dry for one to two days.
5. Allow the celery to cool.
6. Determine the mass of the cooled celery.

Data and Observations

Object	Mass (g)
Empty beaker	
Beaker plus fresh celery	
Beaker plus dried celery	
Amount of water in celery	

Analysis
1. How much water was in the fresh celery?

___

2. **Infer** how much water might be in other fresh fruits and vegetables.

___

Chapter 17
MINILAB 17-2

Determining How Fats Are Emulsified

Procedure
1. Fill two glasses with warm water. Add a large spoonful of cooking oil to each glass.
2. Add a small spoonful of liquid dish-washing detergent to one glass. Stir both glasses.

Analysis
1. Compare what happens to the oil in each glass.

2. How does emulsification change the surface area of the oil drops?

3. How does emulsification speed up digestion?

4. Where in the digestive system does emulsification take place?

5. What is the emulsifier in the digestive system?

Chapter 18
ACTIVITY 18-1

• The Heart as a Pump

Lab Preview

1. How is your pulse related to your heart? _____
   _____

2. Why is it important to know your pulse? _____
   _____

The heart is a pumping organ. Blood is forced through the arteries and causes the muscles of the walls to contract and then relax. This creates a series of waves as the blood flows through the arteries. We call this the pulse. Try this activity to learn about the pulse and the pumping of the heart.

What You'll Investigate
How can you measure heartbeat rate?

Goals
- Observe pulse rate.

Materials
- stopwatch, watch, or clock with a second hand

Procedure
1. **Make** a table like the one shown. Use it to **record** your data.
2. Your partner should sit down and take his or her pulse. You will serve as the recorder.
3. **Find** the pulse rate by placing the middle and index fingers over one of the carotid arteries in the neck. **CAUTION:** *Do not press too hard.*
4. **Calculate** the resulting heart rate. Your partner should count each beat of the carotid pulse silently for 15 s. Multiply the number of beats by four and **record** the number in the data table.
5. Your partner should then jog in place for one minute and take his or her pulse again.
6. **Calculate** this new pulse rate and **record** it in the data table.
7. Reverse roles with your partner. You are now the pulse taker.
8. **Collect** and **record** the new data.

Pulse Rate

Pulse rate	Partner's	Yours
At rest	70	70
After jogging		

97

NAME _____ DATE _____ CLASS _____

Activity (continued)

Conclude and Apply

1. How does the pulse rate change?
   _____
   _____

2. What causes the pulse rate to change?
   _____
   _____

3. What can you **infer** about the heart as a pumping organ?
   _____
   _____

Chapter 18
ACTIVITY 18-2
• Comparing Blood Cells

Lab Preview

1. What makes up the solid part of blood?

   _____

2. What makes up the liquid part of blood?

   _____

Blood is an important tissue for all vertebrates. How do human blood cells compare with those of other vertebrates?

What You'll Investigate
How does human blood compare with the blood of other vertebrates?

Goals
- **Observe** the characteristics of red blood cells, white blood cells, and platelets.
- **Compare** human blood cells with those of other vertebrates.

Safety Precautions

Materials
- prepared slides of human blood
  *photos of human blood
- prepared slides of two other vertebrates' (fish, frog, reptile, bird) blood
  *photos of two other vertebrates' blood
- microscope
  *alternate materials

Procedures

1. Under low power, **examine** the prepared slide of human blood. **Locate** the red blood cells.

2. **Examine** the red blood cells under high power.

3. Make a data table. Draw, count, and **describe** the red blood cells.

4. Move the slide to another position. Find one or two white blood cells. They will be blue or purple due to the stain.

5. Draw, count, and **describe** the white cells in the data table.

6. **Examine** the slide for small fragments that appear blue. These are platelets.

7. Draw, count, and **describe** the platelets on your data table.

8. Follow steps 1 to 7 for each of the other vertebrate cells.

99

Activity (continued)

Data and Observations

Vertebrate type	Blood cell type	Description	Number in field	Drawing
Human	Red			
	White			
	Platelets			
Bird	Red			
	White			
	Platelets			
Frog	Red			
	White			
	Platelets			

Conclude and Apply

1. Does each vertebrate studied have all three cell types?

   _____

2. What might you **infer** about the ability of the different red blood cells to carry oxygen?

   _____
   _____
   _____

3. What is the function of each of the three types of blood cells?

   _____
   _____
   _____

NAME _____ DATE _____ CLASS _____

Chapter 18
MINILAB 18-1

Inferring How Hard the Heart Works

Procedure
1. Take a racquetball and hold it in your outstreched arm.
2. Squeeze the racquetball again and again for one minute.

Analysis
1. How many times did you squeeze the racquetball in one minute? A resting heart beats at approximately 70 beats per minute.

_____
_____
_____

2. What can you do when the muscles of your arm get tired? Explain why cardiac muscle in your heart cannot do the same.

_____
_____
_____

Chapter 18
MINILAB 18-2

Modeling a Blocked Artery

Procedure
1. Insert a dropperful of mineral oil into a piece of clear, narrow, plastic tubing.
2. Squeeze the oil through the tube.
3. Observe how much oil comes out the tube.
4. Next, refill the dropper and squeeze oil through a piece of clear plastic tubing that has been clogged with cotton.

Analysis
1. How much oil comes out of the clogged tube?
   _____
   _____

2. Explain how the addition of the cotton to the tube changed the way the oil flowed through the tube.
   _____
   _____

3. How does this activity demonstrate what takes place when arteries become clogged?
   _____
   _____

Chapter 19
ACTIVITY 19-1

The Effects of Exercise on Respiration

Design Your Own Experiment

Lab Preview

1. What is the function of the respiratory system?

   _____
   _____

2. What is breathing?

   _____
   _____

Breathing rate increases with an increase in physical activity. A bromothymol blue solution changes color when carbon dioxide is bubbled into it. Can you predict whether there will be a difference in the time it takes for the solution to change color before and after exercise?

Recognize the Problem
How will an increase in physical activity affect the amount of carbon dioxide exhaled?

Form a Hypothesis
State a hypothesis about how exercise will affect the amount of carbon dioxide exhaled by the lungs.

Goals
- **Observe** the effects of the amount of carbon dioxide on the bromothymol blue solution.
- **Design** an experiment that tests the effects of a variable, such as the amount of carbon dioxide exhaled before and after exercise, on the rate at which the solution changes color.

Possible Materials
- clock or watch with second hand
- drinking straws
- bromothymol blue solution (200 mL)
- glass cups (12 oz.) (2)
  *beakers (400-mL) (2)
- metric measuring cup
  *graduated cylinder
  *alternate materials

Safety Precautions
Protect clothing from the solution. Wash hands after using the solution. **CAUTION:** *Do not inhale the solution through the straw.*

103

NAME _____ DATE _____ CLASS _____

Activity (continued)

Test Your Hypothesis
Plan

1. As a group, agree upon and **write out** the hypothesis statement.

2. As a group, **list** the steps that you will need to take to test your hypothesis. Consider each of the following factors. How will you introduce the exhaled air into the bromothymol blue solution? How will you collect data on exhaled air before and after physical activity? What kind of activity is involved? How long will it go?

3. **List** your materials. Your teacher will provide instructions on safe procedures for using bromothymol blue.

4. **Design** a data table and **record** it in your Science Journal so that it is ready to use as your group collects data.

5. **Read** over your entire experiment to make sure that all the steps are in logical order.

6. **Identify** any constants, variables, and controls of the experiment.

Do

1. *Make sure your teacher approves your plan before you proceed.*

2. Carry out the experiment as planned.

3. While the experiment is going on, write down any observations that you make and complete the data table in your Science Journal.

Analyze Your Data

1. What caused the bromothymol blue solution to change color? What color was it at the conclusion of each test?
_____

2. What was the control? What was the constant(s)? What was the variable(s)?
_____
_____

3. **Compare** the time it took the bromothymol blue solution to change color before exercise and after exercise. Explain any difference.
_____

4. Prepare a table of your data and **graph** the results.
_____

Draw Conclusions

1. Did exercise affect your rate of respiration? Explain your answer using data from your experiment.
_____
_____

2. Using your graph, **estimate** the time of color change if the time of your physical activity were twice as long.
_____

104 Copyright © Glencoe/McGraw-Hill, a division of The McGraw-Hill Companies, Inc.

NAME   **DATE**   **CLASS**

Chapter 19
ACTIVITY 19-2

• Kidney Structure

Lab Preview

1. What are the safety symbols that you should follow for this activity?

   _____

   _____

2. Why is it important to examine an actual kidney instead of only looking at a drawing?

   _____

   _____

As your body uses nutrients, wastes are created. One role of kidneys is to filter waste products out of the bloodstream and excrete this waste outside the body.

What You'll Investigate
How does the structure of the kidney relate to its function?

Goals
Observe the external and internal structures of a kidney.

Safety Precautions

Materials
- large animal kidney
- scalpel
- hand lens

Procedure
1. **Examine** the kidney supplied by your teacher.
2. If the kidney is still encased in fat, **peel** the fat off carefully.
3. Using a scalpel, carefully **cut** the tissue lengthwise in half around the outline of the kidney. This cut should result in a section similar to the illustrations in your text.
4. **Observe** the internal features of the kidney using a hand lens, or view the features in a model.
5. **Compare** the specimen or model with the kidneys in the illustrations.
6. **Draw** the kidney in your Science Journal, and **label** the structures.

105

Activity (continued)

Conclude and Apply

1. What part makes up the cortex of the kidney? Why is this part red?

2. What is the main function of nephrons?

3. The medulla of the kidney is made up of a network of tubules that come together to form the ureter. What is the function of this network of tubules?

4. How can the kidney be compared to a portable water-purifying system?

Chapter 19
MINILAB 19-1

Measuring Surface Area

Procedure
1. Make a cylinder out of a large sheet of paper. Tape it together.
2. Make cylinders out of small sheets of paper. Place as many as will fit inside the large cylinder without crushing the cylinders.
3. Unroll each cylinder. Place the small sheets next to each other in a rectangle. Lay the large sheet on top.

Analysis
1. Compare the surface area of the large sheet with all the small sheets put together.

2. What do the large sheet and small sheets represent?

3. How does this make gas exchange more efficient?

Chapter 19
MINILAB 19-2

Modeling Kidney Function

Procedure
1. Mix a small amount of soil with water in a cup to make muddy water.
2. Place a funnel into a second clean cup.
3. Place a piece of filter paper into the funnel.
4. Carefully pour the muddy water into the funnel.

Analysis
Compare this filtering process to the function of kidneys inside your body.

_____
_____
_____

Chapter 20
ACTIVITY 20-1

• Reaction Time

Lab Preview

1. What are two major divisions of the human nervous system? _____

2. Which system is used when the body reacts to a stimulus? _____

Your body responds quickly to some kinds of stimuli, and reflexes allow you to react quickly, without even thinking. Sometimes you can improve how quickly you react. Complete this activity to see if you can improve your reaction time.

What You'll Investigate
How can reaction time be improved?

Goals
- **Observe** reflexes.
- **Identify** stimuli and responses.

Materials
- metric ruler

Procedure
1. Review the data table below.
2. Have a partner hold the ruler at the top end.
3. Hold the thumb and finger of your right hand apart at the bottom of the ruler. Do not touch the ruler.
4. Your partner must let go of the ruler without warning you.
5. Try to catch the ruler by bringing your thumb and finger together quickly.
6. Repeat this activity several times and **record** in a data table where the ruler was caught.
7. Repeat this activity with your left hand. **Record** your results.

Where the Ruler Was Caught		
Trial	Right Hand	Left Hand
1		
2		
3		

109

Activity (continued)

Conclude and Apply

1. Identify the stimulus in each activity.

2. Identify the response in each activity.

3. Identify the variable in each activity.

4. Compare the responses of your writing hand and your other hand for both activities.

5. What was your average reaction time for your right hand? For your left hand?

6. **Compare** the response of your writing hand and your other hand for this activity.

7. **Draw a conclusion** about how practice relates to stimulus-response time.

Chapter 20
ACTIVITY 20-2

Investigating Skin Sensitivity

Design Your Own Experiment

Lab Preview
1. What safety symbols are associated with this activity? _____
   _____

2. Where are the receptors that allow you to sense touch located in the skin? _____
   _____

Your body responds to touch, pressure, and temperature. Not all parts of your body are equally sensitive to stimuli. Some areas are more sensitive than others. For example, your lips are sensitive to heat. This protects you from burning your mouth. Now think about touch. How sensitive is the skin on various parts of your body to touch? Which areas can distinguish the smallest amount of distance between stimuli?

Recognize the Problem
What areas of the body are more sensitive to touch?

Form a Hypothesis
Based on your experiences, state a hypothesis about which five areas of the body you believe to be more sensitive than others. Rank the areas from 5 (the most sensitive) to 1 (the least sensitive).

Goals
- **Observe** the sensitivity to touch on various areas of the body.
- **Design an experiment** that tests the effects of a variable, such as the closeness of contact points, to determine which body areas can distinguish between the closest stimuli.

Safety Precautions
Do not apply heavy pressure when using the toothpicks.

Possible Materials
- index cards (3-in. × 5-in.)
- toothpicks
- glue or tape
- metric ruler

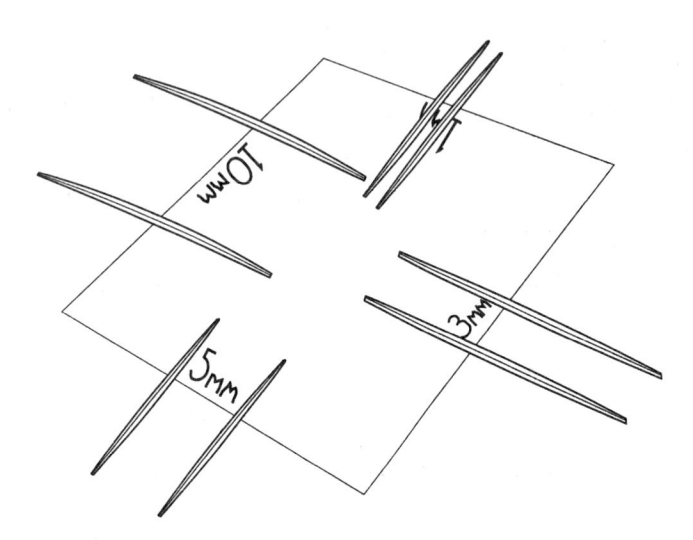

Activity (continued)

Test Your Hypothesis
Plan
1. As a group, agree upon and write out the hypothesis statement.
2. As a group, **list** the steps you need to take to test your hypothesis. Be very specific in describing exactly what you will do at each step. Consider the following factors as you list the steps. How will you know that sight is not a factor? How will you use the card shown on the preceding page to determine **sensitivity** to touch? How will you **determine** and **record** that one or both points of touch are felt? List your materials.
3. **Design** a data table in your Science Journal.
4. **Read** over your entire experiment to make sure that all steps are in order.
5. **Identify** any constants, variables, and controls of the experiment.

Do
1. Make sure your teacher approves the plan before you proceed.
2. **Carry out** the experiment as planned.
3. While the experiment is going on, **write down** any observations that you make and complete the data table in your Science Journal.

Analyze Your Data
1. **Compare** your results with those of other groups.
   _____
   _____

2. **Identify** which part of the body tested can distinguish between the closest stimuli.
   _____

3. **Identify** which part of the body is least sensitive.
   _____

4. **Rank** body parts tested from most to least sensitive. How did your test results **compare** with your hypothesis?
   _____
   _____

Draw Conclusions
1. Based on your answers to questions 2 and 3, what can you **infer** about the distribution of touch receptors in the skin?
   _____
   _____
   _____

2. What other parts of your body would you **predict** to be less sensitive? Explain your predictions.
   _____
   _____

NAME DATE CLASS

Chapter 20
MINILAB 20-1

Observing Balance Control

Procedure
1. Place two narrow strips of paper on the wall to form two parallel vertical lines. Have a student stand between them, as still and straight as possible without leaning on the wall, for three minutes.
2. Observe how well balance is maintained.
3. Have the student close his or her eyes and repeat standing within the lines for three minutes.

Analysis
1. When was balance more difficult to maintain?

___

2. What other factors might cause a person to lose the sense of balance?

___

Chapter 20
MINILAB 20-2

Comparing Sense of Smell

Procedure
1. Design an experiment to test your classmates' abilities to recognize the odors of different foods, colognes, or household products.
2. Record their responses in a data table according to the gender of the individuals tested.

Data and Observations

Male/Female	Substance	Responses

Analysis
1. Compare the numbers of correctly identified odors for both males and females.

2. What can you conclude about the differences between males and females in their ability to recognize odors?

NAME _____ DATE _____ CLASS _____

Chapter 21

ACTIVITY 21-1

Interpreting Diagrams

Lab Preview
1. What happens during menstruation? _____
   _____
2. At what age does menstruation usually begin? _____
   _____

Starting in adolescence, the hormone estrogen causes changes in the uterus. These changes prepare the uterus to accept a fertilized egg that may embed itself in the uterine wall.

What You'll Investigate
What happens to the uterus during a female's monthly cycle?

Materials
- paper and pencil

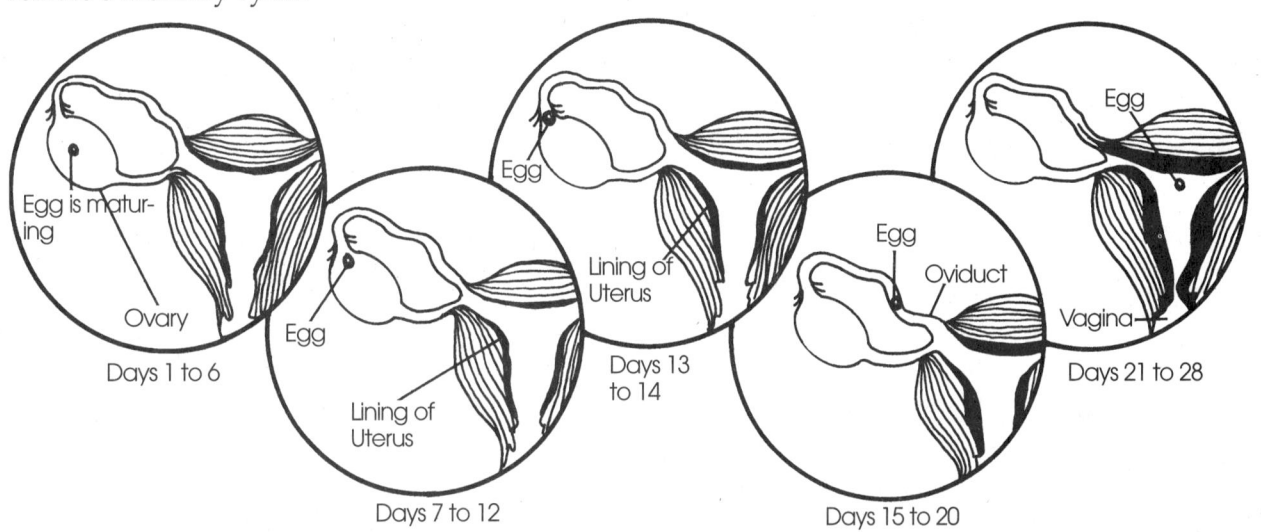

Days 1 to 6 — Egg is maturing, Ovary

Days 7 to 12 — Egg, Lining of Uterus

Days 13 to 14 — Egg, Lining of Uterus

Days 15 to 20 — Egg, Oviduct

Days 21 to 28 — Egg, Vagina

Goals
- **Observe** the stages in a diagram of the menstrual cycle.
- **Relate** the process of ovulation to the cycle.

Procedure
1. The diagrams above show what is explained in the previous section on the menstrual cycle.
2. **Study** the diagrams and their labels.
3. **Use** the information in the previous section and the diagrams above to complete a table like the one shown.
4. **How** are the diagrams different?
5. On approximately what day in a 28-day cycle is egg released from the ovary?

Menstruation Cycle

Days	Condition of uterus	What happens
1–6		
7–12		
13–14		
15–28		

Copyright © Glencoe/McGraw-Hill, a division of The McGraw-Hill Companies, Inc.

NAME	DATE	CLASS

Activity (continued)

Conclude and Apply
1. How long is the average menstrual cycle? _____
2. How many days does menstruation usually last? _____
3. On what days does the lining of the uterus build up? _____
4. **Infer** why this process is called a cycle. _____
   _____
   _____
5. **Calculate** how many days before menstruation ovulation usually occurs. _____
6. **Interpret** the diagram to explain the menstrual cycle. _____
   _____
   _____

Chapter 21
ACTIVITY 21-2
Average Growth Rate in Humans

Lab Preview
1. What are the five stages of growth described in Chapter 21?
   _____
2. What is puberty? _____
   _____

An individual's growth is dependent upon both the effects of hormones and his or her genetic makeup.

What You'll Investigate
Is average growth rate the same in males and females?

Goals
- **Analyze** the average growth rate of young males and females.
- **Compare and contrast** their growth rates.

Materials
- graph paper
- red and blue pencils

Procedure
1. **Construct** a graph similar to graph A. **Plot** mass on the vertical axis and age on the horizontal axis.
2. **Plot** the data given under Data and Observations for the average female growth in mass from ages eight to 18. **Connect** the points with a red line.
3. On the same graph, **plot** the data for the average male growth in mass from ages eight to 18. **Connect** the points with a blue line.
4. **Construct** a separate graph similar to graph B. **Plot** height on the vertical axis and age on the horizontal axis.
5. **Plot** the data for the average female growth in height from ages eight to 18. **Connect** the points with a red line. **Plot** the data for the average male growth in height from ages eight to 18. **Connect** the points with a blue line.

Averages for Growth in Humans		
Age	Mass (kg)	
	Female	Male
8	25	25
9	28	28
10	31	31
11	35	37
12	40	38
13	47	43
14	50	50
15	54	57
16	57	62
17	58	65
18	58	68

Averages for Growth in Humans		
Age	Height (cm)	
	Female	Male
8	123	124
9	129	130
10	135	135
11	140	140
12	147	145
13	155	152
14	159	161
15	160	167
16	163	172
17	163	174
18	163	178

Activity (continued)

Data and Observations

Conclude and Apply

1. Up to what age is average growth in mass similar in males and females?

2. Up to what age is average growth in height similar in males and females?

3. When does the mass of females generally change most?

4. How can you explain the differences in growth between males and females?

5. **Interpret** the data to find whether the average growth rate is the same in males and females.

Chapter 21
MINILAB 21-1

Interpreting Embryo Development

Procedure
1. Interpret the data in the table of embryo development below.
2. On a piece of paper, draw a line the length of the unborn baby at each date.
3. Using reference materials, find out what developmental events happen at each date.

End of month	Length
3	8 cm
4	15 cm
5	25 cm
6	30 cm
7	35 cm
8	40 cm
9	51 cm

Data and Observations

Age (mos.)	Developmental Events
3	
4	
5	
6	
7	
8	
9	

Analysis
1. During which month does the greatest increase in length occur?

_____

2. What size is the unborn baby when movement can be felt by the mother?

_____

_____

Chapter 21
MINILAB 21-2

Investigating Immunizations

Procedure
1. Find out what immunizations are usually given to babies and young children.
2. Compare these to what vaccines are required for children to enter your school.

Analysis
1. What booster shots are given to school children?

   _____
   _____

2. Investigate what immunizations are required to travel to foreign countries.

   _____
   _____
   _____

Chapter 22
ACTIVITY 22-1

• Microorganisms and Disease

Lab Preview
1. Which safety symbols are associated with this activity? _____
   _____
2. Read the procedure below. What is the source of microorganisms in this activity? _____
   _____

Microorganisms are all around us. They are on the surfaces of everything we touch. Try this experiment to see how microorganisms are involved in spreading infections.

What You'll Investigate
How do microorganisms cause infection?

Goals
- **Observe** the transmission of microorganisms.
- **Relate** microorganisms to infections.

Materials
- fresh apples (6)
- rotting apple
- alcohol (5 mL)
- self-sealing plastic bags (6)
- labels and pencil
- paper towels
- sandpaper
- cotton ball
- soap and water

Procedure
1. **Label** the plastic bags 1 through 6. **Put** a fresh apple in bag 1 and seal it.
2. **Rub** the rotting apple over the entire surface of the remaining five apples. This is your source of microorganisms. **CAUTION:** *Always wash your hands after handling microorganisms.* **Put** one apple in bag 2.
3. **Hold** one apple 1.5 m above the floor and drop it. **Put** this apple into bag number 3.
4. **Rub** one apple with sandpaper. **Place** this apple in bag number 4.
5. **Wash** one apple with soap and water. **Dry** it well. **Put** this apple in bag number 5.
6. **Use** a cotton ball to spread alcohol over the last apple. Let it air dry. Place it in bag number 6.
7. **Place** all of the apples in a dark place for three days. Then, wash your hands.
8. **Write** a **hypothesis** to explain what you think will happen to each apple.
9. At the end of three days and again on day 7, **compare** all of the apples. **Record** your observations in the following data table. **CAUTION:** *Give all apples to your teacher for proper disposal.*

121

Activity (continued)

Apple Data

Apple	Condition of the apple	Observations Day 3	Day 7
1	Fresh apple		
2	Untreated apple		
3	Dropped apple		
4	Apple rubbed with sandpaper		
5	Apple washed with soap and water		
6	Apple covered with alcohol		

Conclude and Apply

1. Did you **observe** changes in apples number 5 and 6?

2. Why is it important to clean a wound?

3. Were your hypotheses supported?

4. **Relate** microorganisms to infections on your skin.

NAME _____ DATE _____ CLASS _____

Chapter 22
ACTIVITY 22-2

Microorganism Growth

Design Your Own Experiment

Lab Preview
1. What safety symbols are associated with this activity? _____
   _____
   _____

2. What could you use as a source of microorganisms in this activity? _____
   _____

Infections are caused by microorganisms. Without cleanliness, the risk of getting an infection from a wound is high. Disinfectants are chemicals that kill or remove disease organisms from objects. Antiseptics are chemicals that kill or prevent growth of disease organisms on living tissues. You will test the effect of these chemicals by growing microorganisms in petri dishes filled with agar. Agar is a gel that provides the ideal nutrients for growing microorganisms.

Recognize the Problem
What conditions do microorganisms need to grow? How can they be prevented from growing?

Form a Hypothesis
Based on your knowledge of disinfectants and antiseptics, **state a hypothesis** about methods that will prevent the growth of microorganisms.

Goals
- **Observe** the effects of antiseptics and disinfectants on microorganism growth in petri dishes.
- **Design** an experiment that will test the effects of chemicals on microorganisms growing in contaminated petri dishes.

Safety Precautions

Handle the forceps carefully. When you complete the experiment, give your sealed petri dishes to your teacher for proper disposal.

Possible Materials
- sterile petri dishes with agar (5)
- filter paper (2-cm squares)
- test chemicals (disinfectant, hydrogen peroxide, mouthwash, alcohol)
- transparent tape
- pencil and labels
- scissors
- metric ruler
- forceps
- small jars for chemicals (4)
- cotton balls

Copyright © Glencoe/McGraw-Hill, a division of The McGraw-Hill Companies, Inc.

123

Activity (continued)

Test Your Hypothesis
Plan
1. As a group, agree upon and write out a hypothesis statement.
2. To test disinfectants, first introduce microorganisms to the agar by rubbing your finger gently over each dish. Then, soak a different square of filter paper in each of the disinfectants. Place each square on the agar and seal the dishes with tape. Never break the seal. Look for bacteria growth under and around each square.
3. As a group, list the steps that you will need to take to test your hypothesis. Consider what you learned about how infections are stopped. **List** your materials.
4. **Design** a data table and record it in your Science Journal so that it is ready to use as your group collects data.
5. Read over your entire experiment to make sure that all steps are in logical order.
6. **Identify** any **constants, variables,** and the **control** of the experiment.

Do
1. Make sure your teacher approves your plan before you proceed.
2. Carry out the experiment as planned.
3. While the experiment is going on, write down any **observations** that you make and complete the **data table** in your Science Journal.

Analyze Your Data
1. **Compare** your results with those of other groups.

2. How did you **compare** growth beneath and around each chemical-soaked square in the petri dishes?

3. **Interpret the data** to determine what substances appeared to be most effective in preventing microorganism growth. What substances appeared to be least effective?

Draw Conclusions
1. What methods prevent the growth of microorganisms?

2. How does the growth of microorganisms on the control compare with their growth on the variables?

Chapter 22
MINILAB 22-1

Detecting Bacteria

Procedure
1. Methylene blue is used to detect bacteria. The faster the color fades, the more bacteria are present.
2. Use the food samples provided by your teacher. Label four test tubes 1, 2, 3, and 4.
3. Fill three test tubes half full of the food samples.
4. Fill the fourth with water.
5. Add 20 drops of methylene blue and 2 drops of mineral oil to each tube.
6. Place the tubes into a warm-water bath for 20 minutes.
7. Record the time and your observations.

Data and Observations

Test Tube	Food Sample	Time	Observation
1			
2			
3			
4	water		

Analysis
1. Compare how long it takes each tube to lose its color.

   _____
   _____

2. What was the purpose of tube 4?

   _____
   _____

3. Why is it important to eat and drink only the freshest food?

   _____
   _____
   _____
   _____

Chapter 22
MINILAB 22-2

Determining Reproduction Rates

Procedure
1. Make a chart like the one below.
2. Complete the chart up to the fifth hour. Assume that the bacteria divide every 20 minutes if conditions are favorable.
3. Graph your data.

Data and Observations

Time	Number of Bacteria	Time	Number of Bacteria
0 hours 0 minutes	1	3 hours 0 minutes	
20 minutes	2	20 minutes	
40 minutes	4	40 minutes	
1 hour 0 minutes	8	4 hours 0 minutes	
20 minutes	16	20 minutes	
40 minutes	32	40 minutes	
2 hours 0 minutes		5 hours 0 minutes	
20 minutes		20 minutes	
40 Minutes		40 minutes	

Analysis
1. How many bacteria are present after five hours?

2. Why is it important to take antibiotics promptly if you have an infection?

Chapter 23
ACTIVITY 23-1

Reflection from a Plane Mirror

Lab Preview

1. Do the properties of a reflecting surface change the way a light ray is reflected?
   _____
   _____

2. What is a plane mirror? _____
   _____

A light ray strikes the surface of a plane mirror and is reflected. Is there a relationship between the direction of the incoming light ray and the direction of the reflected light ray?

What You'll Investigate
How does the angle of incidence compare with the angle of reflection for a plane mirror?

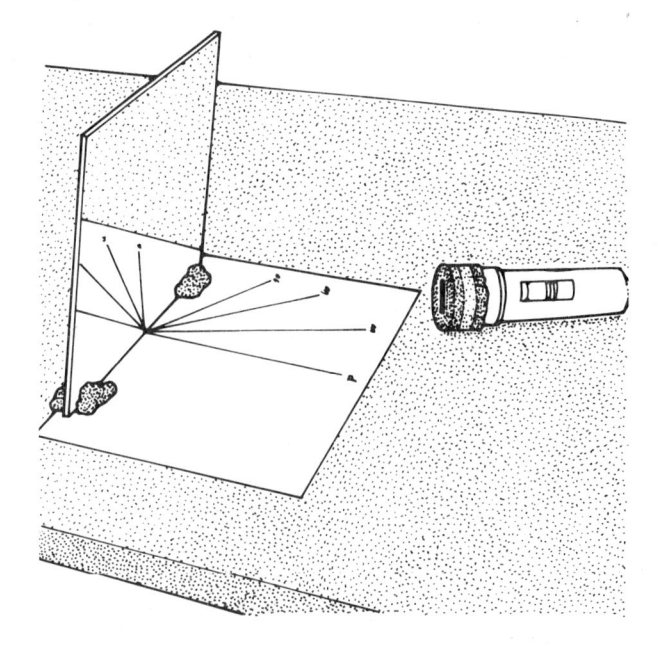

Goals
- **Measure** the angle of incidence and the angle of reflection for a light ray incident on a plane mirror.

Materials
- flashlight
- small plane mirror, at least 10 cm on a side
- protractor
- metric ruler
- scissors
- black construction paper
- tape
- modeling clay

Procedure
1. With the scissors, **cut** a slit in the construction paper and **tape** it over the flashlight lens. Make sure the slit is centered on the lens.
2. **Place** the mirror at one end of the unlined paper. Push the mirror into the lump of clay so it stands vertically, and tilt the mirror so it leans slightly toward the table.
3. **Measure** with the ruler to find the center of the bottom edge of the mirror and mark it. Then, use the protractor and the ruler to **draw** a line on the paper perpendicular to the mirror from the mark. Label this line P.
4. Using the protractor and the ruler, **draw** lines on the paper outward from the mark at the center of the mirror at angles of 30°, 45°, and 60° to line P.
5. Turn on the flashlight and place it so the beam is along the 60° line. This is the angle of incidence. **Locate** the reflected beam on the paper, and **measure** the angle the reflected beam makes with line P. **Record** this angle in your data table. This is the angle of reflection. If you cannot see the reflected beam, slightly increase the tilt of the mirror.

127

Activity (continued)

Data Table—Reflection in Plane Mirrors

Angle of incidence	Angle of reflection
0°	
30°	
45°	
60°	

6. Repeat step 5 for the 30° and 45° lines.

Conclude and Apply

1. What happened to the beam of light when it was shone along line P?

_____

_____

2. What can you **infer** about the relationship between the angle of incidence and the angle of reflection?

_____

_____

Chapter 23

ACTIVITY 23-2

Image Formation by a Convex Lens

Lab Preview

1. What is a convex (or converging) lens?
   _____
   _____

2. If an object is closer than one focal length to a convex lens, how will the image's size compare to the size of the object? Will the image be upside-down or right-side-up?
   _____
   _____

The type of image formed by a convex lens or a converging lens is related to the distance of the object from the lens. This distance is called the object distance. The location of the image is also related to the distance of the object from the lens. The distance from the lens to the image is called the image distance. What happens to the position of the image as the object gets nearer or farther from the lens?

What You'll Investigate
How are the image distance and object distance related for a convex lens?

Goals
- **Measure** the image distance as the object distance changes.
- **Observe** the type of image formed as the object distance changes.

Safety Precautions

Materials
- convex lens
- modeling clay
- meterstick
- flashlight
- masking tape
- cardboard with white surface, about 20-cm square

Procedure

1. **Design** a data table in which to record your data. You will need three columns in your table. One column will be for the object distance, another will be for the image distance, and the third will be for the type of image.

2. **Use** the modeling clay to make the lens stand vertically upright on the lab table.

3. **Form** the letter F on the glass surface of the flashlight with masking tape.

4. Turn on the flashlight and place it 1 m from the lens. **Position** the flashlight so the flashlight beam is shining through the lens.

5. **Record** the distance from the flashlight to the lens in the object distance column in your data table.

6. Hold the cardboard vertically upright on the other side of the lens, and move it back and forth until a sharp image of the letter F is obtained.

7. **Measure** the distance of the card from the lens using the meterstick, and **record** this distance in the image distance column in your data table.

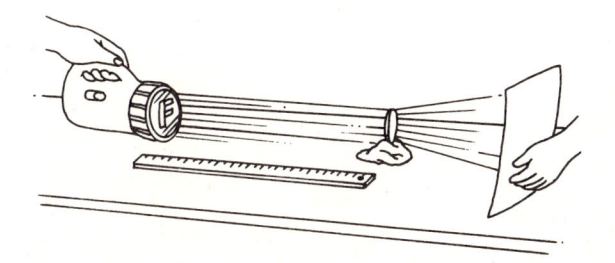

Activity (continued)

8. **Record** in the third column of your data table whether the image is upright or inverted, and smaller or larger.

9. Repeat steps 6–9 for an object distance of 50 cm and 25 cm.

Data and Observations

Conclude and Apply

1. How did the image distance change as the object distance decreased?
   _____
   _____

2. How did the image change as the object distance decreased?
   _____
   _____

3. What would happen to the size of the image if the flashlight were much farther away than 1 m?
   _____
   _____
   _____

NAME _____ DATE _____ CLASS _____

Chapter 23
MINILAB 23-1

Viewing Colors Through Color Filters

Procedure

1. Obtain sheets of red, green, and blue construction paper.
2. Obtain a piece of red cellophane and green cellophane.
3. Look at each sheet of paper through the red cellophane and record the color of each sheet.

   _____

4. Look at each sheet of colored paper through the green cellophane and record the color of each sheet.

   _____

5. Hold both pieces of cellophane together and look at each sheet of colored paper. Record the color of each sheet.

   _____

Analysis
Explain why the sheets of paper changed color when you looked at them through the pieces of cellophane.

_____

_____

Chapter 23
MINILAB 23-2

Forming an Image with a Lens

Procedure

1. Fill a glass test tube with water and seal it with a stopper.

2. Write your name on a 3 × 5 card. Lay the test tube on the card and observe the appearance of your name. Record your observations.

   _____
   _____

3. Hold the test tube about 1 cm above the card and observe the appearance of your name. Record your observations.

   _____
   _____

4. Now, observe what happens to your name as you slowly move the test tube away from the card. Record your observations.

   _____
   _____

Analysis

1. Is the water-filled test tube a concave lens or a convex lens?

   _____

2. Compare the image formed when the test tube was close to the card with the image formed when the test tube was far from the card.

   _____
   _____
   _____

Chapter 24
ACTIVITY 24-1

• Time Trials

Lab Preview

1. Explain why making observations and predictions is an important part of scientific investigations. _____

2. If a prediction is proven incorrect for an experiment, should the experiment be considered a failure? _____

Before a big car race, all the contestants must pass the time trials. Time trials are races against the clock instead of against other cars.

What You'll Investigate
Can time trials be used to predict the winner of a race?

Goals
- **Conduct** time trials.
- **Test** speed and distance predictions from the results of time trials.

Materials
- metersticks (2)
- stopwatch or watch that measures in seconds
- toy cars
- masking tape

Procedure
1. **Set up** a straightaway using two metersticks as curbs. Use the tape to make a starting line at the beginning of the track.

2. **Test** the track with one car. If the car runs into the metersticks, move them farther apart or devise some other remedy.

3. Wind up or push the first car, starting with the front of the car on zero of the meterstick. Time its trip to the end of the metersticks.

4. Repeat this at least three times for each car, and **record** your distance and time measurements in a table on the next page.

5. **Calculate** the average time and distance.

6. **Calculate** the average speed using the averages for the time and distance.

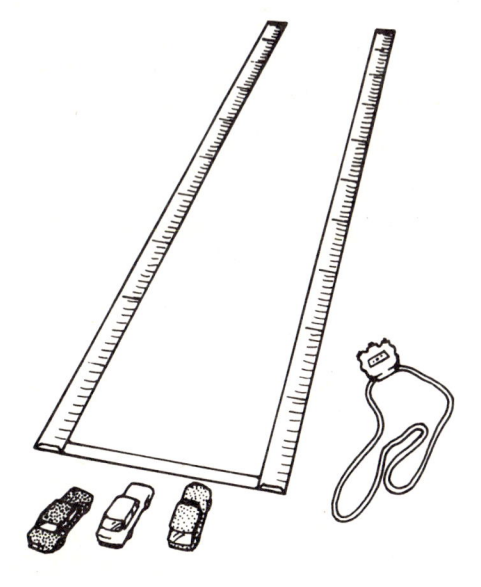

133

Activity (continued)

Time Trials Data

Car	Time (s)	Distance (m)
Trial 1		
Trial 2		
Trial 3		
Average		

Conclude and Apply

1. **Compare** the average speed of your car with those of your classmates.
   _____
   _____

2. **Predict** which car should win a 1-m race based on the time trials. Test your prediction.
   _____
   _____

3. **Predict** which car will travel farthest based on your measurements and observations. Test your prediction.
   _____
   _____
   _____

4. **Explain** whether time trials accurately predict which car will win the race. Were you able to predict which car would travel the farthest? **Explain** why or why not.
   _____
   _____

Chapter 24
MINILAB 24-1

Inferring Free Fall

Procedure
1. Attach a clothespin to either side of a rubber band. If the rubber band has bends, put the clothespins elsewhere on the band.
2. Hold one clothespin. Observe the shape of the band.
3. Drop the clothespin and observe the shape of the band as it falls.

Analysis
1. What did the rubber band look like as it fell? What does the shape mean?

   _____
   _____
   _____
   _____

2. Did the clothespins still have weight when they were falling? Why or why not?

   _____
   _____
   _____
   _____

Chapter 24
MINILAB 24-2

Measuring Friction

Procedure

1. Use your ring binder or a book for a slope.
2. Place a metal washer on the cover. Slowly lift the cover and stop when the washer just starts to move. Measure this angle with a protractor.
3. Repeat step 2 with a rubber washer.
4. Change the surface of your binder by taping a piece of plain, waxed, or sandpaper to it. Repeat steps 2 and 3.

Analysis

1. Which surface required the smallest angle to get the washer to move? What makes this combination different from the others?

2. What could you do to make the angle even smaller?

3. Compare and contrast the friction of the metal and rubber washers.

Chapter 25
ACTIVITY 25-1

Building the Pyramids

Lab Preview

1. In a scientific sense, what is positive work? Give an example. _____
   _____
   _____

2. How is work measured? What units are used? _____
   _____
   _____

The workers who built the Great Pyramid at Giza needed to move 2.3 million blocks of limestone. Each block weighed more than 1 metric ton. The designers knew how to use ramps to reduce the force needed to lift the blocks into place.

What You'll Investigate
How does the force needed to lift a block a certain height depend on the distance traveled?

Goals
- **Model** the method that was probably used to build the pyramids.
- **Compare** the force needed to lift a block straight up with the force needed to pull it up a ramp.

Materials
- wood block
- tape
- spring scale
- ruler
- 3-ring binder
- books
- meterstick

Procedure
1. Use a pile of books to **model** a half-completed pyramid. **Measure** the height.

2. The wooden block **models** a block of stone. Attach it to the spring scale and **measure** the force needed to lift it straight up the side of the books.

3. Use a binder to **model** a ramp. **Measure** the ramp. **Measure** the force needed to pull the block up the ramp. Be sure to pull parallel to the ramp. Repeat the experiment with at least two other ramp lengths. Fill in the table.

Ramp Data

Distance (cm)	Force (N)	Work (J)
40		
30		

Copyright © Glencoe/McGraw-Hill, a division of The McGraw-Hill Companies, Inc.

137

Activity (continued)

Conclude and Apply

1. What happens to the force needed as the distance increases?

2. **Compare and contrast** your results for each case.

3. **Calculate** the work in each case.

4. How could you modify your setup to use less force?

Chapter 25
ACTIVITY 25-2

Pulley Power
Design Your Own Experiment

Lab Preview

1. What is a pulley?

2. Why is it important to use safety goggles and to be careful when using a pulley?

It would have taken decades to build the Sears Tower without the aid of a pulley system attached to a crane. Hoisting the 1-ton I beams to a maximum height of 110 stories required tremendous lifting forces and precise control of the beam's movement.

Recognize the Problem
How can you use a pulley system to reduce the force needed to lift a load?

Form a Hypothesis
Write a hypothesis about how pulleys can be combined to make a system of pulleys to lift a heavy load, such as a building block. Consider the efficiency of your system.

Goals
- **Design** a pulley system.
- **Measure** the mechanical advantage and efficiency of the pulley system.

Safety Precautions
The brick could be dangerous if it falls. Don't stand under it.

Possible Materials
- single- and multiple-pulley systems
- nylon rope
- steel bar to support the pulley system
- meterstick
  * *metric tape measure*
- variety of weights to test pulleys
- force spring scale
- a brick
- balance or scale
  alternate materials

139

Activity (continued)

Test Your Hypothesis
Plan
1. **Decide** how you are going to support your pulley system.
2. How will you measure the effort force and the resistance force? How will you determine the mechanical advantage? How will you measure efficiency?

   _____
   _____

3. Experiment by lifting small weights with a single pulley, double pulley, and so on. How efficient are the pulleys?

4. Use the results of step 3 to **design** a pulley system to lift the building block.

Do
1. Make sure your teacher has approved your plan before you proceed.
2. **Assemble** the pulley system you designed. You may want to **test** it with a smaller weight before attaching the brick.
3. **Measure** the force needed to lift the brick. How much rope must you pull to raise the brick 10 cm?

Analyze Your Data
1. **Calculate** the theoretical mechanical advantage of your pulley system. (You can refer to the *Field Guild to Machines* at the end of this chapter.)

   _____
   _____

2. **Calculate** the actual mechanical advantage of your pulley system.

   _____
   _____

3. **Calculate** the efficiency of your pulley system.

   _____
   _____

Draw Conclusions
1. **Explain** how increasing the number of pulleys increases the mechanical advantage.

   _____
   _____

2. How could you modify the pulley system to lift a weight twice as heavy with the same effort force used here?

   _____
   _____

3. **Compare** this real machine with an ideal machine.

   _____
   _____

NAME _____ DATE _____ CLASS _____

Chapter 25
MINILAB 25-1

Measuring Work and Power

Procedure
1. Measure the mass of a book.
2. Go to a ramp or stairway. Measure the vertical height of the ramp or stairs.
3. Time yourself walking slowly up with the book.
4. Time yourself running quickly up with the book.

Analysis
1. Calculate and compare the work done on the book in each case.

   _____

2. Calculate and compare the power used to lift the book in each case.

   _____

3. Would it always require twice as much power to lift twice as much mass up the stairs? Explain.

   _____

Chapter 25
MINILAB 25-2

Observing Mechanical Advantage—Pulleys

Procedure
1. Give broomsticks or dowels to two students to hold. Tie a 3-m long rope to the middle of one stick. Wrap the rope around both sticks four times, leaving about 0.5-m gap between the sticks. The broomsticks are now pulleys.
2. Give the end of the rope to a third student.
3. While the two students pull the broomsticks apart, have the third student pull on the rope.
4. Observe what happens. Repeat using only two wraps of the rope and then using eight wraps.

Analysis
1. Describe what you observed. Could the students hold the stick apart?

   _____
   _____
   _____

2. Compare and contrast the results with two, four, and eight turns of the rope around the pulleys.

   _____
   _____
   _____

3. With four turns of the rope, what length of rope must be pulled to move the pulleys 10 cm closer together? What is the mechanical advantage of this pulley system?

   _____
   _____
   _____

Chapter 26
ACTIVITY 26-1
A Model for Voltage and Current

Lab Preview
1. What safety symbols are associated with this activity?

   _____

2. What is the unit of measure of electric potential energy?

   _____

The flow of electrons in an electric circuit is something like the flow of water. By raising or lowering the height of a water tank, you can increase or decrease the potential energy of the water. In this activity, you will use a water system to investigate how the flow of water in a tube depends on the height of the water and the diameter of the tube the water flows through.

What You'll Investigate
How is the flow of water through a tube affected by changing the height of a container of water and the diameter of the tube?

Goals
- **Make a model** for the flow of current in a simple circuit.

Materials
- plastic funnel
- rubber or plastic tubing of different diameters (1 m each)
- meterstick
- ring stand with ring
- stop watch
  *clock displaying seconds
- hose clamp
  *clothespin
- beakers (500-mL) (2)
  *alternate materials

Procedure
1. **Design** a data table similar to the example on the next page in which to record your data.

2. **Connect** the tubing to the bottom of the funnel and place the funnel in the ring of the ring stand.

3. **Measure** the diameter of the rubber tubing. **Record** your data.

4. Place a 500-mL beaker at the bottom of the ring stand, and lower the ring so the open end of the tubing is in the beaker.

5. Use the meterstick to **measure** the height from the top of the funnel to the bottom of the ring stand. **Record** your data.

6. **Pour** water into the funnel fast enough to keep the funnel full but not overflowing. **Measure** the time needed for 100-mL of water to flow into the beaker. Use the hose clamp to start and stop the flow of water. **Record** your data.

7. **Connect** tubing with a different diameter to the funnel and repeat steps 2–6.

8. **Reconnect** the original piece of tubing and repeat steps 4–6 for several lower positions of the funnel, lowering the height by 10 cm each time.

9. **Calculate** the rate of flow for each trial by dividing 100-mL by the measured time.

143

Activity (continued)

Flow Rate Data

Trial number	Height (cm)	Diameter of tubing (cm)	Time (s)	Rate of flow (mL/s)
1				
2				
3				
4				

Conclude and Apply

1. **Make a graph** to show how the rate of flow depends on the funnel height.

2. How does the rate of flow depend on the diameter of the tubing?

3. Which of the variables that you changed in your trials corresponds to the voltage in a circuit? Which variable corresponds to the resistance in a circuit? What part of a circuit would the hose clamp correspond to?

4. Based on your results, how would the current in a circuit depend on the voltage? How would the current depend on the resistance?

NAME _____ DATE _____ CLASS _____

Chapter 26
ACTIVITY 26-2

• Current in a Parallel Circuit

Lab Preview

1. Describe a series circuit.
   _____
   _____

2. Describe a parallel circuit.
   _____
   _____
   _____

In this activity you will investigate how the current in a circuit changes when two or more lightbulbs are connected in parallel. Because the brightness of a lightbulb increases or decreases as more or less current flows through it, the brightness of the bulbs in the circuits can be used to determine which circuit has more current.

What You'll Investigate
How does connecting devices in series or parallel affect the electric current in a circuit?

Goals
- **Observe** how the current in a parallel circuit changes as more devices are added.

Safety Precautions

Materials
- lightbulbs (1.5V) (4)
- batteries (1.5V) (2)
- pieces of insulated wire, each about 10 cm long (8)
- battery holders (2)
- minibulb sockets (4)

Procedure
1. **Connect** one lightbulb to the battery in a complete circuit. After you've made the bulb light, disconnect the bulb from the battery to keep the battery from running down. This series circuit will be the brightness tester.

2. **Make** a parallel circuit by connecting two bulbs together as shown in the diagram. **Reconnect** the bulb in the brightness tester and compare its brightness with the brightness of the two bulbs in the parallel circuit. **Record** your observations.

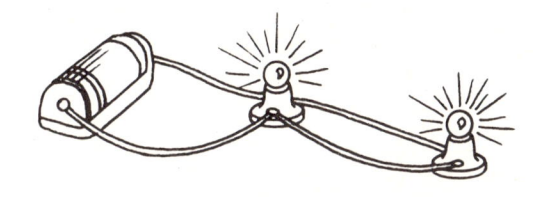

   _____
   _____
   _____
   _____

3. Add another bulb to the parallel circuit as shown in the figure. How does the brightness of the bulbs change? **Record** your observations.

   _____
   _____
   _____

Copyright © Glencoe/McGraw-Hill, a division of The McGraw-Hill Companies, Inc.

NAME	DATE	CLASS

Activity (continued)

4. **Disconnect** one bulb in the parallel circuit. What happens to the brightness of the remaining bulbs?

   _____

   _____

   _____

Conclude and Apply

1. Compared to the brightness tester, is the current in the parallel circuit more or less?

   _____

   _____

2. How does adding additional devices affect the current in a parallel circuit?

   _____

   _____

3. Are the electric circuits in your house wired in series or parallel? How do you know?

   _____

   _____

   _____

Chapter 26
MINILAB 26-1

Analyzing Electric Forces

Procedure
1. Rub a glass rod with a piece of silk.
2. Quickly separate the glass rod and the silk, and then slowly bring them close together.
3. Charge two pieces of silk by rubbing each on a glass rod.
4. Bring the two charged pieces of silk together slowly.

Analysis
Which materials have the same charge? Which have different charges? How do you know?

Chapter 26
MINILAB 26-2

Lighting a Bulb with One Wire

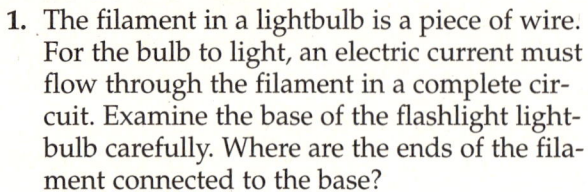

Procedure
1. The filament in a lightbulb is a piece of wire. For the bulb to light, an electric current must flow through the filament in a complete circuit. Examine the base of the flashlight lightbulb carefully. Where are the ends of the filament connected to the base?

2. Connect a piece of wire, a battery, and a flashlight bulb to make the bulb light. (There are four possible ways to do this.)

Analysis
Draw and label a diagram showing the path followed by electrons in your circuit. Explain your diagram.

Chapter 27
ACTIVITY 27-1

Igneous Rocks

Lab Preview

1. Why does the safety symbol for goggles appear in this activity?
   _____
   _____

2. What does the use of a hand lens tell you about this activity? _____
   _____

One way that rocks can form is from melted rock material, called magma. Some rocks formed in this way cool quickly from lava at or near Earth's surface. Others cool slowly from magma deep inside Earth. How igneous rocks form affects their mineral content and the size of the mineral grains.

What You'll Investigate
How can you determine how igneous rocks were formed?

Goals
- **Observe** and **classify** igneous rocks based on texture and color.
- **Recognize** that the texture of igneous rocks is determined by how fast they cool.
- **Recognize** that the color of igneous rocks is an indication of mineral content and chemical composition.

Materials
- igneous rock samples (5)
- hand lens
- table (Common Igneous Rocks) in the textbook
- Appendices F and G

Procedure

1. **Observe** your samples using the hand lens.
2. **Determine** the texture of each rock sample. If the grains or crystals are large and easy to see, the texture is coarse, and the rocks formed slowly. If the grains or crystals are small and are not easy to see, the texture is described as fine, and the rocks formed quickly.
3. **Separate** your samples into two groups based on texture (coarse or fine grained) of the rocks. **Record** which rocks were in which group in your Science Journal.
4. **Determine** whether any of your samples has both coarse and fine crystals in it.
5. **Classify** your rocks based on chemical composition. Igneous rocks that are dark colored generally have a higher percentage of iron and magnesium in them. Igneous rocks that are light colored generally have a higher percentage of the compound silica (SiO_2) in them. Rocks that are intermediate in color are also intermediate in composition. Record your data in your Science Journal.
6. Can you **infer** what minerals have formed in the light-colored rocks? What about the dark-colored or intermediate-colored rocks? Record your inferences in the data table on the next page.
7. Using the table, Appendices F and G, and the information you have entered in your Science Journal, **fill** in the data table on the next page.

Copyright © Glencoe/McGraw-Hill, a division of The McGraw-Hill Companies, Inc.

149

NAME _____ DATE _____ CLASS _____

Activity (continued)

Igneous Rock Data

Texture*	Color	Minerals present	Rock name

*Glassy and fine-textured rocks may not have visible minerals.

Conclude and Apply

1. Dark-colored igneous rocks are classified as basaltic, light-colored ones as granitic, and intermediate-colored ones as andesitic composition. Based on this, how would yours be **classified**?

2. What minerals might be causing the varying colors found in your rocks?

3. Place your pumice sample in a container of water. What happens? **Explain** the cause of what you observe.

4. What process could form a rock that has large crystals surrounded by small crystals?

150   Copyright © Glencoe/McGraw-Hill, a division of The McGraw-Hill Companies, Inc.

NAME _____ DATE _____ CLASS _____

Chapter 27
ACTIVITY 27-2
• Sedimentary Rocks

Lab Preview

1. What warning does the eye safety symbol in this activity give you? _____
_____

2. How do the materials for classifying sedimentary rocks differ from the materials you used for classifying igneous rocks? _____
_____
_____

Sedimentary rocks are formed by the compaction and cementation of sediment. Because sediment is found in all shapes and sizes, do you think these characteristics could be used to classify detrital sedimentary rocks? Sedimentary rocks also can be classified as chemical or organic.

What You'll Investigate
You will observe how rock characteristics are used to classify rocks as detrital, chemical, or organic.

Goals
- **Observe** sedimentary rock characteristics.
- **Compare** and **contrast** clastic and nonclastic textures.
- **Classify** sedimentary rocks as detrital, chemical, or organic.

Safety Precautions

Materials
- unknown sedimentary rock samples
- marking pen
- 5 percent hydrochloric acid (HCl) or vinegar
- dropper
- goggles
- hand lens
- paper towels
- water

Procedure

1. In your Science Journal, make a Data and Observations chart similar to the one on the next page.

2. **Determine** the types of sediments in each sample. Using the table in this section, classify the sediments in the detrital rocks as gravel, sand, silt, or clay.

3. Put a few drops of HCl or vinegar on each rock sample. Bubbling on a rock indicates the presence of calcite. **CAUTION:** *HCl is an acid and can cause burns. Wear goggles. Rinse spills with water. Wash hands afterward.*

4. Look for fossils and **describe** them if any are present.

5. **Determine** whether each sample has a clastic or nonclastic texture.

6. **Classify** your samples as detrital, chemical, or organic. Identify each rock sample.

151

NAME _____ DATE _____ CLASS _____

Activity (continued)

Data and Observations

Sample	Observations	Minerals or fossils present	Sediment size	Detrital, chemical, or organic	Rock name
A					
B					
C					
D					
E					

Conclude and Apply

1. Why did you test the rocks with acid? What minerals react with acid?
   _____
   _____

2. The mineral halite forms by evaporation. Would you **classify** halite as a detrital, a chemical, or an organic rock?
   _____

3. **Compare** and **contrast** sedimentary rocks with a clastic texture with sedimentary rocks with a non-clastic texture.
   _____
   _____

4. **Explain** how you can classify sedimentary rocks.
   _____
   _____

Chapter 27
MINILAB 27-1

Changing Rocks

Procedure
1. Obtain samples of fine-grained sand and glitter from your teacher.
2. Place the sand and glitter into a flat pan.
3. Mix a solution of water and white glue.
4. Pour the solution into the pan and mix thoroughly with the sand and glitter.
5. Place a layer of waxed paper over the mixture, then place a heavy weight on top of the waxed paper.

Analysis
1. After several days, remove the weight and examine the mixture. _____

2. How is the process used to make the model mixture similar to one part of the rock cycle? _____

3. Describe other processes that might be used to model mixture other parts of the rock cycle.

Chapter 27
MINILAB 27-2

Classifying Sediments

Procedure
1. **CAUTION:** *Use care when handling sharp objects.* Spread different samples of sediment on a sheet of paper.
2. Use the table on the same page as the minilab to determine the size-range of gravel-sized sediment.
3. Use tweezers or a dissecting probe and magnifying lens to separate the gravel-sized sediments.
4. Separate each of these three piles into two more piles based on shape—rounded or angular.

Analysis
1. Compare the different piles of sediments. _____
   _____

2. Describe each pile. _____
   _____
   _____

3. Use the table on the same page as the minilab to determine what rock is probably made from each type of sediment that you have. _____
   _____
   _____

Chapter 28

ACTIVITY 28-1

Is it biodegradable?

Lab Preview

1. Name two types of organisms that act as decomposers. _____
   _____
2. What are solid wastes? _____
   _____

As you probably know, all trash is not the same. One important way in which one waste material may differ from another is whether or not the material is biodegrable. A biodegradable substance is anything that can be broken down by organisms in the environment. After it is broken down, the substance can become part of the environment. Whether a material is biodegrable or not can make a big difference in how it affects the environment.

What You'll Investigate
What kinds of materials are biodegradable?

Goals
- **Distinguish** between biodegradable and nonbiodegradable substances.
- **Observe** the decomposition of biodegradable materials.

Materials
- soft-drink bottles (2-L) (2)
- plastic wrap
- potting soil
- gravel or sand
- labels
- biodegradable and nonbiodegradable waste materials
- hand lens
- plastic teaspoon
- transparent tape
- scissors

Safety Precautions
Wash hands after handling soil or waste materials.

Procedure
1. **Cut** a square about 6 cm × 6 cm in the straight sides of the soft-drink bottles as near the top as possible.
2. **Label** the bottles 1 and 2.
3. **Add** 1 cm of sand or gravel to each bottle and then fill with 4 cm of potting soil.
4. Your teacher will give you ten substances. **Hypothesize** which substances are biodegradable and which ones are not. **Record** your hypotheses in your Science Journal. **Make a table** in your Science Journal to record your observations.
5. **Place** the substances you think are biodegradable in bottle 1 and the others in bottle 2.
6. **Cover** each substance with 1 cm to 2 cm of potting soil.
7. **Sprinkle** water on the top of the soil. Cover the hole in the bottle with plastic wrap and secure it with transparent tape.

Copyright © Glencoe/McGraw-Hill, a division of The McGraw-Hill Companies, Inc.

Activity (continued)

8. **Observe** each bottle at the end of five days. Note any change in the level of the layers. Use the teaspoon to carefully remove the soil from each substance. Use your hand lens to observe the substance and record your observations in the table below. Carefully replace each substance and cover with soil.

9. **Observe** the contents of the bottles after five more days and record your results.

Sample Data Table

Time	Biodegradable substances					Nonbiodegradable substances				
	1	2	3	4	5	1	2	3	4	5
5 days										
10 days										

Conclude and Apply

1. Which substances decomposed?

2. Which substances decomposed partially?

3. Was your hypothesis supported? Why or why not?

4. Describe any organisms you observed.

5. Explain how substances that are biodegradable affect the environment.

6. Explain how substances that are not biodegradable affect the environment.

Chapter 28
ACTIVITY 28-2

Modeling the Greenhouse Effect

Lab Preview

1. Why is it important to place the lamp exactly $\frac{1}{2}$ inch from each container? _____
   _____
2. What is the greenhouse effect? _____
   _____

You can create models of Earth with and without heat-reflecting greenhouse gases, then experiment with the models to observe the greenhouse effect.

What You'll Investigate
How does the greenhouse effect influence temperatures on Earth?

Goals
- **Observe** the greenhouse effect.
- **Describe** the effect that a heat source has on an environment.

Materials
- clear, plastic, 2-L soda bottles with tops cut off and labels removed (2)
- thermometers (2)
- potting soil (4 cups)
- masking tape
- plastic wrap
- rubber band
- lamp with 100-watt lightbulb
- chronometer or watch with a second hand

Procedure
1. Put an equal volume of potting soil in the bottom of each container.
2. Use masking tape to affix a thermometer to the inside of each container. Place the thermometers at the same height relative to the soil. Shield each thermometer bulb by putting a double layer of masking tape over it.
3. Seal the top of one container with plastic wrap held in place with the rubber band.
4. Place the lamp with exposed 100-watt bulb between the two containers and exactly $\frac{1}{2}$ inch from each, as shown in the diagram. Do not turn on the light.
5. Let the apparatus sit undisturbed for five minutes, then record the temperature in each container.
6. Turn on the light. Record the temperature in each container every two minutes for the next 15 to 20 minutes. **Record** your temperature measurements in the data table on the next page.
7. **Plot** the results for each container on a graph.

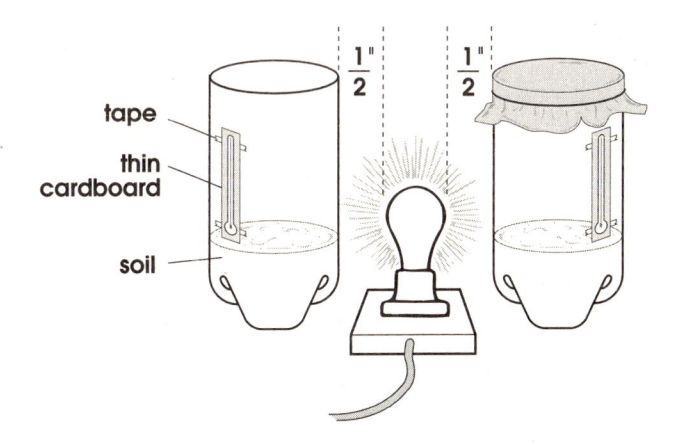

157

Activity (continued)

Data and Observations

Time	Open container temperature	Sealed container temperature
0 minutes		
2 minutes		
4 minutes		
6 minutes		

Conclude and Apply

1. How did the temperature of each container change during the experiment?

2. What was the temperature difference between the two containers at the end of the experiment?

3. What does the lightbulb represent in this experimental model? What does the plastic wrap represent?

4. Describe the ways in which this experimental setup is similar to and different from Earth and its atmosphere.

Chapter 28
MINILAB 28-1

Observing Mineral Mining Effects

Procedure
1. Place a chocolate chip cookie or nut-filled brownie on a paper plate. Pretend the cookie is Earth's crust and the nuts or chips are mineral deposits. **CAUTION:** *Never eat food or put anything in your mouth from an experiment.*
2. Use a toothpick to locate and dig up mineral deposits. Try to disturb the "land" as little as possible.
3. When mining is completed, do your best to restore the land to its original condition.

Analysis
1. Were you able to restore the land to its original condition? Describe the kinds of changes in an ecosystem that might result from a mining operation.

2. How do mining deposits found close to the surface compare with mining deposits found deeper within Earth's crust?

Chapter 28

MINILAB 28-2

Measuring Acid Rain

Procedure
1. Use a container to collect samples of rain.
2. Dip a piece of pH indicator paper into the sample.
3. Compare the color of the paper with the pH chart provided. Record the pH of the rainwater.
4. Use separate pieces of pH paper to test the pH of tap water and distilled water. Record these values.

Data and Observations

	Sample	pH
Rainwater		
Tap water		
Distilled water		

Analysis
1. Is the rainwater acidic, basic, or neutral?

_____

_____

2. How does the pH of the rainwater compare with the pH of tap water? Distilled water?

_____

Chapter 29
ACTIVITY 29-1

• Relative Age Dating

Lab Preview

1. To find out the relative ages of rocks, do you need to know their exact ages? Explain.
   _____
   _____

2. State the principle of superposition. _____
   _____

Can you tell which of two rock layers is older? You don't need to know the exact ages of the layers to tell. Geologists can learn a lot about rock layers simply by studying their arrangement.

What You'll Investigate
Can the relative ages of rocks be determined by studying the rock layers and structures?

Goals
- **Determine** the relative order of events by interpreting illustrations of rock layers.

Materials
- paper
- pencil

Procedure
1. Study Figures A and B. The legend will help you interpret the figures.
2. Determine the relative ages of the rock layers, unconformities, igneous dikes, and faults in each figure.

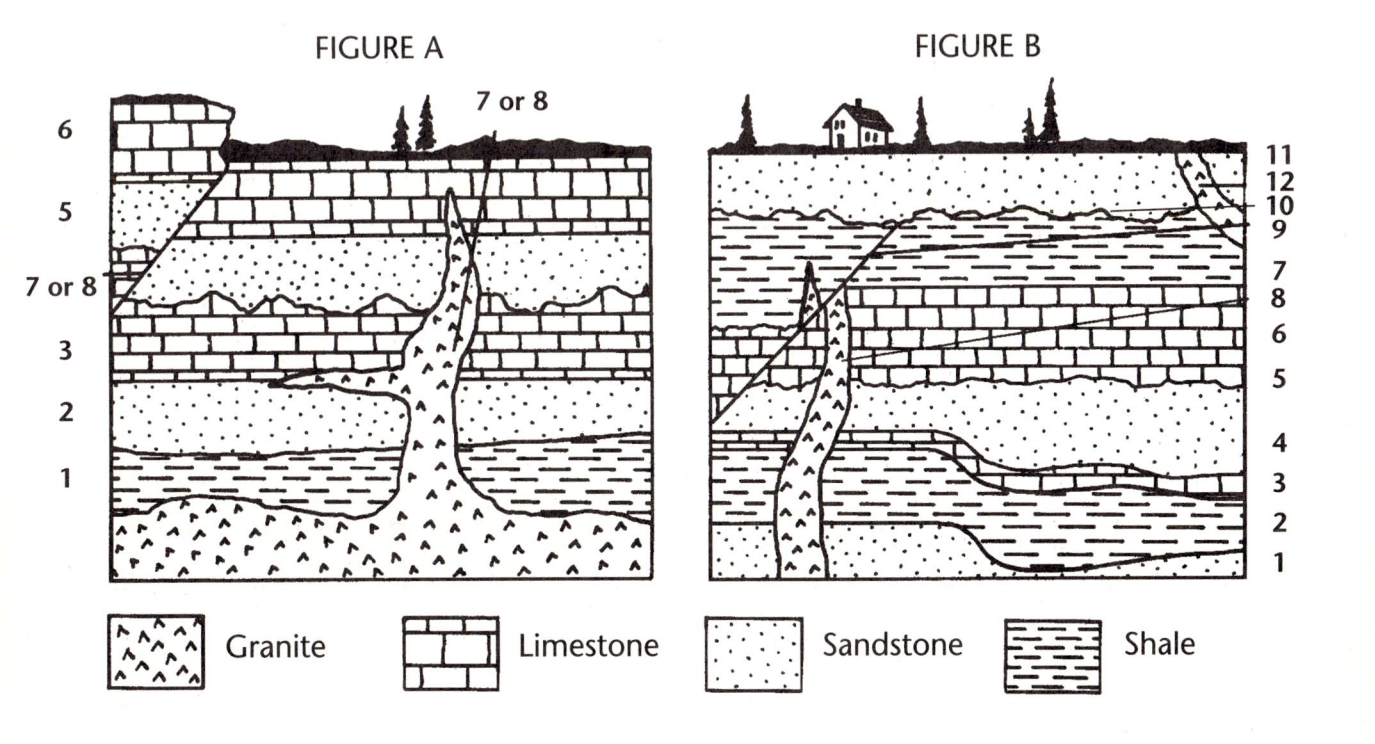

FIGURE A

FIGURE B

Granite   Limestone   Sandstone   Shale

161

NAME	DATE	CLASS

Activity (continued)

Conclude and Apply
Figure A
1. Were any layers of rock deposited after the igneous dike formed? Explain. _____
   _____
   _____

2. What type of unconformity is shown? Is it possible that there were originally more layers of rock than are shown here? Explain. _____
   _____

3. What type of fault is shown? _____

4. Explain how to determine whether the igneous dike formed before or after the fault occurred.
   _____
   _____

Figure B
5. What type of fault is shown? _____

6. Is the igneous dike on the left older or younger than the unconformity near the top? Explain.
   _____
   _____

7. Are the two igneous dikes shown the same age? How do you know? _____
   _____
   _____

8. Which two layers of rock may have been much thicker at one time than they are now? _____
   _____

Interpreting Scientific Illustrations
1. Make a sketch of Figure A. On it, **identify** the relative age of each rock layer, igneous dike, fault, and unconformity. For example, the shale layer is the oldest, so mark it with a *1*. Mark the next-oldest feature with a *2*, and so on.
   _____
   _____

2. Repeat the procedure in question 1 for Figure B.
   _____
   _____

Chapter 29
ACTIVITY 29-2
Radioactive Decay

Lab Preview
1. What do *absolute* and *relative* mean when they refer to the age of a rock?
   _____
   _____

2. What is the half-life of an isotope?
   _____

Radioactive isotopes decay into their daughter elements in a certain amount of time. The rate of decay varies for each individual isotope. This rate can be used to determine the age of rocks that contain the isotopes under study. In this activity, you will develop a model that demonstrates how the half-life of certain radioactive isotopes can be used to determine absolute ages.

What You'll Investigate
What materials can be used to model age determination using radioactive half-lives?

Goals
- **Model** radioactive half-lives using listed materials.
- **Model** absolute age determination using the half-lives of radioactive isotopes.

Materials
- shoe box with lid
- brass fasteners (100)
- paper clips (100)
- graph paper
- pennies (100)
- colored pencils (2)

Procedures
1. Place 100 pennies into the shoe box with all heads up.
2. Place the lid on the box and shake it one time.
3. Remove the lid. Replace the pennies that are now tails up with paper clips. Record the number of pennies remaining in the box in a data table similar to the one shown on the next page.
4. Repeat steps 2 and 3 until all the pennies have been removed.
5. Remove the paper clips from the box. Put an "X" on one of the shorter sides of the box. Place 100 fasteners in the box.
6. Repeat step 2.
7. Remove the lid. Replace the fasteners that point toward the "X" with paper clips. Record the number of fasteners remaining in the box in a data table similar to the one shown on page 114.
8. Repeat steps 2 and 7 until all the fasteners have been removed.
9. **Plot** both sets of data on the same graph. Graph the "shake number" on the horizontal axis and the "number of pennies or fasteners remaining" on the vertical axis. Be sure to use a different colored pencil for each set of data.

163

Activity (continued)

Data and Observations

Shake number	Number remaining	
	Pennies	Fasteners
0		
1		
2		
12		
13		
14		
15		

Conclude and Apply

1. In this model of radioactive decay, what do the coins and fasteners represent? The paper clips? The box? Each shake?

2. What was the half-life of the pennies? The fasteners?

3. How does the difference between the two objects affect the half-life? Compare the objects to the differences among radioactive elements.

4. Suppose you could make only one shake in 100 years. How many years would it take to have 25 coins and 75 paper clips remaining? To have 25 fasteners and 75 paper clips remaining?

5. How can the absolute age of rocks be determined?

Chapter 29
MINILAB 29-1

Predicting Fossil Preservation

Procedure
1. Take a brief walk outside and observe the area near your school or home.
2. Look around and notice what type of litter has been discarded on the school grounds. Note whether there is a paved road near your school. Note anything else that was made by humans.

List of Observations

Analysis
1. **Predict** what human-made or natural objects from our time might be preserved far into the future.

2. **Explain** what conditions would need to exist for these objects to be preserved as fossils.

Chapter 29

MINILAB 29-2

Sequencing Earth's History

Procedure
1. Sequence these events in Earth's history in relative order: Earth forms, first many-celled organisms, first land plants, first mammals, dinosaurs become extinct, first amphibians, first human ancestors, oldest known fossils, first many-celled animals.

2. Make a time line, using these dates: 4.6 billion years, 3.5 billion years, 1.25 billion years, 600 million years, 439 million years, 408 million years, 225 million years, 65 million years, and 4.4 million years ago.

3. Match each event with the absolute date on your time line.

Event	Years before present
Earth forms	4.6 B
oldest known fossils	3.5 B
1st many-celled organisms	1.25 B
1st many-celled animals	600 M
1st plants on land	439 M
1st amphibians	408 M
1st mammals	225 M
dinosaurs extinct	65 M
1st human ancestors	4.4 M

Analysis
1. Check your time line with your teacher.

2. Did you correctly list the events in relative order? _____

3. How does the age of Earth compare with the presence of humans on the time line? _____

Chapter 30
ACTIVITY 30-1
• Changing Species

Lab Preview
Name three traits that would help identify a type of animal. _____
_____

In this activity, you will observe how adaptation within a species might cause the evolution of a particular trait, leading to the development of a new species.

What You'll Investigate
How might adaptation within a species cause the evolution of a particular trait?

Goals
- Model adaptation within a species.

Materials
- deck of playing cards

Procedure
1. **Remove** all of the kings, queens, jacks, and aces from a deck of playing cards.

2. Each remaining card represents an individual in a population of animals called "varimals." The number on each card represents the height of the individual. For example, the 5 of diamonds is a varimal that's 5 units tall.

3. **Calculate** the average height of the population of varimals represented by your cards.

4. Suppose varimals eat grass, shrubs, and leaves from trees. A drought causes many of these plants to die. All that's left are a few tall trees. Only varimals at least 6 units tall can reach the leaves on these trees.

5. All the varimals under 6 units leave the area to seek food elsewhere or die from starvation. **Discard** all of the cards with a number value less than 6. **Calculate** the new average height of the population of varimals.

6. Shuffle the deck of remaining cards.

7. **Draw** two cards at a time. Each pair represents a pair of varimals that will mate and produce offspring.

8. The offspring of each pair reaches a height equal to the average height of his or her parents. **Calculate** and **record** the height of each offspring.

9. Repeat by discarding all parents and offspring under 8 units tall. Now **calculate** the new average height of varimals. Include both the parents and offspring in your calculation.

Conclude and Apply
1. How did the average height of the population change over time? _____
_____

2. If you hadn't discarded the shortest varimals, would the average height of the population have changed as much? **Explain.** _____
_____

3. What trait was selected for? _____
_____

167

Activity (continued)

4. Why didn't every member of the original population reproduce? _____
_____
_____

5. If there had been no varimals over 6 units tall in step 5, what would have happened to the population? _____
_____

6. If there had been no variation in height in the population before the droughts occurred, would the species have been able to evolve into a taller species? Explain. _____
_____
_____
_____
_____

7. How does this activity **demonstrate** that traits evolve in species? _____
_____
_____
_____
_____

Chapter 30
MINILAB 30-1

Interpreting Rock Layers

Procedure
1. Draw a sequence of three sedimentary rock layers.
2. Number the rock layers 1 through 3, bottom to top.
3. Identify the fossils in each layer as follows: Layer 1 contains fossils B and A; layer 2 contains fossils A, B, and C; layer 3 contains only fossil C.
4. Assign each of the fossils to one or more geologic periods. For example, fossil A lived from the Cambrian period through the Devonian periods. Fossil C lived from the Devonian through the Permian periods, and so on.
5. Analyze the fossils' occurence in each layer to help you determine the ages of each rock layer.

Data and Observations

Period	Fossil A	Fossil B	Fossil C
Permian			
Pennsylvanian			
Mississippian			
Devonian			
Silurian			
Ordovician			
Cambrian			

Analysis
1. Which layer or layers were you able to date to a specific period? _____

2. Why isn't it possible to determine during which specific period the other layers formed?
_____
_____

3. What is the age or possible age of each layer? _____
_____
_____

NAME _____ DATE _____ CLASS _____

Chapter 30
MINILAB 30-2

Measuring Seafloor Spreading

Procedure

1. On a globe or world map, measure the distance in kilometers between a point near the east coast of South America and a corresponding point on the west coast of Africa.

2. Assuming that the rate of spreading has been about 3.5–4.0 cm per year, calculate how many years it took to create the present Atlantic Ocean if the continents were once joined.

3. Measure the distance across the Atlantic Ocean in several other locations and calculate the average of your results.

4. Check your calculations with the information provided in the geological time scale at the beginning of the chapter.

Data and Observations

Points selected		Distance (cms)	Time (years)
in South America	in Africa		
1			
2			
3			

Analysis

1. Did the values used to obtain your average value vary much? _____
_____
_____
_____

2. How close did your average value come to the accepted estimate for the beginning of the breakup of Pangaea? _____
_____
_____
_____
_____

NAME _____ DATE _____ CLASS _____

Chapter 1
ACTIVITY 1-1 • Using Scientific Methods

Design Your Own Experiment

Lab Preview

1. If an organism lives in the ocean, what can you infer about its dependency on salt?
   A saltwater organism must depend on salt for normal vital body functions.

2. What special precaution should you take when working with live organisms?
   You must be informed about their survival needs, including temperature sensitivity and light tolerance.

You are to use scientific methods to determine how salt affects the growth of brine shrimp. Brine shrimp are tiny organisms that live in the ocean. How can you find out why they live where they do?

Recognize the Problem
How can you use scientific methods to determine how salt affects the hatching and growth of brine shrimp?

Form a Hypothesis
Based on your observations, make a hypothesis about how salt affects the hatching and growth of brine shrimp.

Goals
- **Design** and carry out an experiment using scientific methods.
- **Infer** why brine shrimp live in the ocean.

Safety Precautions 🧤 👁
Protect clothing and eyes. Be careful when working with live organisms.

Possible Materials
- widemouthed, 0.5-L containers (3)
- *clear plastic cups (3)
- brine shrimp eggs
- wooden splint
- distilled water (500-mL)
- weak salt solution (500-mL)
- strong salt solution (500-mL)
- wax pencil
- *labels (3)
- hand lens

alternate materials

Test Your Hypothesis

Plan

1. As a group, agree upon and write out the hypothesis statement.

2. List the steps that you need to take to test your hypothesis. Be specific. **Describe** exactly what you will do at each step. **List** your materials.

3. How will you know whether brine shrimp hatch and grow?

4. **Decide** what data you need to collect during the experiment. **Design** a data table in your Science Journal to **record** your observations.

5. **Identify** the steps in solving a problem that each of your actions presents. For example, what action have you taken that represents stating the problem or gathering information? Make sure you include all the steps needed to reach a conclusion.

6. **Read** over your entire experiment to make sure that all steps are in logical order.

NAME _____ DATE _____ CLASS _____

Activity (continued)

7. Identify any constants, variables, and controls of the experiment.

8. Can you explain what variable you are testing?

9. Decide whether you need to run your tests more than once. Can your data be summarized in a graph?

Do

1. Make sure your teacher approves your plan before you proceed.
2. Carry out the experiment as planned.
3. While the experiment is going on, **write down** any observations that you make and complete the data table.

Sample Data

Day	Water Environment		
	Distilled water	Weak salt solution	Strong salt solution
0	Brine	Brine	Brine
1	shrimp	shrimp	shrimp
2	die	live	live
3			

Analyze Your Data

1. **Compare** your results with those of other groups.
   Student results should be consistent with those of other groups.

2. Was your hypothesis supported by your data? Explain your answer.
   The hypothesis that brine shrimp hatch best in any salt solution was supported. Shrimp will not grow in distilled water.

Draw Conclusions

1. **Describe** how the physical conditions in the container in which the brine shrimp hatched and grew best are similar to those in the ocean.
   The container had salt, water, and oxygen and received light.

2. How did you use scientific methods to solve this problem? Give examples from this activity.
   Students formed a hypothesis, performed an experiment with a variable and a control, recorded data, analyzed data, and drew conclusions. Students should give examples from their activities.

NAME _____ DATE _____ CLASS _____

Chapter 1
MINILAB 1-1

Inferring from Pictures

Procedure

1. Fill in the table below with your observations.

Observations and Inferences

Picture	Observations	Inferences
1		
2		

2. Study the two pictures on the same page in the textbook as this minilab. Write down all your observations in the table.

3. Make inferences based on your observations. Record your inferences.
   Answers will vary.

4. Share your inferences with others in your class.
   Answers will vary.

Analysis

1. Analyze the inferences that you made. Are there other explanations for what you observed? **Answers will vary. Students will probably say that both situations are due to rain. The cause for the wet street in Picture 1 is a street cleaning machine that just passed and used water to clean the street. It did not rain. The cause for the wet puddle in Picture 2 is someone spilling water when he or she watered the plant.**

2. Why must you be careful when making inferences? **You must have all necessary information before making a decision. Otherwise you may assume something occured that may be the most reasonable but not necessarily the true reason why.**

3. Create your own picture and description. Have other students make inferences based on the picture and description. **Pictures and descriptions will vary.**

Copyright © Glencoe/McGraw-Hill, a division of The McGraw-Hill Companies, Inc.

172

NAME _____ DATE _____ CLASS _____

Chapter 1
MINILAB 1-2

Comparing Paper Towels

Procedure

1. Record observations in the data table below.
2. Cut a 5-cm by 5-cm square from each of the three brands of paper towel. Lay each piece on a smooth, level, waterproof surface.
3. Add drop of water to each square.
4. Continue to add drops until the piece of paper towel can no longer absorb the water.
5. Record your observations in your data table and graph your results.

Data and Observations

Paper Towel Absorbency (drops of water/sheet)

Trial	Brand A	Brand B	Brand C
1			
2			
3			
4			

Analysis

1. Did all the squares of paper towels absorb equal amounts of water? **No; the students should use their data to support their answers.**

2. If one brand of paper towel absorbs more water than the others, can you conclude that it is the towel you should buy? Explain. **No; the towel may be poor at absorbing oil or too expensive.**

3. Which scientific methods did you use to answer the question of which paper towel is most absorbent? **experimentation using quantitative data, observing, and comparing and contrasting**

4.

Copyright © Glencoe/McGraw-Hill, a division of The McGraw-Hill Companies, Inc.

Chapter 2
ACTIVITY 2-1

Comparing Light Microscopes

Design Your Own Experiment

Lab Preview

1. Describe a compound light microscope. **In a compound microscope, light passes through an object and then through two or more lenses. There is a single eyepiece.**
2. Describe a stereoscopic light microscope. **A stereoscopic microscope has two eyepieces, so that it provides a three-dimensional image. It is used to view things that are too thick for light to pass through or too large to fit the stage of a compound microscope.**

You're a technician in a police forensic laboratory. You use stereoscopic and compound light microscopes in the laboratory. A detective just returned from a crime scene with bags of evidence. You must examine each piece of evidence under a microscope. How do you decide which microscope is the best tool to use?

Recognize the Problem

Compare the items to be examined under the microscopes. Which microscope will be used for each item?

Form a Hypothesis

Microscopes are very useful tools for scientists. Stereoscopic and compound light microscopes are used for many tasks. What things are better viewed with a compound light microscope? What things are better viewed with a stereoscopic microscope?

Goals

- **Learn** how to use a stereoscopic microscope and a compound light microscope.
- **Compare** the uses of the stereoscopic and compound light microscopes.

Possible Materials

- a compound light microscope
- a stereoscopic light microscope
- any eight items from the classroom; include some living or once-living items
- microscope slides and coverslips
- plastic petri dishes
- distilled water
- dropper

Safety Precautions

Thoroughly wash your hands when you have completed this experiment.

Test Your Hypothesis

Plan

1. As a group, decide how you will test your hypothesis.
2. **List** the steps that you will need to complete this experiment. Be specific, describing exactly what you will do at each step. Make sure the steps are in a logical order. Remember that you must place an item in the bottom of a plastic petri dish to **examine** it under the stereoscopic microscope. You must **make a wet mount** of any item to be examined under the compound light microscope.
3. If you need a data or observation table, **design** one in your Science Journal.

Activity (continued)

Do

1. Make sure your teacher approves the objects you'll examine, your plan, and your data table before you proceed.
2. Carry out the experiment as planned.
3. While doing the experiment, **record** your observations and **complete** the data table.

Analyze Your Data

1. Compare the items you examined with those of your classmates. **Answers will vary.**

2. Based on this experiment, classify the eight items you observed. **Answers will vary, but large items should be classified together and items small enough to fit on a slide should be grouped together.**

Draw Conclusions

1. Infer which microscope a scientist might use to examine a blood sample, fibers, and live snails. **A scientist might use a stereomicroscope to examine live snails and a compound light microscope to examine blood and fibers.**

2. If you examined an item under both microscopes, how would the images differ? **Differences include size and orientation. The image of a compound light microscope is inverted and reversed left to right. The stereomicroscope's image is not.**

3. List five careers that require people to use a stereomicroscope.
   a. **surgeons, botanists, entomologists, geologists, and gemologists**
   b. _____
   c. _____
   d. _____
   e. _____

4. List five careers that require people to use a compound light microscope.
   a. **Answers will vary but may include lab technicians, forensic scientists, and cell biologists.**
   b. _____
   c. _____
   d. _____
   e. _____

Chapter 2
ACTIVITY 2-2
Comparing Plant and Animal Cells

Lab Preview

1. Why do you use the low power objective to locate cells on a slide?
   With the lower magnification, a larger area of the slide is visible.

2. What is a chloroplast?
   an organelle in plant cells in which light energy is changed into chemical energy

If you were to compare a goldfish with a rose bush, you would find the two to be different. However, when the individual cells of these organisms are compared, will they be as different? Try this activity to see how plant and animal cells compare.

What You'll Investigate
In this exercise, you will observe an animal cell, a human cheek cell, and a plant cell, *Elodea*, under a compound light microscope.

Goals
- **Compare and Contrast** an animal cell and a plant cell.

Safety Precautions

Materials
- microscope
- microscope slide
- coverslip
- forceps
- dropper
- *Elodea* plant
- prepared slide of human cheek cells

Procedure

1. Copy the data table in your Science Journal. Check off the cell parts as you observe them.

2. Follow the directions in your textbook for using low and high power objectives on your microscope and for making a wet-mount slide.

3. Using forceps, **make** a wet-mount slide of a young leaf from the tip of an *Elodea* plant.

4. **Observe** the leaf on low power. Focus on the top layer of cells. Carefully focus down through the top layer of cells to observe other layers of cells.

5. Switch to high power and focus on one cell. Does the center of the cell appear empty? This is the central vacuole that contains water and stores cell products. **Observe** the chloroplasts in the cytoplasm, the green disk-shaped objects moving around the central vacuole. Try to find the cell nucleus. It looks like a clear ball.

6. Make a drawing of the *Elodea* cell. **Label** the cell wall, cytoplasm, chloroplasts, central vacuole, and nucleus. Return to low power and remove the slide.

7. Place a prepared slide of cheek cells on the microscope stage. Locate the cells under low power.

8. Switch to high power and **observe** the cell nucleus. **Draw** and **label** the cell membrane, cytoplasm, and nucleus.

Activity (continued)

Data and Observations

Cell part	*Elodea*	Cheek
cytoplasm		
nucleus		
chloroplasts		
cell wall		
cell membrane		

Diagrams of cells:

Conclude and Apply

1. How many cell layers could you see in the *Elodea* leaf?
   usually two layers

2. Compare and contrast the shape of the cheek cell and the *Elodea* cell.
   The *Elodea* cell is oblong and rectangular; the cheek cell is oval.

3. What can you conclude about the differences between plant and animal cells?
   Plant and animal cells differ by the presence or absence of a cell wall. Students may also say that animal cells have no chloroplasts.

NAME _____ DATE _____ CLASS _____

Chapter 2
MINILAB 2-1

Observing Magnified Objects

Procedure
1. Look at a newspaper through both the curved side and the flat bottom of an empty, clear glass.
2. Look at the newspaper through a clear glass bowl filled with water and then look at the newspaper with a magnifying glass.

Data and Observations

Sample data

Tools	Observations
flat bottom of glass	not much magnification
curved side of glass	more than flat surface
bowl filled with water	magnifies
magnifying glass	Magnification depends on quality of lens.

Analysis
1. In your Science Journal, compare how well you can see the newspaper through each of the objects.

   Each of the objects magnifies the newsprint.

2. What did early scientists learn by using such tools?

   Early scientists learned that cells existed, and they began to infer that living things were made of cells.

NAME _____ DATE _____ CLASS _____

Chapter 2
MINILAB 2-2

Modeling Cytoplasm

Procedure
1. Fill a beaker with 100 mL water.
2. Add unflavored gelatin and stir.
3. Shine a flashlight through the beaker.

Analysis
1. Describe what you see.

   Particles represent organelles suspended in the cytoplasm.

2. How does a model help you understand what a real thing looks like?

   A model is used to help explain a concept that is not easy to see or understand.

Chapter 3
ACTIVITY 3-1 • Observing Osmosis

Lab Preview
1. What safety symbols are associated with this activity? __eye safety, clothing protection safety, and disposal alert__
2. What is osmosis? __diffusion of water through a membrane__

It is difficult to see osmosis occurring in cells because most cells are so small. However, a few cells can be seen without the aid of a microscope. Try this activity to see how osmosis occurs in a large cell.

What You'll Investigate
How does osmosis occur in an egg cell?

Goals
- Observe osmosis in an egg cell.
- Determine what affects osmosis.

Materials
- egg
- containers (500-mL) with covers (2)
- white vinegar (250 mL)
- light corn syrup (250 mL)
- graduated cylinder (100-mL)
- labels (A and B)
- small bowl
- spoon

Procedure
1. Copy the tables below and use them to record your data and observations.
2. Place label A on one of the 500-mL containers and label B on the other. Pour the vinegar into container A and the syrup into container B. **Record** data on the table. Cover container B.
3. Place the egg in container A and cover the container.
4. **Observe** the egg after 30 minutes, then again in two days. After each observation, **record** the egg's appearance on the table.

Volume Data

	Beginning volume	Ending volume
Vinegar	250 mL	220 mL
Syrup	250 mL	290 mL

Egg Observations

After 30 minutes	bubbles on shell
After 2 days	eggshell has dissolved
After 3 days	egg has shrunk

Activity (continued)

5. After the second observation, **remove** container A's cover. Carefully **remove** the egg from the liquid with a spoon, and gently rinse the egg in a slow stream of cool tap water.
6. **Remove** the cover from container B. Carefully **place** the egg in the syrup and replace the cover.
7. **Measure** the volume of liquid in container A and **record** its appearance on the table.
8. **Observe** the egg the next day and **record** its appearance on the table.
9. **Remove** container B's cover. Gently remove the egg and allow the syrup to drain back into container B. Then, place the egg in the small bowl. **Measure** the volume of syrup and record on the table.

Conclude and Apply
1. What caused the change in volume of container A and container B?
   __More water was outside the egg in the vinegar in container A. More water was inside the egg in container B than in the syrup, so the water diffused from the egg into the syrup.__

2. Calculate the amount of water that moved into and out of the egg.
   __Answers may vary. About 30 mL of water entered the egg from the vinegar, and about 40 mL of water left the egg when it was placed in the syrup.__

3. **Infer** what part of the egg controlled what moved into and out of the cell.
   __cell membrane__

Chapter 3
ACTIVITY 3-2
Photosynthesis and Respiration

Lab Preview
1. What safety symbols are associated with this activity?
   chemical, eye, clothing protection, and plant safety
2. What is photosynthesis? Photosynthesis is a process whereby producers change light energy into chemical energy.

Every living cell carries on many chemical processes. Two important chemical processes are respiration and photosynthesis. Every cell, including the ones in your body, carries on respiration. But, some plant cells, unlike your cells, carry on both. In this experiment, you will investigate when these processes occur in plant cells.

What You'll Investigate
When do plants carry on photosynthesis and respiration?

Goals
- Observe green water plants in the light and dark.
- Determine if green plants carry on both photosynthesis and respiration.

Safety Precautions
Protect clothing and eyes and be careful using chemicals. Do not get chemicals on your skin.

Materials
- test tubes, 16-mm × 150-mm with stoppers (4)
  small, clear-glass baby food jars with lids (4)
- test-tube rack
- stirring rod
- balance scale
- scissors
- sodium hydrogen carbonate
- bromothymol blue solution in dropping bottle
- aged tap water
  distilled water
- pieces of Elodea (2)
  other water plants
  alternate materials

Procedure
1. Label each test tube using the numbers 1, 2, 3, and 4. Pour 5 mL aged tap water into each test tube.
2. Add 10 drops of carbonated water to test tubes 1 and 2.
3. Add 10 drops of bromothymol blue to each test tube. Bromothymol blue turns green to yellow in the presence of an acid.
4. Cut two 10-cm pieces of *Elodea*. Place one piece of *Elodea* in the liquid in test tube 1 and one piece in the liquid in test tube 3. Stopper the test tubes.
5. Copy the Test Tube Data Table on the next page in your Science Journal. Record the color of the solution in each of the four test tubes in your Science Journal.
6. Place test tubes 1 and 2 in bright light. Place test tubes 3 and 4 in the dark. Observe the test tubes at the end of 30 minutes or until there is a color change. Record the colors.

13

Activity (continued)

Data and Observations
Sample data

Test tube	Color at start	Color after 30 minutes
1	yellow	some greenish-blue
2	yellow	yellow
3	blue	some yellow
4	blue	blue

Conclude and Apply
1. What is indicated by the color of the water in all four test tubes at the start of the activity?
   Yellow indicates the presence of carbonic acid; blue indicates no acid present. Test tubes 1 and 2 contained carbon dioxide.

2. Infer what happened in the test tube or tubes that changed color after 30 minutes.
   Green plants use carbon dioxide in photosynthesis and release carbon dioxide during respiration.

3. What can you conclude about the test tube or tubes that didn't change color after 30 minutes?
   There was no change in the acidity of the solution. Photosynthesis or respiration did not occur in these test tubes.

4. Describe the purpose of test tubes 2 and 4.
   Test tubes 2 and 4 were controls.

5. Does this experiment show that both photosynthesis and respiration occur in plants? Explain.
   Yes the experimental results showed that both processes happen in plant cells.

14

NAME _____ DATE _____ CLASS _____

Chapter 3
MINILAB 3-1

Determining How Enzymes Work

Procedure
1. Make a mark on one of two clean test tubes. Place them in a test-tube rack, then fill each halfway with milk.
2. Place a tablet of rennin, an enzyme, in a small plastic bowl. Crush the tablet using the back of a metal spoon. Add the crushed tablet to the marked test tube.
3. Let both test tubes stand undisturbed during your class period.
4. Observe what happens to the milk.

Analysis
1. What effect did the rennin have on the milk?
   The milk curdles.
2. Predict what would eventually happen to the milk without rennin.
   The milk would spoil (curdle).
3. Infer how rennin's effect on milk might be useful to the dairy industry.
   It decreases the time it takes to produce cheeses and other dairy products.

NAME _____ DATE _____ CLASS _____

Chapter 3
MINILAB 3-2

Observing the Rate of Diffusion

Procedure
1. Use two beakers of equal size. Label one "hot," then fill it halfway with hot water. Label the other "cold," then fill it halfway with cold water. **CAUTION:** *Do not spill hot water on your skin.*
2. Add one drop of food coloring to each beaker. Carefully release the drop just above the water's surface to avoid splashing and disturbing the water.
3. Observe the beakers and record your observations. Repeat your observations after 10 minutes and record them again.

Data and Observations

Beaker	Initial Observations	After 10 minutes
cold water		
hot water		

Analysis
1. Describe what happens when food coloring is added to each beaker.
   The food coloring spreads in each beaker. It spreads faster in hot water.
2. How does temperature affect the rate of diffusion?
   Heat increases the rate of diffusion.

NAME _____ DATE _____ CLASS _____

Chapter 4
ACTIVITY 4-1 • Mitosis in Plant and Animal Cells

Lab Preview
1. What is mitosis? **Mitosis is the process in which a cell divides to form two identical cells. This nucleus divides into two nuclei, each of which contains the same number and type of chromosomes as the parent cell.**
2. Why is mitosis necessary? **Cells have to reproduce to replace worn-out cells and to provide cells as an organism grows.**

Reproduction of cells in plants and animals is accomplished by mitosis. In this activity, you will study prepared slides of onion root-tip cells and whitefish embryo cells. These slides are used because they show cells in the various stages of mitosis.

What You'll Investigate
How mitosis in a plant cell is different from mitosis in an animal cell.

Materials
- Prepared slide of an onion root tip
- Prepared slide of a whitefish embryo
- Microscope

Goals
- **Compare** the sizes of the whitefish embryo cells and the onion root-tip cells.
- **Observe** the chromosomes of the whitefish embryo and onion root tip.

Procedure
1. **Obtain** prepared slides of onion root-tip cells and whitefish embryo cells.
2. Set your microscope on low power and **examine** the onion root tip. Move the slide until you can see the area just behind the root tip. Turn the nosepiece to high power.
3. Use the figure to help you find a cell in prophase. **Draw** and **label** the parts of the cell you observe.
4. Repeat step 3 for metaphase, anaphase, and telophase.
5. Turn the microscope back to low power. Remove the onion root-tip slide.
6. Place the whitefish embryo slide on the microscope stage under low power. Focus and find a region of dividing cells. Switch to high power.
7. Repeat steps 3 and 4 using the whitefish embryo slide.
8. Return the nosepiece to low power. Remove the whitefish embryo slide from the microscope stage.

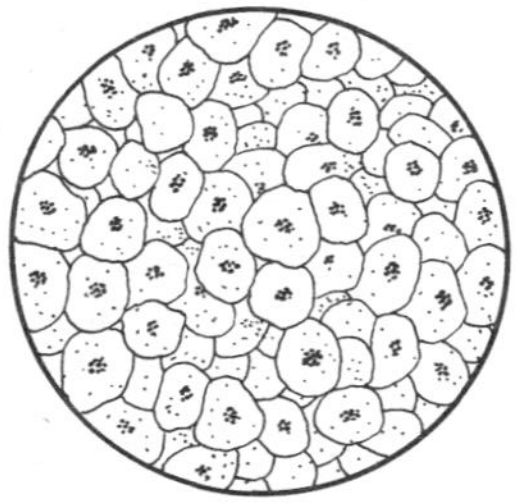

Whitefish embryo cells

Onion root-tip cells

NAME _____ DATE _____ CLASS _____

Activity (continued)

Conclude and Apply
1. Compare the cells in the region behind the onion root tip to those in the root tip. **The cells behind the root tip are larger than those in the root tip. Mitosis is not happening as much in cells behind the root tip.**
2. Describe the shapes of the cells in the onion root tip and the whitefish embryo. **Onion root-tip cells are rectangular; whitefish embryo cells are almost round.**
3. Infer why embryo cells and root-tip cells are used to study mitosis. **Cells in embryos and root tips undergo rapid and frequent cell division. As a result, the phases of mitosis can be seen easily.**
4. Copy the following statements in your Science Journal, then fill in each blank with the name of the correct phase of mitosis.

   telophase _____ Nuclear membrane re-forms.
   metaphase _____ Chromosomes move to the center of the cell.
   prophase _____ Spindle fibers appear.
   anaphase _____ Chromosomes move in opposite directions.

Chapter 4
ACTIVITY 4-2 • Modeling of DNA

Lab Preview
1. What safety symbols are associated with this activity?
   sharp object safety, eye safety
2. What are the parts of a DNA molecule?
   sugar-phosphate strands held apart with nitrogen bases

Bits of metal, pieces of wire, and cardboard cutouts are not usually considered scientific equipment. But, that's what Nobel prize winners James Watson and Francis Crick used to construct their model of DNA. In this lab you will use colored construction paper to make a model of DNA.

What You'll Investigate
You will examine the structure of a DNA molecule.

Goals
- **Design and construct** a model of DNA that is four base pairs long.

Safety Precautions
Use scissors carefully.

Materials
- 6 colors of construction paper (8" × 11") (2 of each color)
- scissors
- 2 cardboard patterns, a circle and a pentagon
- tape

Procedure
1. **Plan** your DNA molecule. Write down the four base pairs and enter them in your Science Journal.
2. **Assign** one color of paper to represent each of the following: phosphate groups, sugar molecules, guanines, adenines, thymines, and cytosines.
3. Using the circle pattern for each phosphate group and the pentagon pattern for each sugar molecule, **trace and cut out enough** figures to make the sugar-phosphate sides of your DNA molecule.
4. **Tape** a circle to each pentagon, as seen in illustration A.
5. Use the pentagon pattern to make the nitrogen bases. For each adenine and guanine **trace and cut out** two pentagons of the same color and tape them together, as seen in illustration B. Trace and cut out just one pentagon for each thymine and each cytosine.
6. **Tape** a nitrogen base to each sugar-phosphate unit.
7. **Construct** the DNA molecule that you planned in step 1 by taping the correct nitrogen bases together.

Activity (continued)

Conclude and Apply
1. Compare your models with those of other groups. Were the molecules your group created the same as those of other groups?
   The model of each of the groups will probably be different from those of other groups.
2. Compile a list of all the DNA sequences made and enter them in your Science Journal.
3. Based on your observations of the DNA molecule model, infer why a DNA molecule seldom copies itself incorrectly.
   Because A always bonds with T and C with G, DNA seldom copies itself incorrectly.
4. Explain why models are useful to scientists.
   Models help to explain concepts visually.

A.

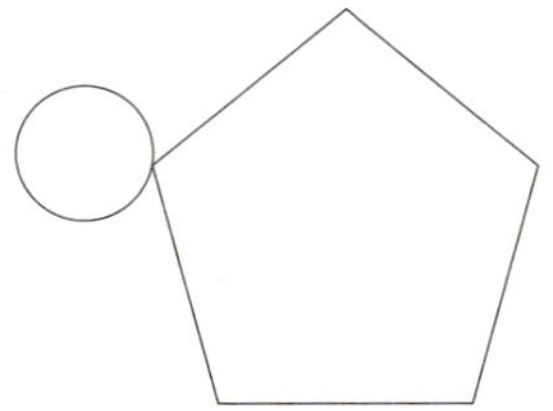

B.

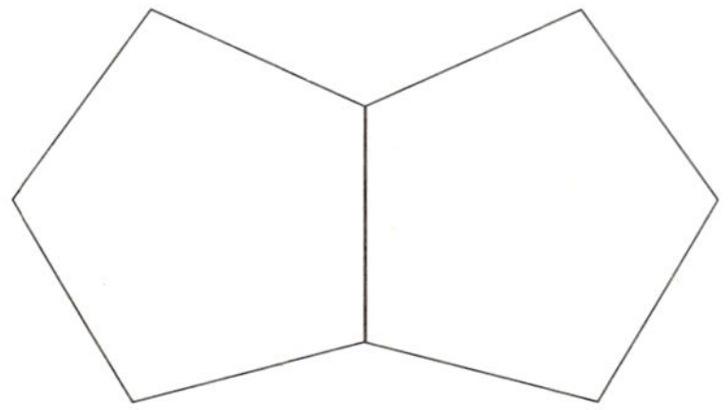

NAME _____ DATE _____ CLASS _____

Chapter 4
MINILAB 4-1

Modeling Mitosis

Procedure
1. Make models of cell division using materials supplied by your teacher.
2. Use four chromosomes in your model.
3. When finished, arrange the models in the order in which mitosis occurs.

Analysis
1. In which steps is the nucleus visible?

   prophase and telophase

2. How many cells does a dividing cell form?

   two new cells

NAME _____ DATE _____ CLASS _____

Chapter 4
MINILAB 4-2

Comparing DNA Sequences

Procedure
1. Suppose you have a segment of DNA that is six nitrogen base pairs in length. In the space below, using the letters A, T, C, and G, write down a combination of six pairs remembering that A and T are always a pair and C and G are always a pair.

2. Now replicate your segment of DNA. On paper, diagram how this happens and show the new DNA segments.

Analysis
Compare the order of bases of the original DNA to the new DNA molecules.

Answers will vary with the bases chosen, but bases should be the same as the original DNA.

181

Chapter 5
ACTIVITY 5-1 • Comparing Mosses, Liverworts, and Ferns

Lab Preview
1. Why is it important to be careful when using coverslips?
   A coverslip is fragile and may break easily.
2. What do mosses and liverworts have in common?
   They are both seedless, nonvascular plants.

Mosses and liverworts make up the division of plants called bryophytes. Ferns make up the division Pterophyta and are called pteridophytes (tuh RIH duh fites). Try this activity to observe the similarities and differences in these groups of plants.

What You'll Investigate
How are the gametophyte and sporophyte stages of liverworts, mosses, and ferns similar and different?

Goals
- **Describe** the sporophyte and gametophyte forms of liverworts, mosses, and ferns.
- **Identify** the spore-producing structures of liverworts, mosses, and ferns.

Materials
- live mosses, liverworts, and ferns with gametophytes and sporophytes
- hand lens
- forceps
- dropper
- microscope slide and coverslip
- microscope
- dissecting needle
- pencil with eraser

Procedure
1. Obtain a gametophyte of each plant. With a hand lens, **observe** the rhizoids, leafy parts, and stemlike parts, if any are present.
2. Obtain a sporophyte of each plant, and use a hand lens to **observe** it.
3. Locate the spore structure on the moss plant. **Remove** it and place it in a drop of water on the slide. Place a coverslip over it. Use the eraser of a pencil to gently push on the coverslip to release the spores.
   CAUTION: *Do not break the coverslip.*
   Observe the spores under low and high power.
4. Make labeled drawings of all observations on the next page.

Activity (continued)
Data and Observations

Conclude and Apply
1. For each plant, compare the gametophyte's appearance to the sporophyte's appearance.
   The gametophyte of a moss is a green, low-growing structure with leaves in a whorl around a stalk; that of the liverwort is a green, flat, leaflike form. Sporophytes of mosses are a nongreen stalk with a capsule containing spores at the top of the gametophyte. In liverworts, the sporophytes form on the gametophyte as nongreen umbrella-like structures with spores in cases underneath. Fern gametophytes are green, heart-shaped structures. Fern sporophytes are familiar green plants.
2. List the structure(s) common to all three plants.
   Spores, leaflike structures, and rootlike structures are common to all three.
3. Form a hypothesis about why each plant produces a large number of spores.
   Many spores do not land where conditions are right for growth. The greater the number of spores produced, the greater the chances that some will grow.

NAME _____ DATE _____ CLASS _____

Chapter 5
ACTIVITY 5-2 • Germination Rate of Seeds

Design Your Own Experiment

Lab Preview
1. What happens to a seed during germination?
   The embryo uses the endosperm for food until it can produce food on its own.
2. What safety symbols are associated with this activity?
   disposal alert, biological hazard, electrical safety, clothing protection safety, and eye safety

Many environmental factors affect the germination rate of seeds. Among these are soil temperature, air temperature, moisture content of soil, and salt content of soil. What happens to the germination rate when one of these variables is changed? Can you determine a way to predict the best conditions for seed germination?

Recognize the Problem
How does an environmental factor affect seed germination?

Form a Hypothesis
Based on your knowledge of seed germination, state a hypothesis about how environmental factors affect germination rates.

Goals
- **Design** an experiment to test the effect of an environmental factor on seed germination rate.
- **Compare** germination rates under different conditions.

Safety Precautions
Some kinds of seeds are poisonous. Do not place any seeds in your mouth. Be careful when using any electrical equipment to avoid shock hazards.

Possible Materials
- seeds
- water
- salt
- potting soil
- plant trays or plastic cups
- *seedling warming cables*
- thermometer
- graduated cylinder
- beakers
- *alternate materials*

Test Your Hypothesis
Plan
1. As a group, agree upon and **write** out the hypothesis statement.
2. As a group, list the steps that you need to take to test your hypothesis. Be specific, and **describe** exactly what you will do at each step. List your materials.
3. **Identify** any constants, variables, and controls of the experiment.
4. What measurements will you take? What data will you collect? How often will you collect data? If you need a data table, **design** one in your Science Journal so that it is ready to use as your group collects data. Will the data be summarized in a graph?
5. **Read** over your entire experiment to make sure that all steps are in logical order. How many tests will you run?

25

NAME _____ DATE _____ CLASS _____

Activity (continued)

Do
1. Make sure your teacher approves your plan before you proceed.
2. Carry out the experiment as planned.
3. While the experiment is going on, **record** any observations that you make and complete the data table in your Science Journal.

Analyze Your Data
1. **Compare** your results with those of other groups. Explain.
   Group results should be similar for the same variable.
2. Did changing the variable affect germination rates? Explain.
   Germination rates decrease in high concentrations of salt and cold temperatures.
3. In the space below, **graph** your results using a bar graph, placing germination rate on the y-axis and the environmental variables on the x-axis.
   Graph should accurately reflect experimental data.

Draw Conclusions
1. **Interpret** your graph to estimate the conditions that give the best germination rate.
   Student graph will vary, but each graph should indicate a range for the best germination of the variable tested.
2. What things affect the germination rate?
   Answers will vary, but may include water quality, amount of water, planting depth.

26

183

NAME _____ DATE _____ CLASS _____

Chapter 5
MINILAB 5-1

Observing Gymnosperm Cones

Procedure
1. Using a hand lens, look at the parts of a gymnosperm cone.
2. On a large paper towel, open the cone and note where the seeds are located.

Analysis
1. Make a drawing of the cone and seeds in the space below. **Drawings will vary.**

2. Where are the seeds located?
   Seeds are found at the base of a woody scale near the center of a cone.

3. Predict how this location is an advantage for the tree species.
   Because these seeds are not inside a fruit, this location ensures that they are protected until released from the cone.

184

NAME _____ DATE _____ CLASS _____

Chapter 5
MINILAB 5-2

Identifying How Seeds Disperse

Procedure
1. Make a list of ten different seeds, including some mentioned in the textbook.
2. Research each of the ten seeds to determine how they are dispersed.

Data and Observations

Answers will vary.

Type of seed	Dispersal method
1.	
2.	
3.	
4.	
5.	
6.	
7.	
8.	
9.	
10.	

Analysis
1. How are the seeds of each plant on your list dispersed—by wind, water, insects, birds, or mammals?
   Answers will vary depending on the seeds listed.

2. Identify features that tell you how each kind of seed is dispersed.
   Features will vary but may include wings, parachutes, or similar features.

28

NAME _____ DATE _____ CLASS _____

Chapter 6
ACTIVITY 6-1
Expected and Observed Results

Lab Preview
1. What are alleles? _different genetic forms for a trait_
2. What is probability? _Probability is a branch of mathematics that helps you determine the chance that something will happen._

Could you predict how many white flowers would result from crossing two heterozygous red flowers if you knew that white color was a recessive trait? Try this experiment to find out.

What You'll Investigate
How does chance affect combinations of genes?

Goals
- **Model** chance events in heredity.
- **Compare** and **contrast** predicted and actual results.

Materials
- paper bags (2)
- red beans (100)
- white beans (100)

Safety Precautions
CAUTION: Do not taste, eat, or drink any materials used in lab.

Procedure
1. Place 50 red beans and 50 white beans into a paper bag. Place 50 red beans and 50 white beans into a second bag. Each bean represents an allele for flower color.
2. **Label** one of the bags "female" for the female parent. **Label** the other bag "male" for the male parent.
3. Without looking, remove one bean from each bag. The two beans represent the alleles that combine when sperm and egg join.
4. Use a Punnett square to **predict** how many red/red, red/white, white/white combinations are possible.
5. Use a data table to **record** the combination of the beans each time you remove two beans. Your table will need to accommodate 100 picks. After recording, return the beans to their original bags.
6. **Count** and **record** the total numbers of combinations in your data table.
7. Compile and record the class totals.

Gene Combinations   Sample data

Beans	Red/Red	Red/White	White/White
Your total	22	54	24
Class total	200	400	200

NAME _____ DATE _____ CLASS _____

Activity (continued)

Predicted outcome: Female Parent

Male Parent [Punnett square]

R/R __25__ %
R/W __50__ %
W/W __25__ %

Conclude and Apply
1. Which combination occurred most often? _red/white_
2. Calculate the ratio of red/red to red/white to white/white. Results should show a generally close ratio of 1:2:1.
3. Compare your predicted (expected) results with your observed (actual) results. _Answers will vary according to the individual numbers of the various color combinations chosen, but should reflect a generally close following of the expected results._
4. Does chance affect allele combination? Explain. _Each time an allele is chosen, there is a 50/50 chance it or its corresponding other allele will be chosen._
5. How do the results of a small sample compare with the results of a large sample? _The larger the sample, the more nearly accurate the results._
6. Hypothesize how you could get predicted results to be closer to actual results. _by increasing the size of the sample_

Chapter 6
ACTIVITY 6-2
Determining Polygenic Inheritance

Lab Preview
1. What is polygenic inheritance?
   It occurs when a group of gene pairs act together to produce a single trait.
2. What are some traits polygenic inheritance controls?
   height; weight; shape of eyes, lips, and ears; eye and hair color; skin color

When several genes at different locations on chromosomes act together to produce a single trait, a wide range of phenotypes for the trait can result. By measuring the range of phenotypes and graphing them, you can determine if a trait is produced by polygenic inheritance. How would graphs differ if traits were inherited in a simple dominant or recessive pattern?

What You'll Investigate
How can the effect of polygenic inheritance be determined?

Goals
- **Measure** the heights of students to the nearest centimeter.
- **Create** a bar graph of phenotypes for a polygenic trait.

Safety Precautions
Always obtain the permission of any person included in an experiment on human traits.

Materials
- meterstick
- graph paper
- pencil

Procedure
1. **Form a hypothesis** about what a bar graph that shows the heights of the students in your class will look like.
2. **Measure** and **record** the height of every student in the class to the nearest centimeter.
3. **Design** a table on the next page like the one shown. Count the number of students for each interval and complete the table.

Height in cm	Number of students
A 101 – 110	1
B 111 – 120	2
C 121 – 130	5
D 131 – 140	6
E 141 – 150	6
F 151 – 160	2
G 161 – 170	2
H 171 – 180	1

4. **Plot** the results from the table on a bar graph in the space on the next page. The height should be graphed on the horizontal axis and the number of students of each height along the vertical axis. If you need help, refer to Making and Using Graphs in the **Skill Handbook**.
5. The *range* of a set of data is the difference between the greatest measurement and the smallest measurement. The *median* is the middle number when the data are placed in order. The *mean* is the sum of all the data divided by the sample size. The *mode* is the number that appears most often in the measurements. Calculate each of these numbers and record them on the next page.

Activity (continued)

Data and Observations

Conclude and Apply
1. How does the bar graph differ from one that would be produced for a trait controlled by a single gene?
   It shows several bars forming a "bell shape" instead of a graph with only two or three bars.
2. How can you tell if a trait is controlled by more than one gene?
   The more genes that control a trait, the more bars that should appear when the data are graphed.
3. Can you **infer** from your data that height is controlled by more than two genes? Explain why or why not.
   Yes, the graph has several bars.

NAME _____ DATE _____ CLASS _____

Chapter 6
MINILAB 6-1

Comparing Common Traits

Procedure
1. Always obtain the permission of any person included in an experiment on human traits.
2. Survey ten students in your class or school for the presence of freckles, dimples, cleft or smooth chins, and attached or detached earlobes.
3. A data table below lists each of the traits.
4. Fill in the table.

Data and Observations *Data will vary.*

Trait	Number of students
Freckles	
Dimples	
Cleft Chin	
Attached Earlobes	

Analysis
1. Compare the number of people who have one form of a trait with those who have the other form. How do those two groups compare?

   Answers will vary.

2. What can you conclude about the number of variations you noticed?

   There are as many variations as people because each person is unique.

NAME _____ DATE _____ CLASS _____

Chapter 6
MINILAB 6-2

Interpreting Fingerprints

Procedure
1. Look at the figure on the same page in the textbook as the minilab.
2. With a pencil lead, rub a spot large enough for your finger onto a piece of paper.
3. Rub your finger in the pencil markings.
4. Stick clear tape to your finger.
5. Remove the tape and stick it to the paper. **CAUTION:** *Wash hands after taking fingerprints.*
6. Using a magnifying lens, observe your fingerprints to see if you can find a whorl, arch, or loop pattern.

Analysis
1. What patterns did you find?

   Answers will vary.

2. Are fingerprints inherited as a simple Mendelian pattern or as a more complex pattern?

   Fingerprints are more complex because each finger shows different patterns.

187

Chapter 7
ACTIVITY 7-1

Recognizing Variation in a Population

Design Your Own Experiment

Lab Preview
1. What is a species?
   A species is a group of organisms that can mate with one another to produce fertile offspring.
2. Name some variations found in seeds.
   size, shape, color, texture

When you first see a group of plants or animals of one species, they may all look alike. However, when you look closer, you will notice minor differences in each characteristic. Variations must exist in a population for evolution to occur. What kinds of variations have you noticed among species of plants or animals?

Recognize the Problem
How can you measure variation in a plant or animal population?

Form a Hypothesis
Make a hypothesis about the amount of variation in seeds, leaves, or flowers of one species of plant.

Goals
- Design an experiment that will allow you to collect data about variation in a population.
- Observe, measure, and analyze variations in a population.

Possible Materials
- leaves, flowers, and seeds from one species of plant
- metric ruler
- magnifying glass
- graph paper

Safety Precautions
Do not put any seeds, flowers, or plant parts in your mouth. Wash your hands after handling plant parts.

Activity (continued)

Test Your Hypothesis

Plan
1. As a group, agree upon and write out the hypothesis statement.
2. List the steps you need to take to test your hypothesis. Be specific. Describe exactly what you will do at each step. List your materials.
3. Decide what characteristic of seeds, leaves, or flowers you will study. For example, you could measure the length of seeds, the width of leaves, or the number of petals on the flowers of plants.
4. Design a data table in your Science Journal to collect data about one variation. Use the table to record the data your group collects as you complete the experiment.
5. Identify any constants, variables, and controls of the experiment.
6. How many seeds, leaves, or flowers will you examine? Will your data be more accurate if you examine larger numbers?
7. Summarize the data in a graph or chart.

Do
1. Make sure your teacher approves your plan before you proceed.
2. Carry out the experiment as planned.
3. While the experiment is going on, write down any observations that you make and complete the data table in your Science Journal.

Analyze Your Data
1. Compare your results with those of other groups.
   Results should be similar for the same measured variables.
2. How did you determine the amount of variation present?
   The amount of variation is determined by the range of measurements.

Draw Conclusions
1. Graph your results, placing the *range* of variation on the x-axis and the number of organisms that had that measurement on the y-axis.
   Graphs will be a bell-shaped curve for most variables.
2. Calculate the *mean* and *range* of variation in your experiment.
   Means and ranges will vary depending on the seeds used and the variables measured.
   The *range* in a set of data is the difference between the greatest measurement and the smallest measurement. The *mean* is the sum of all the data divided by the sample size.

Chapter 7
ACTIVITY 7-2 • A Model of Natural Selection

Lab Preview
1. What is a fossil?
   Fossils are any remains of life from an earlier time.
2. Why do scientists study fossils?
   Fossils provide evidence of geological changes and of evolution.

Natural selection has been observed in a variety of organisms in nature. Studying natural selection takes a long time because natural selection occurs in populations that may take years to produce a new generation. However, the process occurs in a way that can be explained by a simple model.

What You'll Investigate
What is the result of natural selection?

Safety Precautions
Caution: *Do not taste or eat any material used in the lab.*

Materials
- red beans and white beans
- paper bags
- pencils and paper

Procedure
Part A
1. Take a paper bag and write "Rabbit Gene Pool" on it.
2. Place 10 red beans and 10 white beans in the bag.
3. Make a table that you can use to record the genetics in the population. Assume that pairs of beans are rabbits. A pair of red beans makes a brown rabbit. A red bean and a white bean make a gray rabbit, and a pair of white beans makes a white rabbit.
4. Without looking into the bag, take out two beans to represent an offspring. Do not return the beans to the bag. Write the colors of the beans on the chart.
5. Continue taking the beans out of the bag two at a time until all beans are removed. Write the results on the chart.

Part B
1. To model selection, assume that predators eat all of the white rabbits and one half of the gray rabbits.
2. For each brown rabbit from Part A, put 14 red beans (two beans for the brown rabbit and 12 beans representing six baby brown rabbits) into the bag.
3. For each remaining gray rabbit from Part A, put 7 red beans and 7 white beans (one of each color for the remaining gray rabbit and six of each color for six baby gray rabbits) into the bag.
4. Repeat steps 3–5 of Part A.

Activity (continued)
Data and Observations

Rabbit Offspring

Rabbit #	Bean colors		Rabbit color
1	red	white	gray
2	red	red	brown
3	white	red	gray
4	white	white	white
5	red	red	brown
6	red	white	gray
7	red	white	gray
8	white	red	gray
9	white	white	white
10	red	white	gray

Analysis
1. How did the rabbit gene pool change during the activity?
   The number of white beans in the gene pool decreased. The number of red beans increased, and the overall number of rabbits increased.

2. What eventually happens to the white rabbits?
   The white rabbits died out as a result of natural selection by predators.

3. Describe how this model is similar to the way natural selection occurs in nature.
   The model is similar to natural selection because there is an overpopulation of rabbits (the population continued to grow even with predation). Predation removed certain individuals but not others.

4. How is this model unlike the way natural selection occurs in nature?
   The model is unlike natural selection because the predation was 100% against white rabbits and 0% against brown rabbits. This does not usually occur in nature. Also, in nature, some populations tend to remain fairly stable and do not continue to increase.

NAME _____ DATE _____ CLASS _____

Chapter 7
MINILAB 7-1

Relating Evolution to Species

Procedure
1. On a piece of paper, print the alphabet in lowercase letters.
2. Order the letters into three groups. Put all of the vowels in the first group. Place all of the consonants that do not drop below the line into the second group and all of the consonants that do drop below the line in the third group.

Analysis
1. How are the three groups of letters similar to each other? Answers will vary. Students may indicate that they are all letters of the alphabet or are all lowercase letters.

2. If the letters were organisms, how would scientists know how closely related the letters were to each other? Evolution changes species into different forms using the same mechanism, just as different strokes of a pen make changes in letters.

NAME _____ DATE _____ CLASS _____

Chapter 7
MINILAB 7-2

Living Without Thumbs

Procedure
1. Tape your thumb securely to your hand. Do this for both hands.
2. Leave your thumbs taped down for at least two hours. During this time, do the following activities: eat a meal, change clothes, and brush your teeth. Be careful not to try anything that could be dangerous.
3. Write about your experience in the space below.

Data and Observations

Analysis
1. Did not having usable thumbs significantly affect the way you did things? Explain. Answers will vary.

2. Infer how having opposable thumbs may have influenced primate evolution. Have students explain their responses. Accept all reasonable answers.

Chapter 8
ACTIVITY 8-1 • Classifying Seeds

Design Your Own Experiment

Lab Preview
1. What is a seed?
   A seed is the reproductive part of a plant, which contains a plant embryo and stored food.
2. Name a seed plant.
   Answers will vary, but may include flowers or vegetables students have seen on seed packets.

Scientists have developed classification systems to show how organisms are related. How do they determine what features they will use to classify organisms? Can you learn to use the same methods?

Recognize the Problem
You are given several kinds of seeds and are asked to classify them into groups of similar seeds. How would you begin?

Form a Hypothesis
Make a hypothesis about the traits or physical features that may be used to help classify various kinds of seeds.

Goals
- **Observe** the seeds provided and notice their distinctive features.
- **Classify** seeds using your model.

Possible Materials
- packets of seeds (10 different kinds)
- hand lens
- metric ruler
- sheets of paper (2)

Safety Precautions
Do not eat any seeds or put them in your mouth. Some may have been treated with chemicals.

Sample Model

Test Your Hypothesis
Plan
1. As a group, list the steps that you need to take to classify seeds. Be specific, and describe exactly what you will do at each step. List your materials.
2. **Classify** your seeds by making a model.
3. Make a key to identify your seeds.
4. Read over your entire experiment to make sure that all steps are in logical order.

Do
1. Make sure your teacher approves your model before you proceed.
2. Carry out the experiment as planned.
3. While you are working, write down any observations that you make that would cause you to change your model.
4. Complete the plan.

Analyze Your Data
1. Compare your key and branching model with those made by other groups. **Comparisons may or may not result in agreement.**
2. Check your key by having another group use it. **If one group can use another group's key, the second group was successful.**

Draw Conclusions
1. In what ways can groups of different types of seeds be classified? **shape, texture, how they are attached to the plant**
2. Why is it an advantage for scientists to use a standardized system to classify organisms? What observations did you make to support your answer? **Different classification systems could result in confusion and differing interpretations of scientific observations. Answers will vary but should be based on the observation that not every student classified the seeds in the same way.**

Chapter 8
ACTIVITY 8-2 • Using a Dichotomous Key

Lab Preview
1. What is binomial nomenclature?
   a system of classification that gives a two-word scientific name to organisms
2. Who introduced binomial nomenclature?
   Carolus Linnaeus

Scientists who classify organisms have made many keys that allow you to identify unknown organisms. Try this activity to see how it is done.

What You'll Investigate
How a dichotomous key can be used to identify native cats in the United States.

Goals
- Learn to use a dichotomous key.
- Identify two native cats of North America.

Materials
- paper and pencil

Procedure
1. **Observe** the cats pictured below.
2. Begin with 1 of the key to the right. **Identify** the cat labeled A.
3. On your paper, write the common and scientific name for the cat and list all of its traits given in the key.
4. Use the same procedure to **identify** the species of the cat labeled B.

Key to Native Cats of North America

1. Tail length
   a. short, go to 2
   b. long, go to 3
2. Cheek ruff
   a. no cheek ruff; long ear tuffs tipped with black; coat distinctly mottled; lynx, *Lynx canadensis*
   b. broad cheek ruffs; ear tuffs short; coat with indistinct spots; bobcat, *Lynx rufus*
3. Coat
   a. plain colored, go to 4
   b. patterned, go to 5
4. Coat color
   a. yellowish to tan above with white to buff below; mountain lion, *Felis concolor*
   b. all brown or black; jaguarundi, *Felis yagouaroundi*
5. Coat pattern
   a. lines of black-bordered brown spots; ocelot, *Felis pardalis*
   b. irregular tan and black, go to 6
6. Animal size
   a. large cat; rows of black rosettes or rings unevenly distributed; jaguar, *Panthera onca*
   b. small cat; four dark-brown stripes on the back and one on the neck; some irregularly shaped spots; margay, *Felis wiedii*

Activity (continued)

Conclude and Apply
1. According to the key, how many species of native cats reside in North America?
   seven different species
2. How do you know that this key doesn't contain all the species of native cats in the world?
   The title of the key specifies that it is a key to cats of North America.
3. Infer why you couldn't identify a lion using this key.
   Lions are not found in North America.
4. Explain why it wouldn't be a good idea to begin in the middle of a key instead of with the first step.
   Beginning with the first pair of descriptions, and then continuing with those that follow, will lead to the correct identification.

NAME _____ DATE _____ CLASS _____

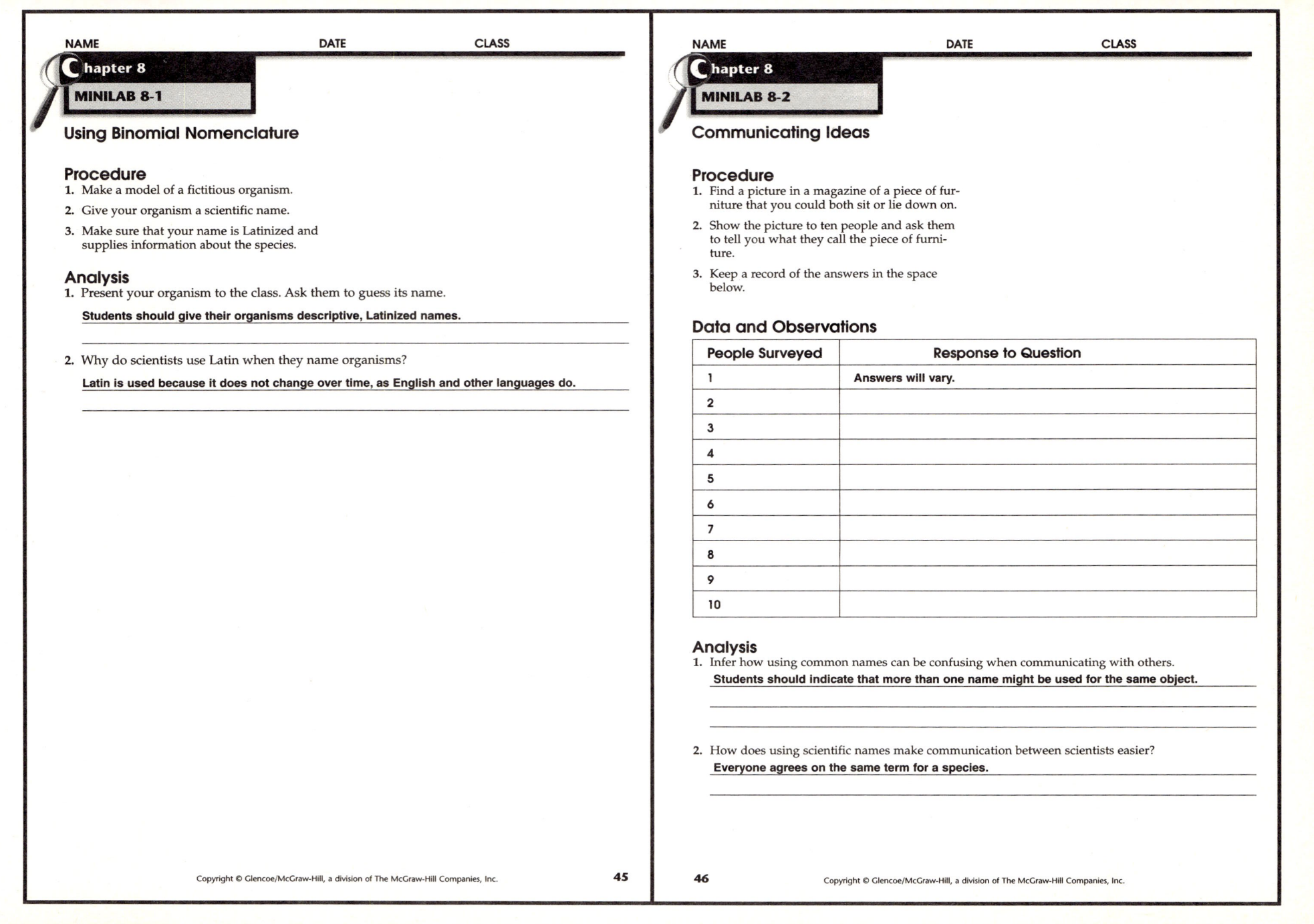

Chapter 8
MINILAB 8-1

Using Binomial Nomenclature

Procedure
1. Make a model of a fictitious organism.
2. Give your organism a scientific name.
3. Make sure that your name is Latinized and supplies information about the species.

Analysis
1. Present your organism to the class. Ask them to guess its name.

   Students should give their organisms descriptive, Latinized names.

2. Why do scientists use Latin when they name organisms?

   Latin is used because it does not change over time, as English and other languages do.

NAME _____ DATE _____ CLASS _____

Chapter 8
MINILAB 8-2

Communicating Ideas

Procedure
1. Find a picture in a magazine of a piece of furniture that you could both sit or lie down on.
2. Show the picture to ten people and ask them to tell you what they call the piece of furniture.
3. Keep a record of the answers in the space below.

Data and Observations

People Surveyed	Response to Question
1	Answers will vary.
2	
3	
4	
5	
6	
7	
8	
9	
10	

Analysis

1. Infer how using common names can be confusing when communicating with others.

   Students should indicate that more than one name might be used for the same object.

2. How does using scientific names make communication between scientists easier?

   Everyone agrees on the same term for a species.

Chapter 9
ACTIVITY 9-1 • Observing Cyanobacteria

Lab Preview

1. What safety symbols are associated with this activity? <u>disposal alert, biological hazard, eye safety, clothing protection safety</u>

2. What is the common name for cyanobacteria? <u>blue-green bacteria</u>

You can obtain many species of cyanobacteria from ponds. When you look at these organisms under a microscope, you will find that they have many similarities but that they are also different from each other in important ways. In this activity, you will compare and contrast species of cyanobacteria.

What You'll Investigate
What do cyanobacteria look like?

Materials
- micrograph photos
- *microscope
- *prepared slides of Gloeocapsa and Anabaena
- *alternate materials

Goals
- Observe several species of cyanobacteria.
- Describe the structure and function of cyanobacteria.

Procedure

1. Indicate whether each cyanobacterium sample is in colony form or filament form. Write a *yes* or *no* in the data table for the presence or absence of each characteristic in each type of cyanobacterium.

2. Observe photos or prepared slides, if available, of *Gloeocapsa* and *Anabaena*. If using slides, observe under the low and high power of the microscope. Notice the difference in the arrangement of the cells. Draw and label a few cells of each species of cyanobacterium.

3. Observe photos of *Nostoc* and *Oscillatoria*. In your Science Journal, draw and label a few cells of each.

47

Activity (continued)

Cyanobacteria Observations

Sample data

Structure	*Anabaena*	*Gloeocapsa*	*Nostoc*	*Oscillatoria*
Filament or colony	filament	colony	filament	filament
Nucleus	no	no	no	no
Chlorophyll	yes	yes	yes	yes
Gel-like layer	yes	yes	yes	yes

Conclude and Apply

1. How does the color of cyanobacteria compare with the color of leaves on trees? What can you infer from this?
   <u>Cyanobacteria are bluer than leaves but contain chlorophyll. Therefore, they can undergo photosynthesis.</u>

2. How can you tell by observing them that cyanobacteria belong to Kingdom Eubacteria?
   <u>Cyanobacteria are small cells without visible nuclei that contain chlorophyll.</u>

3. Describe the general appearance of cyanobacteria.
   <u>Cyanobacteria appear blue-green in color and may form slimy colonies in water.</u>

48

Chapter 9
ACTIVITY 9-2 • Are there bacteria in foods?

Lab Preview
1. What is an indicator?
   An indicator is a substance that changes color in the presence of another substance.
   A color change indicates that the other substance is present.
2. Why are separate droppers and craft sticks used in this activity?
   Separate droppers and craft sticks are used to avoid mixing the samples and possibly obtaining false results.

You've learned that bacteria are too small to be seen without a microscope, but is there some way that you can tell if they are present in foods? Because bacteria respire by producing carbon dioxide like other living things, a chemical test that indicates the respiration of bacteria can be used to tell if bacteria are growing in foods you eat.

What You'll Investigate
Is there bacteria in the food you eat?

Goals
- Observe color changes in test tubes containing food.
- Determine which foods contain the most bacteria

Safety Precautions

Materials
- 6 test tubes
- 6 stoppers
- test-tube rack
- felt-tip marker
- 3 droppers
- 3 craft sticks
- milk, buttermilk, cottage cheese, yogurt, sour cream, water
- bromothymol blue solution (150 mL)

Procedure
1. Use the marker to label the test tubes 1 through 6 and place them in the test-tube rack.
2. Add 25 mL of bromothymol blue-indicator solution to each test tube.
3. Using a different dropper each time, add four drops of water to tube 1, four drops of milk to tube 2, and four drops of buttermilk to tube 3. Be careful not to let the drops go down the sides of the tubes.
4. Using a different craft stick each time, add an amount of yogurt about the size of a green pea to tube 4, the same amount of cottage cheese to tube 5, and the same amount of sour cream to tube 6.
5. Loosely place a stopper in each tube and record the color of the contents of each tube in the data table below.
6. Leave the tubes undisturbed until the end of the class period. Record the color of the contents of the tubes in the data table below.
7. The next time you arrive in class, record the color of the contents of the tubes again.

Activity (continued)
Data and Observations

Data Table for Test of Bacteria in Food

Tube	Contents	Color at Start	Color at End of Class	Color One Day Later	Test + or −	Bacteria Present?
1	Water	blue	blue	blue	−	No
2	Milk	blue	green	green	+	Yes
3	Buttermilk	blue	green	green	+	Yes
4	Yogurt	blue	yellow	green	+	Yes
5	Cottage cheese	blue	yellow	green	+	Yes
6	Sour cream	blue	yellow	green	+	Yes

Conclude and Apply
1. Why was water added to tube 1?
   Water acted as a control so that the negative effect on bromothymol blue could be observed and compared.

2. What color does bromothymol turn if carbon dioxide is present?
   Bromothymol turns yellow or green if carbon dioxide is present.

3. Using strength of the color change as a guide, judge which tubes contain the most bacteria.
   Students may have varying answers depending on the colors present in their tubes, but buttermilk and yogurt usually have the highest concentrations of bacteria present.

NAME _____ DATE _____ CLASS _____

Chapter 9
MINILAB 9-1

Observing Bacterial Growth

Procedure

1. Obtain two or three dried beans.
2. Break them into halves and place the halves into 10 mL of distilled water in a glass beaker.
3. Observe how many days it takes for the water to become cloudy and develop an unpleasant odor.
4. Use methylene blue to dye a drop of water from the beaker and observe it under the microscope.

Analysis

1. How long did it take for the water to become cloudy?
   It usually takes three or four days.
2. What did you observe on the slide that would make the water cloudy?
   bacteria
3. What do you think the bacteria were feeding on?
   beans

NAME _____ DATE _____ CLASS _____

Chapter 9
MINILAB 9-2

Making Yogurt

Procedure

1. Bring a liter of milk almost to a boil in a saucepan. **CAUTION:** *Always be careful when using a stove or hot plate. Do not eat food used in a classroom activity.*
2. Remove the pan from the burner and allow it to cool until it is lukewarm.
3. Add one or two heaping tablespoons of yogurt starter with live cultures and stir.
4. Pour the mixture into a clean thermos and put on the lid.
5. Let stand for six hours and then refrigerate overnight.

Analysis

1. What do you think was in the yogurt starter?
   bacteria
2. Infer why you let the milk cool before adding the starter.
   Yogurt culture is alive and excess heat can kill the bacteria. The bacteria culture grows well when lukewarm.

Chapter 10
ACTIVITY 10-1 • Comparing Algae and Protozoans

Lab Preview
1. How do plant cells that, like algae, contain chloroplasts differ from animal cells? **They can make their own food.**
2. How many cells do protozoans have? **They are one-celled organisms.**

Algae and protozoan cells have characteristics that are similar enough to place them within the same kingdom. However, the variety of forms within Kingdom Protista is great. In this activity, you can observe many of the differences that make organisms in Kingdom Protista so diverse.

What You'll Investigate
What are the differences between algae and protozoans?

Goals
- Draw and label the organisms you examine.
- Observe the differences between algae and protozoans.

Safety Precautions
Make sure to wash your hands after handling algae and protozoans.

Materials
- cultures of *Paramecium*, *Amoeba*, *Euglena*, and *Spirogyra*
- *prepared slides of above organisms
- prepared slide of slime mold
- coverslips (5)
- *stereomicroscope
- microscope
- dropper
- microscope slides (5)
- *alternate materials

Procedure
1. Record your drawings and observations in the table on the next page.
2. Make a wet mount of the *Paramecium* culture. If you need help doing this, refer to Appendix D.
3. Observe the wet mount first under low and then under high power. Draw and label the organism.
4. Repeat steps 2 and 3 with the other cultures. Return all preparations to your teacher and wash your hands.
5. Observe the slide of slime mold under low and high power. Record your observations.

53

Activity (continued)
Protist Observations

	Paramecium	*Amoeba*	*Euglena*	*Spirogyra*
Drawing	Student drawings should resemble illustration in the textbook.	Student drawings should resemble illustration in the textbook.	Student drawings should resemble illustration in the textbook.	Student drawings should resemble illustration in the textbook.

Conclude and Apply
1. For each organism that could move, label the structure that enabled the movement. *Paramecium*—cilia; *Amoeba*—psuedopods; *Euglena*—flagella
2. Which protists make their own food? Explain how you know that they make their own food. **Spirogyra and Euglena make their own food. We know they make their own food because they contain chloroplasts and, therefore, use light to photosynthesize food.**
3. Identify those protists with animal characteristics. **Paramecium, Amoeba, and Euglena are animal-like because they obtain their food from other sources and move.**

54

Chapter 10
ACTIVITY 10-2 • Comparing Types of Fungi

Lab Preview
1. What safety symbol is associated with this activity?
   disposal, eye safety, and irritant

2. Name three ways in which fungi benefit people.
   Fungi decompose organic material, provide medicine (penicillin), and are necessary for the production of bread.

Fungi differ mainly in their reproductive structures. The diversity of these structures allows scientists to classify fungi as zygote fungi, club fungi, sac fungi, or imperfect fungi. In this activity, you will compare the reproductive structures in cultures of fungi.

What You'll Investigate
How do reproductive structures of fungi compare?

Goals
- **Observe** the appearance of fungi colonies.
- **Compare** the reproductive structures of fungi cultures.
- **Draw, label,** and **identify** different types of fungi.

Safety Precautions
Make sure to wash your hands after handling fungi.

Materials
- cultures of fungi (bread mold, mushrooms, yeasts, lichens, or *Penicillium*)
- cellophane tape
- microscope
- microscope slides
- coverslips
- magnifying lens

Procedure
1. **Design** a data table in your Science Journal with columns labeled *Fungus, Colony Appearance, Reproductive Structures,* and *Fungi Division.*
2. **Compare** and **contrast** the cultures of fungi in drawings that you labeled.
3. Your teacher will demonstrate how to collect the reproductive structures of fungi with cellophane tape by gently touching the tape to your samples.
4. Place the tape, adhesive side up, on a microscope slide, and cover it with a coverslip.
5. **Draw** and **label** the reproductive structures.
6. Repeat this procedure for each culture of fungus.

Activity (continued)

Conclude and Apply
1. Write a description of the reproductive structures you observed. Include relative numbers, shape of cells, and size.
   Students descriptions will be based on the cultures observed. Students should describe spores as being small, spherical objects of varying colors. The numbers will range from hundreds to thousands, depending on how many spores they collected from each specimen.

2. From your descriptions, explain why fungi are classified based on their reproductive structures.
   Many reproductive structures of the major groups of fungi are unique and distinctive.

3. List the four divisions of fungi, and give an example of each division.
   The four phyla of fungi should be listed with a representative from each phylum.

Data and Observations

Sample Data

Fungi Observations

Fungus	Colony appearance	Reproductive structures	Fungi division
mushroom	rounded stalks with club-like caps	basidia	club fungi
bread mold	fuzzy with black spots (spore cases)	sporangia	zygote fungi
Penicillium	blue-green flattened colonies growing in circles	none observed	imperfect fungi

NAME _____ DATE _____ CLASS _____

Chapter 10
MINILAB 10-1

Observing Slime Molds

Procedure

1. Obtain live specimens of the slime mold *Physarum polycephaalum* from your teacher.
2. Observe the mold for four days.

Analysis

1. Make daily drawings and observations of the mold as it grows. Use a magnifying glass. **Drawings will vary depending on observations.**
2. Predict the conditions under which the slime mold will change from the amoeboid form to the spore-producing form. **Lower temperatures and reduced humidity or food will result in the growth of the spore-producing form.**

Data and Observations

Observations will vary.

Day	Drawings	Observation
1		
2		
3		
4		

NAME _____ DATE _____ CLASS _____

Chapter 10
MINILAB 10-2

Interpreting Spore Prints

Procedure

1. Obtain several mushrooms from the grocery store and let them age until the undersides look brown.
2. Remove the stems and arrange the mushroom caps with the gills down on a piece of unlined white paper.
3. Let the mushroom caps sit undisturbed overnight and remove them from the paper the next day.

Analysis

1. Draw and label a sketch of the results in the space below. **Sketches will vary.**

2. Describe the marks on the page and what made them. **Brown lines will be parallel or concentric rings made by falling spores.**

3. How could you estimate the number of new mushrooms that could be produced from one mushroom cap? **Count a few in one area and multiply by the total area of spore production.**

199

Chapter 11
ACTIVITY 11-1 • Comparing Seedless Plants

Lab Preview
1. What are the two categories of seedless plants?
   nonvascular and vascular

2. What is the name of the threadlike roots that hold mosses and liverworts in place?
   rhizoids

Liverworts, mosses, ferns, horsetails, and club mosses have at least one common characteristic—they reproduce by spores. But, do they have other things in common? In this activity, discover their similarities and differences.

What You'll Investigate
How are seedless plants alike and how are they different?

Goals
- Observe types of seedless plants.
- Compare and contrast seedless plants.

Materials
One living example of each of these plants:
- moss
- liverwort
- club moss
- horsetail
- fern

*detailed photographs of the above plant types
*alternate material

Procedure
1. Review the Plant Observations table on the next page.
2. Examine each plant and fill in the table using the following guidelines:
   Color—green or not green
   Growth—mostly flat and low or mostly upright
   Root Type—small and fiberlike or rootlike
   Leaf Form—needlelike, scalelike, or leaflike

Activity (continued)
Plant Observations

Plant	Color	Growth	Root Type	Leaf Form
Moss	green	mostly flat and low	small and fiberlike	leaflike
Liverwort	green	mostly flat and low	small and fiberlike	leaflike
Club moss	green	mostly flat and low	small and fiberlike	scalelike or needlelike
Horsetail	green	mostly upright	rootlike	leaflike
Fern	green	mostly upright	rootlike	leaflike

Conclude and Apply
1. Observe and infer what characteristics seedless plants have in common.
   All the seedless plants reproduce by spores, possess specialized photosynthesizing structures, and have structures that hold the plants in the ground.

2. Hypothesize about the differences in growth.
   Upright plants possess vascular tissue; flat and low-growing plants do not.

3. Compare and contrast the seedless plants.
   Mosses and liverworts are nonvascular and grow low to the ground; ground pines, horsetails, and ferns have vascular tissue and are taller.

Chapter 11

ACTIVITY 11-2 • Comparing Monocots and Dicots

Lab Preview

1. What safety symbols are associated with this activity?
   clothing protection, fumes, toxic, eye safety, and sharp objects

2. What is a seed?
   A seed is a reproductive structure of gymnosperms and angiosperms containing an embryo and stored food.

You have read that monocots and dicots are similar because they are both groups of flowering plants. However, you have also learned that these two groups are different. Try this activity to compare and contrast monocots and dicots.

What You'll Investigate
How do the characteristics of monocots and dicots compare?

Goals
- **Observe** similarities and differences between monocots and dicots.
- **Classify** plants as monocots or dicots based on flower characteristics.
- **Infer** what type of food is stored in seeds.

Safety Precautions

Materials
- monocot and dicot flowers
- monocot and dicot seeds
- scalpel
- forceps
- iodine solution

Procedure

1. Use the Data and Observations table on page 76 to record your observations.

2. **Observe** the leaves on the stem of each flower. In your Science Journal, describe the monocot and the dicot leaf.

3. **Examine** the monocot and the dicot flower. For each flower, remove and count the outer row of sepals. Enter this number on your table. Do the same with the petals.

4. Locate, remove, and **observe** the structures inside each flower. Notice that there are two different types of structures. How many of each kind are there? Enter these numbers in the "Other Observations" column.

5. Examine the two seeds. **Cut** the seeds lengthwise and **observe** the two halves. Try to **identify** the embryo and cotyledon(s).

6. Test the seeds for starch by placing a drop of iodine on different parts of the seed. A blue-black color indicates the presence of starch. **CAUTION:** *Iodine is poisonous and may stain or burn the skin.*

Activity (continued)

Data and Observations

Sample data

	Number of sepals	Number of petals	Number of cotyledons	Other observations
Monocot	multiple of 3	multiple of 3	1	pistil—1 stamen—multiple of 3
Dicot	multiple of 4 or 5	multiple of 4 or 5	2	pistil—multiple of 4 or 5 stamen—multiple of 4 or 5

Conclude and Apply

1. Compare the numbers of sepals and petals of monocot and dicot flowers.
   Monocot flowers have petals and sepals in multiples of three. Dicot flowers have petals and sepals in multiples of four or five.

2. What characteristics are the same for monocot and dicot flowers?
   Both kinds of flowers have stigmas, styles, ovaries, filaments, anthers, pollen, petals, and sepals.

3. Distinguish between a monocot and a dicot seed.
   Dicot seeds have two cotyledons, and monocot seeds have only one cotyledon.

4. What type of food stored in monocot and in dicot seeds?
   starch

Chapter 11
MINILAB 11-1

Measuring Water Absorption by a Moss

Procedure

1. Place a few teaspoons of *Sphagnum* moss on a piece of cheesecloth. Twist the cheesecloth to form a ball and tie it securely.
2. Weigh the ball.
3. Put 200 mL of water in a container and add the ball.
4. Predict how much water the ball will absorb.
5. Wait 15 minutes. Remove the ball and drain the excess water back into the container.

Analysis

1. Weigh the ball and measure the amount of water left in the container.
   About 100 mL will be left.
2. In your Science Journal, calculate how much water the *Sphagnum* moss absorbed.
   Sphagnum moss will soak up about 100 g of water.

Chapter 11
MINILAB 11-2

Observing Water Moving in a Plant

Procedure

1. Into a clear container, about 10 cm tall and 4 cm in diameter, pour water to a depth of 1.5 cm. Add 15 drops of red food coloring to the water.
2. Put the root end of a whole green onion in the colored water in the container. Do not cut the onion in any way.
3. Let the onion stand overnight.
4. The next day, examine the outside of the onion. Peel off the layers of leaves and examine them.

Analysis

1. Compare the appearance of the onion before and after it was in the colored water.
   Before the onion was placed in the colored water it appeared to be white at the bottom with green leaves. The next day, the onion was pinkish and colored stripes appeared in its leaves.
2. Describe the location of red color inside the onion.
   There are red, vertical stripes in the onion and its leaves.
3. Infer how the red color inside the onion might be related to vascular tissue.
   The location is the xylem tubes of the vascular tissue.

Chapter 12
Activity 12-1 • Garbage-eating Worms

Design Your Own Experiment

Lab Preview
1. What safety symbols are associated with this activity?
   animal safety, eye safety, toxic substance, and clothing protection
2. How do earthworms use the soil they live in? **Earthworms eat the soil to get energy from the bits of leaves and other living matter in the soil. They excrete undigested soil along with waste material.**

You know that soil conditions can influence the growth of plants. You are trying to decide what factors might improve the soil in your back-yard garden. A friend suggests that earthworms improve the quality of the soil. Does the presence of earthworms have any value in improving soil conditions?

Recognize the Problem
How does the presence of earthworms change the condition of the soil?

Form a Hypothesis
Based on your reading and observations, state a hypothesis about how earthworms might improve the conditions of soil.

Goals
- **Design an experiment** that compares the condition of soil in two environments, one with earthworms and one without.
- **Observe** the change in soil conditions for two weeks.

Possible Materials
- worms (red wigglers)
- plastic containers with drainage holes (4-L) (2)
- soil (7 L)
- chopped food scraps including fruit and vegetable peels, pulverized eggshells, tea bags, and coffee grounds
- shredded newspaper
- spray bottle

Safety Precautions
Be careful when working with live animals. Always keep your hand wet when handling earthworms. Dry hands will remove the mucus from the earthworms.

Test Your Hypothesis
Plan
1. As a group, agree upon the hypothesis and decide how you will test it. **Identify** what results will confirm the hypothesis.
2. **List** the steps you will need to take to test your hypothesis. Be specific. **Describe** exactly what you will do in each step. **List** your materials.
3. Prepare a data table in your Science Journal to **record** your observations.
4. **Read** over the entire experiment to make sure all steps are in logical order.
5. **Identify** all constants, variables, and controls of the experiment.

Do
1. Make sure your teacher approves your plan and your data table before you proceed.
2. Carry out the experiment as planned.
3. While doing the experiment, **record** your observations and complete the data table in your Science Journal.

Activity (continued)

Analyze Your Data
1. Compare the changes in the two sets of soil samples.
   There should be less food scraps in the container with worms, and the soil should have a darker appearance.
2. Compare your results with those of other groups.
   Student results should be similar to those of other groups.
3. What was your control in this experiment?
   The control in this experiment was a container filled with soil, chopped food, and shredded newspapers. It was treated in the same manner as the container with worms in it.
4. What were your variables?
   The variable was the presence of worms in one container.

Draw Conclusions
1. Did the result support your hypothesis? Explain.
   Answers will be determined by student hypotheses.
2. Describe what effect you think rain would have on the soil and worms.
   Rain would compact the soil, and too much rain could drown the worms.

Chapter 12
ACTIVITY 12-2
Observing Complete Metamorphosis

Lab Preview
1. What safety symbols are associated with this activity?
   eye safety, clothing protection, and animal safety
2. Do you expect to see a nymph stage during this activity? Why or why not?
   No. The nymph stage is part of incomplete metamorphosis.

Many insects go through the four stages of complete metamorphosis during their life cycles. Chemicals that are secreted by the body of the animal control the changes. How different do the body forms look between the stages of metamorphosis?

What You'll Investigate
What do the stages of metamorphosis look like for a darkling beetle?

Goals
- Observe the stages of metamorphosis of mealworms to adult darkling beetles.
- Compare the physical appearance of the beetles as they go through two stages of metamorphosis.

Safety Precautions

Materials
- large-mouth jar or old fishbowl
- bran or oatmeal
- dried bread or cookie crumbs mixed with flour
- slice of apple or carrot
- paper towel
- cheesecloth
- mealworms
- rubber band

Procedure
1. Set up a habitat for the mealworms by placing a 1-cm layer of bran or oatmeal on the bottom of the jar. Add a 1-cm layer of dried bread or cookie crumbs mixed with flour. Then, add another layer of bran or oatmeal.
2. Add a slice of apple or carrot as a source of moisture. Replace the apple or carrot daily.
3. Place 20 to 30 mealworms in the jar. Add a piece of crumpled paper towel.
4. Cover the jar with a piece of cheesecloth. Use the rubber band to secure the cloth to the jar.
5. Observe the mealworms daily for two to three weeks. **Record** daily observations in your Science Journal.

Activity (continued)

Conclude and Apply
1. In your Science Journal, draw and describe the mealworms' metamorphoses to adults.
   Answers will vary.
2. Identify the stages of metamorphosis that mealworms go through to become adult darkling beetles.
   eggs, larva, pupa and adult
3. Which of these stages did you not see during this investigation?
   egg
4. What are some of the advantages of an insect's young being different from the adult form?
   Larval forms often eat different things from what the adults eat.
5. Based on the food you placed in the habitat, **infer** where you might find mealworms or adult darkling beetles in your house.
   kitchen cabinets with cereals, flour, etc.
6. Why do you think pet stores would stock and sell mealworms?
   as food for fish, reptiles, and amphibians

Chapter 12
MINILAB 12-1

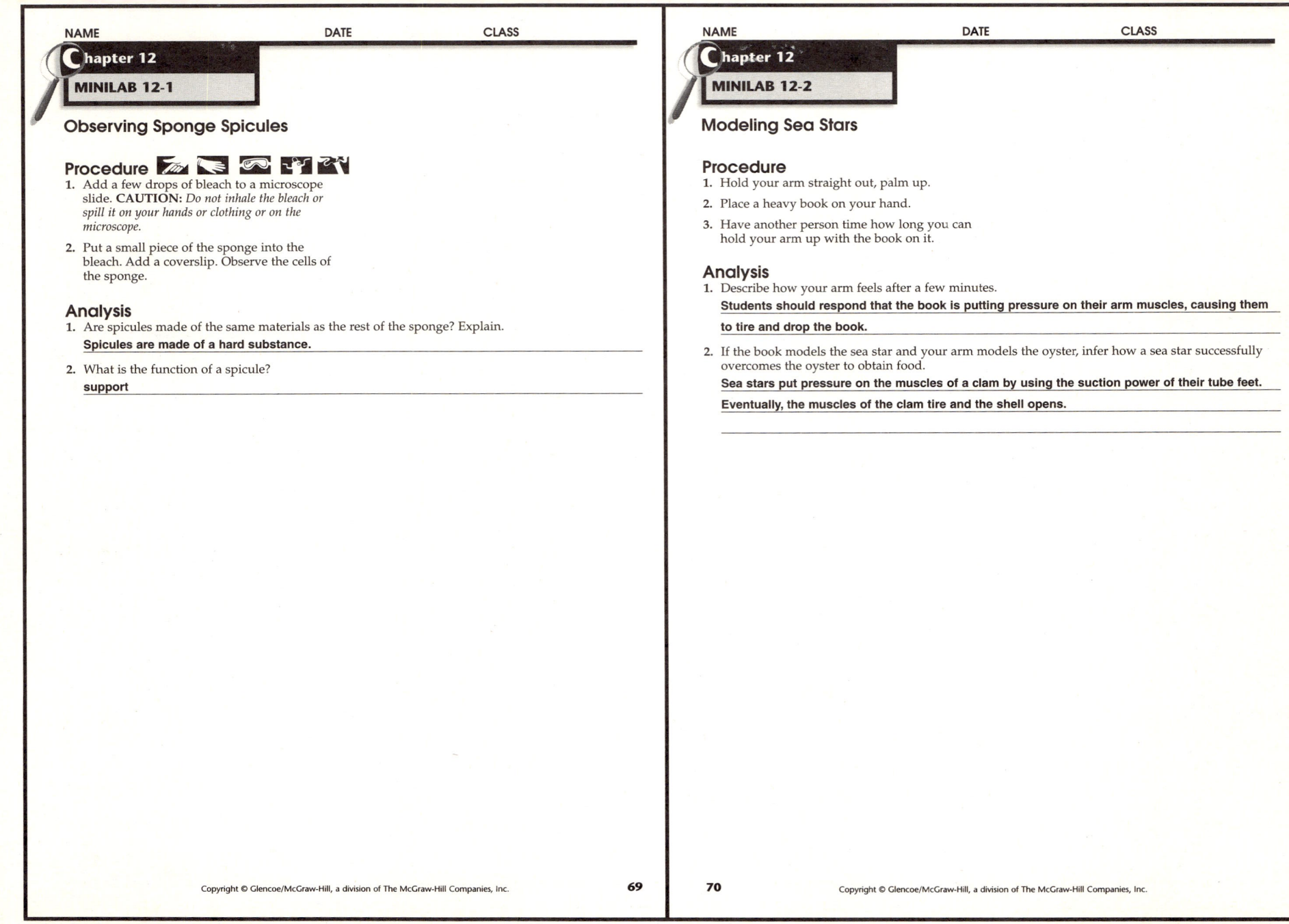

Observing Sponge Spicules

Procedure
1. Add a few drops of bleach to a microscope slide. **CAUTION:** *Do not inhale the bleach or spill it on your hands or clothing or on the microscope.*
2. Put a small piece of the sponge into the bleach. Add a coverslip. Observe the cells of the sponge.

Analysis
1. Are spicules made of the same materials as the rest of the sponge? Explain.
   Spicules are made of a hard substance.
2. What is the function of a spicule?
   support

Chapter 12
MINILAB 12-2

Modeling Sea Stars

Procedure
1. Hold your arm straight out, palm up.
2. Place a heavy book on your hand.
3. Have another person time how long you can hold your arm up with the book on it.

Analysis
1. Describe how your arm feels after a few minutes.
   Students should respond that the book is putting pressure on their arm muscles, causing them to tire and drop the book.
2. If the book models the sea star and your arm models the oyster, infer how a sea star successfully overcomes the oyster to obtain food.
   Sea stars put pressure on the muscles of a clam by using the suction power of their tube feet. Eventually, the muscles of the clam tire and the shell opens.

Chapter 13
ACTIVITY 13-1 • Frog Metamorphosis

Lab Preview
1. What safety symbols are associated with this activity? **animal safety, clothing protection, eye safety**
2. What factors affect the rate of amphibian metamorphosis? **the particular species undergoing the metamorphosis, the water temperature, and the amount of available food**

Frogs and other amphibians use external fertilization to reproduce. Female frogs lay hundreds of jellylike eggs in water. Male frogs then fertilize these eggs. Once larvae hatch, the process of metamorphosis begins. Over a period of time, young tadpoles develop into adult frogs.

What You'll Investigate
What changes occur as a tadpole goes through metamorphosis?

Goals
- **Observe** how body structures change as a tadpole develops into an adult frog.
- **Determine** how long metamorphosis takes to be completed.

Materials
- aquarium or jar (4-L)
- frog egg mass
- lake or pond water
- stereoscopic microscope
- watch glass
- small fishnet
- aquatic plants
- washed gravel
- lettuce (previously boiled)
- large rock

Procedure
1. Review the data table on the next page.
2. As a class, use the aquarium, pond water, gravel, rock, and plants to prepare a water habitat for the frog eggs.
3. **Place** the egg mass in the water of the aquarium. Use the fishnet to separate a few eggs from the mass. Place these eggs in the watch glass. The eggs should have the dark side up. **CAUTION:** *Handle the eggs with care.*
4. **Observe** the eggs. **Record** your observations in the data table.
5. **Observe** the eggs twice a week. **Record** any changes that occur.
6. Continue observing the tadpoles twice a week after they hatch. **Identify** the mouth, eyes, gill cover, gills, nostrils, fin on the back, hind legs, and front legs. **Observe** how tadpoles eat boiled lettuce that has been cooled.

Activity (continued)
Frog Metamorphosis

Sample data

Date	Observations
	Observations will vary according to the kind of frog eggs used. Students should note fishlike appearance of tadpoles, disappearance of the tail, and development of legs.

Conclude and Apply
1. How long does it take for the eggs to hatch and the tadpoles to develop legs? **Answers will vary from 8 to 20 days. Legs develop in approximately four weeks, depending on the species.**
2. Which pair of legs appears first? **the hind legs**
3. Explain why the jellylike coating around the eggs is important. **It protects the eggs and keeps them from drying out.**
4. Compare the eyes of young tadpoles with the eyes of older tadpoles. **The eyes of young are on each side of the head, as in fish. In older ones, they are nearer the top of the head.**
5. Calculate how long it takes for a tadpole to change into a frog. **approximately two to four months, depending on the species**

NAME _____ DATE _____ CLASS _____

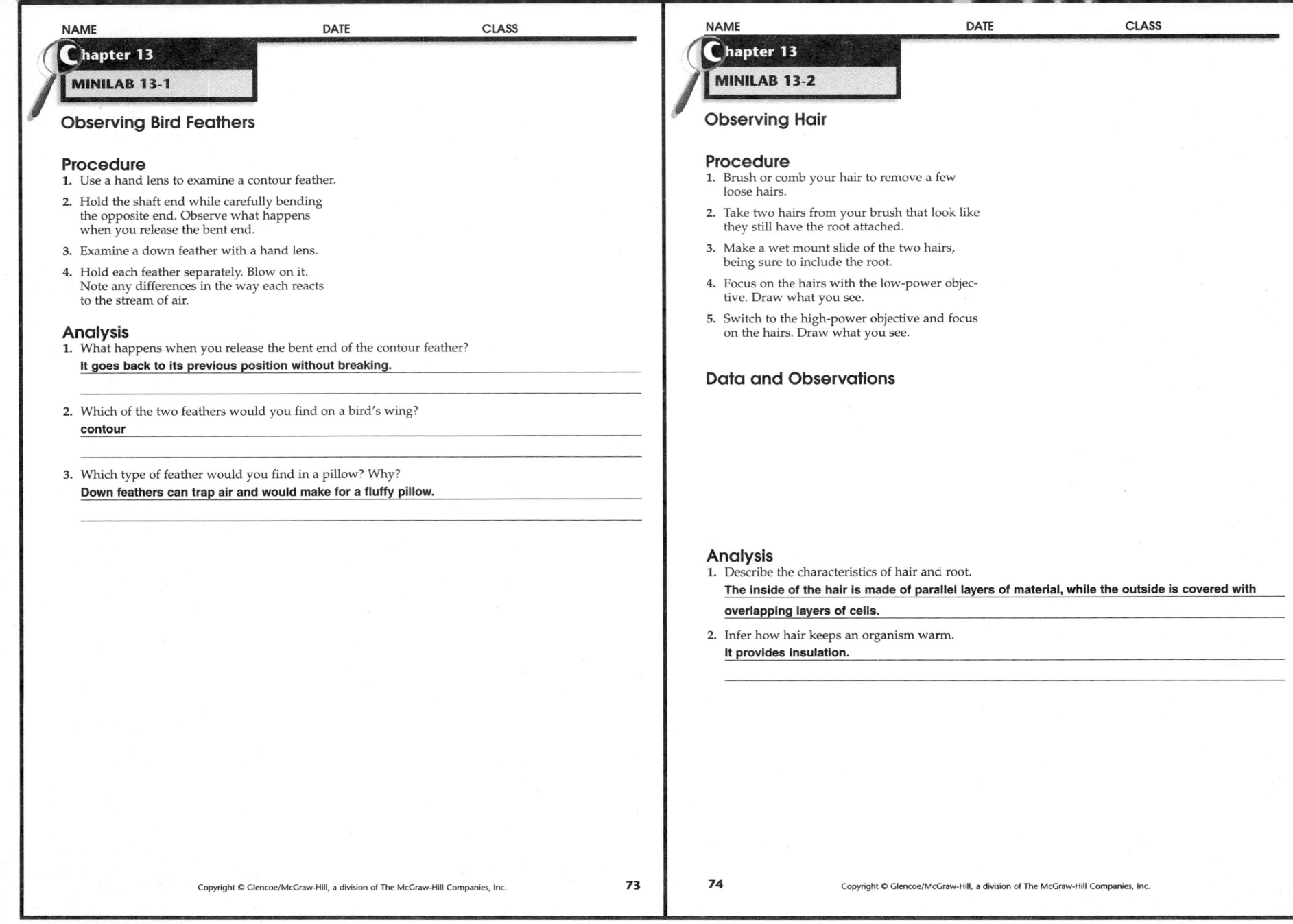

Chapter 13
MINILAB 13-1

Observing Bird Feathers

Procedure
1. Use a hand lens to examine a contour feather.
2. Hold the shaft end while carefully bending the opposite end. Observe what happens when you release the bent end.
3. Examine a down feather with a hand lens.
4. Hold each feather separately. Blow on it. Note any differences in the way each reacts to the stream of air.

Analysis
1. What happens when you release the bent end of the contour feather?
   It goes back to its previous position without breaking.

2. Which of the two feathers would you find on a bird's wing?
   contour

3. Which type of feather would you find in a pillow? Why?
   Down feathers can trap air and would make for a fluffy pillow.

NAME _____ DATE _____ CLASS _____

Chapter 13
MINILAB 13-2

Observing Hair

Procedure
1. Brush or comb your hair to remove a few loose hairs.
2. Take two hairs from your brush that look like they still have the root attached.
3. Make a wet mount slide of the two hairs, being sure to include the root.
4. Focus on the hairs with the low-power objective. Draw what you see.
5. Switch to the high-power objective and focus on the hairs. Draw what you see.

Data and Observations

Analysis
1. Describe the characteristics of hair and root.
   The inside of the hair is made of parallel layers of material, while the outside is covered with overlapping layers of cells.

2. Infer how hair keeps an organism warm.
   It provides insulation.

Chapter 14
ACTIVITY 14-1 • Soil Composition

Lab Preview
1. What are abiotic factors? _nonliving, physical features of the environment_
2. Name at least three abiotic factors.
   Possible answers include water, soil, sunlight, temperature, and air.

Soil is more than minerals mixed with the decaying bodies of dead organisms. It contains other biotic and abiotic factors.

What You'll Investigate
What are the components of soil?

Goals
- Determine what factors are present in soil.

Materials
- 3 small paper cups containing freshly dug soil
- newspaper
- hand lens
- scale
- beaker of water
- jar with lid

Procedure
1. Obtain 3 cups of soil sample from your teacher. **Record** the source of your sample in your Science Journal.
2. **Pour** one of your samples onto the newspaper. **Sort** through the objects in the soil and separate abiotic and biotic items. Use a hand lens to help identify the items. **Describe** your observations in the data table below.
3. Carefully place the second sample in the jar, disturbing it as little as possible. Quickly fill the jar with water and screw the lid on tightly. Without moving the jar, **observe** its contents for several minutes. **Record** your observations in the data table.
4. **Weigh** the third sample. **Record** the weight in the data table. Leave the sample undisturbed for several days, then weigh it again. **Record** the second weight in the data table.

Data and Observations

Cup	Items in soil		Weight	
	Abiotic	Biotic	1st weight	2nd weight
1				
2	Answers will vary.			
3				

Activity (continued)

Conclude and Apply

1. Can you infer the presence of any organisms?
   Students will observe worms, fungi, and other soil organisms.

2. Describe the abiotic factors in your sample. What biotic factors did you observe?
   Abiotic factors include air, water, and minerals. Biotic factors include decaying plants and animals and soil organisms.

3. Did you record any change in the soil weight over time? If so, why?
   The soil weight changed because the water contained in the sample of soil evaporated.

Chapter 14
ACTIVITY 14-2 • Identifying a Limiting Factor
Design Your Own Experiment

Lab Preview
1. What is a limiting factor?
   any factor that limits the number, distribution, reproduction, or existence of organisms
2. What is an abiotic factor?
   a nonliving, physical feature of the environment

Organisms depend on many biotic and abiotic factors in their environment to survive. When these factors are limited or are not available, it can affect an organism's survival. By experimenting with some of these limiting factors, you will see how organisms depend on all parts of their environment.

Recognize the Problem
How do abiotic factors such as light, water, and temperature affect the germination of seeds?

Form a Hypothesis
Based on what you have learned about limiting factors, make a hypothesis about how one specific abiotic factor may affect the germination of a bean seed. Be sure to consider factors that you can change easily.

Goals
- **Observe** the effects of an abiotic factor on the germination and growth of bean seedlings.
- **Design** an experiment that demonstrates whether or not a specific abiotic factor limits the germination of bean seeds.

Safety Precautions
Wash hands after handling soil and seeds.

Possible Materials
- bean seeds
- small planting containers
- soil
- water
- labels
- trowel or spoon
- aluminum foil
- sunny window or other light source
- refrigerator or oven

Test Your Hypothesis
Plan
1. As a group, agree upon and write out a hypothesis statement.
2. Decide on a way to test your group's hypothesis. Keep available materials in mind as you plan your procedure. **List** your materials.
3. **Prepare** a data table on the following page.
4. Remember to **test** only one variable at a time and use suitable controls.
5. **Read** over your entire experiment to make sure that all steps are in logical order.
6. **Identify** any constants, variables, and controls in your experiment.
7. Be sure the factor you test is measurable.

Do
1. Make sure your teacher has approved your plan before you proceed.
2. Carry out the experiment as planned.
3. While the experiment is going on, write down any observations that you make and complete the data table on the following page.

Activity (continued)

Analyze Your Data
1. Compare your results with those of other groups.
   Student results should be consistent with those of other groups using the same variable.
2. Infer how the abiotic factor you tested affected the germination of bean seeds.
   Student answers will vary based on the abiotic factor tested.
3. Graph your results using a bar graph that compares the number of bean seeds that germinated in the experimental container with the number of seeds that germinated in the control container.
   The graph will be determined by the number of seeds used in the experiment.

Draw Conclusions
1. Identify which factor had the greatest effect on the seeds.
   Answers will vary depending on the abiotic factor tested.
2. Determine whether you could substitute one factor for another and still grow the seeds.
   Each different type of abiotic factor is necessary for seeds to germinate.

NAME _____ DATE _____ CLASS _____

Chapter 14
MINILAB 14-1

Observing Symbiosis

Procedure
1. Carefully wash, then examine the roots of a legume plant and a nonlegume plant.
2. Examine a prepared microscope slide of the bacteria that live in the roots of legumes.

Analysis
1. What differences do you observe in the roots of the two plants?
   The legume plant has nodules that contain nitrogen-fixing bacteria.

2. The bacteria help legumes to thrive in poor soil. What type of symbiotic relationship is this? Explain.
   This is mutualism.

79

NAME _____ DATE _____ CLASS _____

Chapter 14
MINILAB 14-2

Modeling the Water Cycle

Procedure
1. With a marker, make a line halfway up on a plastic cup. Fill the cup to the mark with water.
2. Cover the top with plastic wrap and secure it with a rubber band or tape.
3. Put the cup in direct sunlight. Observe the cup for three days. Record your observations.
4. Remove the plastic wrap and observe the cup for a week.

Analysis
1. What parts of the water cycle did you observe in this activity?
   condensation, evaporation, and precipitation

2. What happened to the water level in the cup when the plastic wrap was removed?
   It decreased.

80

210

NAME _____ DATE _____ CLASS _____

Chapter 15
ACTIVITY 15-2
Studying a Land Environment

Lab Preview
1. What is an ecosystem? **An ecosystem consists of communities and the abiotic factors that affect them.**

2. What is a population? **A population is all of the individuals of one species living in the same area at the same time.**

An ecological study includes observation and analysis of living organisms and the physical features of the environment.

What You'll Investigate
How do you study an ecosystem?

Goals
- Observe biotic and abiotic factors of an ecosystem.
- Analyze the relationships among organisms and their environment.

Materials
- graph paper
- thermometer
- tape measure
- hand lens
- notebook
- binoculars
- pencil
- field guides

Procedure
1. **Choose** a portion of an ecosystem near your school or home as your area of study. You might choose to study a pond, a forest area in a park, a garden, or another area.
2. **Decide** the boundaries of your study area.
3. Using a tape measure and graph paper, **make a map** of your study area.
4. Using a thermometer, **measure and record** the air temperature in your study area.
5. **Observe** the organisms in your study area. Use field guides to identify them. Use a hand lens to study small organisms. Use binoculars to study animals you cannot get near. Also, look for evidence (such as tracks or feathers) of organisms you do not see.
6. **Record** your observations in a table like the one shown. Make drawings to help you remember what you see.
7. Visit your study area as many times as you can and at different times of the day for four weeks. At each visit, be sure to make the same measurements and record all observations. Note how biotic and abiotic factors interact.

Environmental Data

Date	Time of day	Temperature	Organisms observed	Observations and comments
		Data will vary.		

81

NAME _____ DATE _____ CLASS _____

Activity (continued)

Conclude and Apply

1. Identify relationships among the organisms in your study area, such as predator-prey or symbiosis.
   Answers will vary depending on the ecosystem chosen by each group.

2. Diagram a food chain or food web for your ecosystem.
   Answers will vary depending on the ecosystem chosen by each group.

3. Predict what might happen if one or more abiotic factors were changed suddenly.
   Populations would be affected by changes in temperature, water, or other abiotic factors. The entire ecosystem could be disrupted.

4. Predict what might happen if one or more populations were removed from the area.
   Other populations could be affected.

82

Chapter 15
MINILAB 15-1
Comparing Tundra and Taiga

Procedure
1. Compare the latitudes where tundra is found in the northern hemisphere with the same latitudes in South America.
2. Compare the latitudes where taiga is found in the northern hemisphere with the same latitudes in South America.

Analysis
Are either of these biomes found in South America? Explain why or why not.

There are no landmasses in the southern hemisphere at the latitudes where these biomes are found in the northern hemisphere.

Chapter 15
MINILAB 15-2
Modeling Freshwater Environments

Procedure
1. Cover the bottom of a self-sealing freezer bag with about 2 cm of gravel, muck, and other debris from the bottom of a pond. If plants are present, add one or two to the bag. Use a dip net to capture small fish, insects, or tadpoles.
2. Carefully pour pond water into the bag until it is about two-thirds full. Seal the bag.
3. Keep the bag indoors at room temperature and out of direct sunlight.

Analysis
1. Using a hand lens, observe as many organisms as possible. Record your observations. After two or three days, return your sample to the original habitat.

Student records will depend on organisms observed.

2. Write a short paper describing the organisms in your sample ecosystem and explaining their interactions.

Answers will depend on what organisms students observe.

Chapter 16
ACTIVITY 16-1 • Observing Bones

A Traditional Experiment

Lab Preview

1. Other than movement, name three functions of bones. **Bones protect internal organs, give shape and support to the body, produce blood cells, and store major quantities of calcium and phosphorus.**

2. Why is the sharp object safety symbol necessary? **because of the danger of cuts or punctures due to the use of a scalpel**

To move, animals must overcome the force of gravity. A skeleton aids in this movement. Land animals need skeletons that provide support against gravity. A flying animal needs a skeleton that provides support yet also allows it to overcome the pull of gravity and fly. Bones are adapted to the functions they perform. Find out if there is a difference between the bones of a land animal and those of a flying animal.

What You'll Investigate
What are the differences in the bone structures of land animals and flying animals?

Goals
- Learn the parts of a bone.
- Observe the differences between the bones of land animals and those of flying animals.

Materials
- beef bones (cut in half lengthwise)
- chicken leg bones (cut in half lengthwise)
- hand lens
- paper towels

Procedure

1. Copy the data table and use it to record your observations.
2. **Obtain a beef bone and a chicken leg bone that have been cut in half along the length from your teacher.**
3. Observe the bones with a hand lens.
4. **Identify the periosteum, compact bone, spongy bone, and the remains of any marrow that may be present.**
5. Draw a diagram of the bones and label their parts on the next page.
6. In the data table, **write down any observations that you make.**
7. Try to bend the bones to determine their flexibility.

Activity (continued)
Data and Observations
Bone Features

Part	Description of beef bone	Description of chicken bone
Periosteum		
Compact bone		
Spongy bone		
Marrow		

Diagrams of bones:

Conclude and Apply

1. Do your data indicate any adaptations for flight in the bones in the bones? **The lighter weight of the chicken bones is an adaptation to flight. Birds known for soaring and gliding flight have very light bones.**

2. Infer which type of bone would require more force to move. Explain why. **The denser, more compact beef bone requires more force to move than the lighter-weight chicken bone does.**

3. How do the structures of the two types of bone tissue aid their function? **The denser, compact beef bone provides support for movement on land; the less-dense, hollow chicken bone is suited for movement through air.**

4. Which type of bone tissue was more flexible? **the chicken bone tissue**

Chapter 16
ACTIVITY 16-2 • Observing Muscle

Lab Preview
1. What safety symbols are associated with this activity?
   sharp object safety, disposal alert, clothing safety, and eye safety
2. Name the three types of muscles.
   cardiac, skeletal, and smooth

Muscles can be identified by their appearance. In this activity, you will make observations to distinguish among the three types of muscle tissue.

What You'll Investigate
You will distinguish between the three types of muscle tissue. What do different types of muscles look like.

Goal
- Examine three types of muscle tissue.
- Examine muscle fibers.

Safety Precautions

Materials
- prepared slides of smooth, skeletal, and cardiac muscles
- *detailed posters of the three types of muscle*
- microscope
- cooked turkey leg or chicken leg
- dissecting pan or cutting board
- dissecting probes (2)
- hand lens
- *alternate materials*

Procedure
1. **Record** your observations in the table on the next page.
2. Using the microscope, first on low power and then on high power, **observe** prepared slides of three different types of muscle.
3. On the data table, **draw** each type of muscle that you **observe**.
4. **Obtain** a piece of cooked turkey leg from your teacher. Muscle tissue is made up of groups of cells held together in fibers, usually by a transparent covering called connective tissue.
5. **Place** the turkey leg in the dissecting pan. Use the forceps to remove the skin. **Locate** and tease apart the muscle fibers.
6. Use a hand lens to examine the muscle fibers and any connective tissue you see in the turkey leg.
7. **Draw** and **measure** five turkey leg fibers and describe the shape of these muscle fibers.

Activity (continued)
Data and Observations

Types of muscle	Diagram of muscle	Length of fibers	Description of fibers
Skeletal	Student drawings should resemble photos in Fig. 11-10.	Lengths will vary. 1 cm, 2.5 cm, 1.5 cm, 0.75 cm	Fibers are long and tapered at the ends.
Cardiac			
Smooth			

Diagrams of turkey leg fibers:

Lengths of turkey leg fibers **Lengths will vary.**
Shape of turkey leg fibers **Fibers are long with tapered ends.**

Conclude and Apply
1. How are muscle fibers arranged in the prepared slides?
   Accept all reasonable descriptions. Most will reply that the fibers lay side by side along the length of the bone.
2. Predict how the shape of a muscle fiber relates to its function.
   The fiber is long and thicker in the center than it is at the ends. When a muscle contracts, it becomes even thicker in the center, but the ends stay about the same.
3. Can you conclude that striations have anything to do with whether a muscle is voluntary or involuntary? Explain.
   No, both cardiac and skeletal are striated; but cardiac is involuntary and skeletal is voluntary.

NAME _____ DATE _____ CLASS _____

Chapter 16
MINILAB 16-1

Observing Muscle Pairs at Work

Procedure
1. Find out which muscles are used to move your arm.
2. Stretch your arm out straight. Bring your hand to your shoulder, then down again.
3. Use the muscles shown in the figure on the same page as the minilab to determine which skeletal muscles in your upper arm enable you to perform this action.

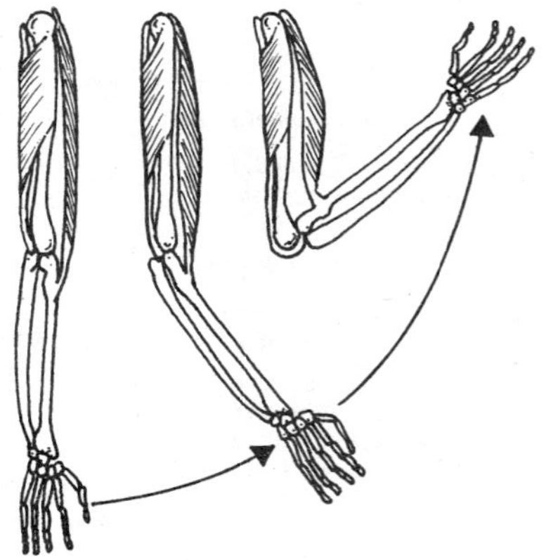

Analysis
1. How many muscles were involved in this action?

   two—biceps and triceps

2. Which muscle contracted to bring the forearm closer to the shoulder?

   the biceps

NAME _____ DATE _____ CLASS _____

Chapter 16
MINILAB 16-2

Recognizing Why You Sweat

Procedure
1. Examine the epidermis and the pores of your skin using a hand lens.
2. Put your hand in a clear plastic bag and taped it closed.
3. Sit quietly for 10 minutes. Observe what happens in the bag.
4. Observe what happened to your hand while it was in the bag.

Analysis
1. Identify what formed inside the bag. Where did this substance come from?

   water; from the skin

2. Why is it necessary for this substance to form, even when you are inactive?

   The evaporation cools the skin surface and helps maintain a constant body temperature.

Chapter 17
ACTIVITY 17-1

Identifying Vitamin C Content

Lab Preview

1. What are vitamins? _Vitamins are essential, organic nutrients that help your body use other nutrients._
2. Why is vitamin C necessary? _It is necessary for strong bones and teeth and for healing wounds._

Vitamin C is found in a variety of fruits and vegetables. In some plants, the concentration is high; in others, it is low. Try this activity to test various juices and find out which contains the most vitamin C.

What You'll Investigate
Which juices contain vitamin C?

Goals
- Observe differences in the vitamin C content of juices.

Materials
- indophenol solution
- graduated cylinder (10-mL)
- *graduated container
- glass-marking pencil
- *tape
- test tubes (10)
- test-tube rack
- *paper cups
- dropper
- dropping bottles (10)
- test substances: water, orange juice, pineapple juice, apple juice, lemon juice, tomato juice, cranberry juice, carrot juice, lime juice, mixed vegetable juice
- *alternate materials

Procedure
1. Make a data table like the example shown to record your observations.
2. Label the test tubes 1 through 10.
3. Predict which juices contain vitamin C. Record your predictions in your table.
4. **Measure 5 mL of indophenol into each of the ten test tubes. CAUTION:** *Wear your goggles and apron. Do not taste any of the juices.* Indophenol is a blue liquid that turns colorless when vitamin C is present. The more vitamin C in a juice, the less juice it takes to turn indophenol colorless.
5. Add 20 drops of water to test tube 1. Record your observations.
6. Begin adding orange juice, one drop at a time, to test tube 2.
7. Record the number of drops needed to turn indophenol colorless.
8. Repeat steps 6 and 7 to test the other juices.

Activity (continued)
Test Results for Vitamin C

Test Tube	Juice	Prediction (yes or no)	Number of drops
1	water	no	5
2	orange	yes	3
3	pineapple	no	4
4	apple	no	4
5	lemon	yes	3
6	tomato	yes	4
7	cranberry	no	5
8	carrot	no	5
9	lime	yes	3
10	vegetable	yes	4

Conclude and Apply

1. What is the purpose of testing water for the presence of vitamin C?
   It was the control.
2. Does the amount of vitamin C vary in fruit juices?
   Yes, the amount of vitamin C is influenced by whether vitamin C has been added; water has been added; or if the juice is fresh, frozen, or canned.
3. Which juice did not contain vitamin C?
   Apple, cranberry, carrot, and vegetable. Answers may vary if juices fortified with vitamins are used.

Chapter 17
ACTIVITY 17-2 • Protein Digestion

Design Your Own Experiment

Lab Preview

1. What safety symbols are associated with this activity?
   eye, chemical, and clothing protection safety

2. Where does chemical digestion take place?
   in the mouth, stomach, and small intestine

You learned that proteins are large, complex, organic compounds necessary for living things to carry out their life processes. To be useful for cell functions, proteins must be broken down into their individual amino acids. The process of chemically breaking apart protein molecules involves several different factors, one of which is the presence of the enzyme pepsin in your stomach.

Recognize the Problem
Under what conditions will the enzyme pepsin begin the digestion of protein?

Form a Hypothesis
Formulate a hypothesis about what conditions are necessary for protein digestion to occur. When making your hypothesis, consider the various contents of the digestive juices that are found in your stomach.

Goals
- Design an experiment that tests the effect of a variable, such as the presence or absence of acid, on the activity of the enzyme, pepsin.
- Observe the effects of pepsin on gelatin.

Safety Precautions
Always use care when working with acid. Wear goggles and an apron. Avoid contact with skin and eyes. Wash your hands thoroughly after pouring the acid.

Possible Materials
- test tubes with gelled, unflavored gelatin (3)
- dropper
- test-tube rack
- pepsin powder
- glass marking pen
- cold water
- dilute hydrochloric acid
- beaker
- watch or clock

Activity (continued)

Test Your Hypothesis

Plan

1. **Decide** how your group will test your hypothesis.

2. Your teacher will supply you with three test tubes containing gelled, unflavored gelatin. Pepsin powder will liquify the gelatin if the enzyme is active.

3. As a group, list the steps you will need to take to test your hypothesis. Consider the following factors as you plan your experiment. Based on information provided by your teacher, how will you use the pepsin and the acid? How will the gelatin be prepared? How often will you make observations? Be specific and describe exactly what you will do at each step.

4. List your materials.

5. **Prepare** a data table and **record** it in your Science Journal so that it is ready to use as your group collects data.

6. **Read** over the entire experiment to make sure that all steps are in logical order.

7. **Identify** any constants, variables, and controls of the experiment.

Do

1. Make sure your teacher approves your plan before you proceed.

2. Carry out the experiment as planned.

3. While the experiment is going on, **write** down any observations that you make and complete the data table in your Science Journal.

Analyze Your Data

1. Compare your results with those of other groups.
   Student results should be consistent with those of other groups.

2. Did you observe a difference in the test tubes?
   Yes, the test tube with acid had more liquid than the one without acid.

3. Identify the constants in this experiment.
   Gelatin and pepsin.

Draw Conclusions

1. Did the acid have any effect on the activity of the pepsin? How does this relate to the activity of this enzyme in the stomach?
   Pepsin is active only in an acid medium. Acid is added to the food material from the walls of the stomach. This allows digestion to occur.

2. Predict the effects of the pepsin on the gelatin if you increased or decreased the concentration of the acid.
   Students might predict that the pepsin is active only in a narrow range of acidity.

3. Is time a factor in the effectiveness of the pepsin on the gelatin? Explain.
   Yes, as more liquid is formed, the acid is diluted and the pepsin will be less effective.

NAME _____ DATE _____ CLASS _____

Chapter 17
MINILAB 17-1

Measuring the Water Content of Food

Procedure
1. Use a pan balance to find the mass of an empty 250-mL beaker.
2. Fill the beaker with sliced celery and find the mass of the filled beaker.
3. Estimate the amount of water you think is in the celery.
4. Put the celery on a flat tray. Leave the celery out to dry for one to two days.
5. Allow the celery to cool.
6. Determine the mass of the cooled celery.

Data and Observations *Data will vary.*

Object	Mass (g)
Empty beaker	
Beaker plus fresh celery	
Beaker plus dried celery	
Amount of water in celery	

Analysis
1. How much water was in the fresh celery?
   The water content will vary with the freshness of the celery used, but students should
   find that vegetables are mostly water. Celery should be about 90% water.

2. Infer how much water might be in other fresh fruits and vegetables.
   Students' answers will vary, but most will likely infer that leafy vegetables will have more water
   than "hard" vegetables such as cauliflower or broccoli.

NAME _____ DATE _____ CLASS _____

Chapter 17
MINILAB 17-2

Determining How Fats Are Emulsified

Procedure
1. Fill two glasses with warm water. Add a large spoonful of cooking oil to each glass.
2. Add a small spoonful of liquid dish-washing detergent to one glass. Stir both glasses.

Analysis
1. Compare what happens to the oil in each glass.
   In the glass with the detergent, the large ring of oil is broken up into smaller globules.

2. How does emulsification change the surface area of the oil drops?
   The surface area is greatly increased.

3. How does emulsification speed up digestion?
   More surface area is available for the chemical action of digestion.

4. Where in the digestive system does emulsification take place?
   in the small intestine

5. What is the emulsifier in the digestive system?
   Bile is the emulsifier in the digestive system.

Chapter 18
ACTIVITY 18-1 • The Heart as a Pump

Lab Preview
1. How is your pulse related to your heart? **Your pulse is the rhythm of your heart beating.**
2. Why is it important to know your pulse? **A healthy heart has a steady, regular rhythm that is not too fast and not too slow. Your pulse tells you what your heart's rhythm is like.**

> The heart is a pumping organ. Blood is forced through the arteries and causes the muscles of the walls to contract and then relax. This creates a series of waves as the blood flows through the arteries. We call this the pulse. Try this activity to learn about the pulse and the pumping of the heart.

What You'll Investigate
How can you measure heartbeat rate?

Goals
- Observe pulse rate.

Materials
- stopwatch, watch, or clock with a second hand

Procedure
1. **Make** a table like the one shown. Use it to **record** your data.
2. Your partner should sit down and take his or her pulse. You will serve as the recorder.
3. **Find** the pulse rate by placing the middle and index fingers over one of the carotid arteries in the neck. CAUTION: *Do not press too hard.*
4. **Calculate** the resulting heart rate. Your partner should count each beat of the carotid pulse silently for 15 s. Multiply the number of beats by four and **record** the number in the data table.
5. Your partner should then jog in place for one minute and take his or her pulse again.
6. **Calculate** this new pulse rate and **record** it in the data table.
7. Reverse roles with your partner. You are now the pulse taker.
8. **Collect** and **record** the new data.

Pulse Rate

Pulse rate	Partner's	Yours
At rest	70	70
After jogging		

Activity (continued)

Conclude and Apply
1. How does the pulse rate change?
   The pressure in the brachial is temporarily closed off, then released.
2. What causes the pulse rate to change?
   The exercise increases the pulse rate so the heart can supply the extra oxygen that working cells require.
3. What can you infer about the heart as a pumping organ?
   Answers will vary, but students should understand that pulse rate varies according to the body's needs.

Chapter 18
ACTIVITY 18-2 • Comparing Blood Cells

Lab Preview
1. What makes up the solid part of blood?
   red blood cells, white blood cells, and platelets
2. What makes up the liquid part of blood?
   plasma, which is mostly water

Blood is an important tissue for all vertebrates. How do human blood cells compare with those of other vertebrates?

What You'll Investigate
How does human blood compare with the blood of other vertebrates?

Goals
- **Observe** the characteristics of red blood cells, white blood cells, and platelets.
- **Compare** human blood cells with those of other vertebrates.

Safety Precautions

Materials
- prepared slides of human blood
- *photos of human blood
- prepared slides of two other vertebrates' (fish, frog, reptile, bird) blood
- *photos of two other vertebrates' blood
- microscope
- *alternate materials

Procedures
1. Under low power, **examine** the prepared slide of human blood. **Locate** the red blood cells.
2. **Examine** the red blood cells under high power.
3. Make a data table. Draw, count, and **describe** the red blood cells.
4. Move the slide to another position. Find one or two white blood cells. They will be blue or purple due to the stain.
5. Draw, count, and **describe** the white cells in the data table.
6. **Examine** the slide for small fragments that appear blue. These are platelets.
7. Draw, count, and **describe** the platelets on your data table.
8. Follow steps 1 to 7 for each of the other vertebrate cells.

Activity (continued)
Data and Observations

Vertebrate type	Blood cell type	Description	Number in field	Drawing
Human	Red	Round biconcave; no nucleus	200	
	White	Round or oval with nucleus	0–4	
	Platelets	Cell fragments	10–12	
Bird	Red	Oval; nucleus	*	
	White	Round-oval; nucleus		
	Platelets	Spindle-shaped; nucleus		
Frog	Red	Oval; nucleus	*	
	White	Round-oval; nucleus		
	Platelets	Spindle-shaped; nucleus		

* Numbers will vary; white cells are one percent of number of red cells.

Conclude and Apply
1. Does each vertebrate studied have all three cell types?
   Yes
2. What might you infer about the ability of the different red blood cells to carry oxygen?
   Accept all reasonable responses. Students might infer that red cells without nuclei can carry more oxygen.
3. What is the function of each of the three types of blood cells?
   Red blood cells carry oxygen and carbon dioxide. White blood cells ingest foreign substances and dead cells. Platelets help clot blood.

Chapter 18
MINILAB 18-1

Inferring How Hard the Heart Works

Procedure
1. Take a racquetball and hold it in your outstretched arm.
2. Squeeze the racquetball again and again for one minute.

Analysis
1. How many times did you squeeze the racquetball in one minute? A resting heart beats at approximately 70 beats per minute.

   Answers will vary.

2. What can you do when the muscles of your arm get tired? Explain why cardiac muscle in your heart cannot do the same.

   Students can stop or change arms. The heart must continue and not fatigue in order to maintain the body's activities.

Chapter 18
MINILAB 18-2

Modeling a Blocked Artery

Procedure
1. Insert a dropperful of mineral oil into a piece of clear, narrow, plastic tubing.
2. Squeeze the oil through the tube.
3. Observe how much oil comes out the tube.
4. Next, refill the dropper and squeeze oil through a piece of clear plastic tubing that has been clogged with cotton.

Analysis
1. How much oil comes out of the clogged tube?

   The rate of flow of the oil through the tube should be less.

2. Explain how the addition of the cotton to the tube changed the way the oil flowed through the tube.

   The oil had greater resistance to flow and moved more slowly.

3. How does this activity demonstrate what takes place when arteries become clogged?

   An inference can be made that fatty deposits in an artery will reduce the bloodflow.

NAME _____ DATE _____ CLASS _____

Chapter 19
ACTIVITY 19-1 • The Effects of Exercise on Respiration

Design Your Own Experiment

Lab Preview
1. What is the function of the respiratory system?
   The respiratory system delivers oxygen to the blood and removes carbon dioxide waste from the blood.
2. What is breathing?
   Breathing is the process whereby fresh air moves into the lungs and stale air moves out of the lungs, that is, the process of inhaling and exhaling.

Breathing rate increases with an increase in physical activity. A bromothymol blue solution changes color when carbon dioxide is bubbled into it. Can you predict whether there will be a difference in the time it takes for the solution to change color before and after exercise?

Recognize the Problem
How will an increase in physical activity affect the amount of carbon dioxide exhaled?

Form a Hypothesis
State a hypothesis about how exercise will affect the amount of carbon dioxide exhaled by the lungs.

Goals
- **Observe** the effects of the amount of carbon dioxide on the bromothymol blue solution.
- **Design** an experiment that tests the effects of a variable, such as the amount of carbon dioxide exhaled before and after exercise, on the rate at which the solution changes color.

Possible Materials
- clock or watch with second hand
- drinking straws
- bromothymol blue solution (200 mL)
- glass cups (12 oz.) (2)
  beakers (400-mL) (2)
- metric measuring cup
  graduated cylinder
  alternate materials

Safety Precautions
Protect clothing from the solution. Wash hands after using the solution. CAUTION: *Do not inhale the solution through the straw.*

NAME _____ DATE _____ CLASS _____

Activity (continued)

Test Your Hypothesis
Plan
1. As a group, agree upon and write out the hypothesis statement.
2. As a group, list the steps that you will need to take to test your hypothesis. Consider each of the following factors. How will you introduce the exhaled air into the bromothymol blue solution? How will you collect data on exhaled air before and after physical activity? What kind of activity is involved? How long will it go?
3. List your materials. Your teacher will provide instructions on safe procedures for using bromothymol blue.
4. Design a data table and record it in your Science Journal so that it is ready to use as your group collects data.
5. Read over your entire experiment to make sure that all the steps are in logical order.
6. Identify any constants, variables, and controls of the experiment.

Do
1. *Make sure your teacher approves your plan before you proceed.*
2. Carry out the experiment as planned.
3. While the experiment is going on, write down any observations that you make and complete the data table in your Science Journal.

Analyze Your Data
1. What caused the bromothymol blue solution to change color? What color was it at the conclusion of each test?
   the presence of carbon dioxide; yellow
2. What was the control? What was the constant(s)? What was the variable(s)?
   The control was breathing into beaker A, which contained the bromothymol blue solution, before exercising. Constant—amount of bromothymol blue; variable—amount of exercise
3. Compare the time it took the bromothymol blue solution to change color before exercise and after exercise. Explain any difference.
   Bromothymol blue takes less time to change color after exercise. Exercise produces more carbon dioxide.
4. Prepare a table of your data and graph the results.
   The table should contain all the data collected. The graph should accurately reflect the data.

Draw Conclusions
1. Did exercise affect your rate of respiration? Explain your answer using data from your experiment.
   Answers will vary, but they should show a change in the rate. Students active in physical activities may show less of a rate change. Students should use data from activity to defend their answers.
2. Using your graph, estimate the time of color change if the time of your physical activity were twice as long.
   Estimates will vary, but should indicate that it would take less time for a color change if the physical activity were twice as long.

Chapter 19
ACTIVITY 19-2 • Kidney Structure

Lab Preview
1. What are the safety symbols that you should follow for this activity?
   The symbols are special disposal required, tools that can puncture or slice skin, wear safety goggles, and wear protective clothing.

2. Why is it important to examine an actual kidney instead of only looking at a drawing?
   Answers will vary but students should realize that working with the actual three-dimensional organ will present a more accurate picture of a kidney than they can get from a drawing.

As your body uses nutrients, wastes are created. One role of kidneys is to filter waste products out of the bloodstream and excrete this waste outside the body.

What You'll Investigate
How does the structure of the kidney relate to its function?

Goals
Observe the external and internal structures of a kidney.

Safety Precautions

Materials
- large animal kidney
- scalpel
- hand lens

Procedure
1. **Examine** the kidney supplied by your teacher.
2. If the kidney is still encased in fat, **peel** the fat off carefully.
3. Using a scalpel, carefully **cut** the tissue lengthwise in half around the outline of the kidney. This cut should result in a section similar to the illustrations in your text.
4. **Observe** the internal features of the kidney using a hand lens, or view the features in a model.
5. **Compare** the specimen or model with the kidneys in the illustrations.
6. **Draw** the kidney in your Science Journal, and **label** the structures.

Activity (continued)

Conclude and Apply
1. What part makes up the cortex of the kidney? Why is this part red?
   The mass of nephron units; the color is due to the blood in the nephrons.

2. What is the main function of nephrons?
   filters blood within the kidney

3. The medulla of the kidney is made up of a network of tubules that come together to form the ureter. What is the function of this network of tubules?
   The network of tubules moves the fluid from the nephrons. As the fluid is moved along, some water, sugar, and salt are reabsorbed into the bloodstream. Eventually, the fluid collects in the bladder.

4. How can the kidney be compared to a portable water-purifying system?
   Both serve as filtering mechanisms.

Chapter 19
MINILAB 19-1

Measuring Surface Area

Procedure
1. Make a cylinder out of a large sheet of paper. Tape it together.
2. Make cylinders out of small sheets of paper. Place as many as will fit inside the large cylinder without crushing the cylinders.
3. Unroll each cylinder. Place the small sheets next to each other in a rectangle. Lay the large sheet on top.

Analysis
1. Compare the surface area of the large sheet with all the small sheets put together.

   Answers will vary depending on student construction techniques, but will usually indicate at least a twofold increase in surface area.

2. What do the large sheet and small sheets represent?

   The large piece of paper represents a lung; the smaller pieces represent alveoli sacs.

3. How does this make gas exchange more efficient?

   More gas can be exchanged because there is greater surface area within the same space.

Chapter 19
MINILAB 19-2

Modeling Kidney Function

Procedure
1. Mix a small amount of soil with water in a cup to make muddy water.
2. Place a funnel into a second clean cup.
3. Place a piece of filter paper into the funnel.
4. Carefully pour the muddy water into the funnel.

Analysis
Compare this filtering process to the function of kidneys inside your body.

The filter removes the dirt and particles. Only the liquid goes through. The filter is like a nephron, through which all liquid passes. The nephrons keep waste from passing through.

NAME _____ DATE _____ CLASS _____

Chapter 20
ACTIVITY 20-1 • Reaction Time

Lab Preview

1. What are two major divisions of the human nervous system? **central (CNS) and peripheral (PNS)**

2. Which system is used when the body reacts to a stimulus? **Both are used.**

Your body responds quickly to some kinds of stimuli, and reflexes allow you to react quickly, without even thinking. Sometimes you can improve how quickly you react. Complete this activity to see if you can improve your reaction time.

What You'll Investigate
How can reaction time be improved?

Goals
- Observe reflexes.
- Identify stimuli and responses.

Materials
- metric ruler

Procedure

1. Review the data table below.
2. Have a partner hold the ruler at the top end.
3. Hold the thumb and finger of your right hand apart at the bottom of the ruler. Do not touch the ruler.
4. Your partner must let go of the ruler without warning you.
5. Try to catch the ruler by bringing your thumb and finger together quickly.
6. Repeat this activity several times and record in a data table where the ruler was caught.
7. Repeat this activity with your left hand. Record your results.

Sample Data for left-handed person

Where the Ruler Was Caught

Trial	Right Hand	Left Hand
1	30	20
2	20	10
3	15	10

NAME _____ DATE _____ CLASS _____

Activity (continued)

Conclude and Apply

1. Identify the stimulus in each activity. **the ruler falling**

2. Identify the response in each activity. **catching the ruler**

3. Identify the variable in each activity. **which hand is used**

4. Compare the responses of your writing hand and your other hand for both activities. **Answers will vary.**

5. What was your average reaction time for your right hand? For your left hand? **To find the average, students should add all reaction times and divide by the number of trials.**

6. Compare the response of your writing hand and your other hand for this activity. **Answers will vary. Generally, the writing hand reacts faster.**

7. Draw a conclusion about how practice relates to stimulus-response time. **With practice, stimulus-response time will probably improve.**

Chapter 20
ACTIVITY 20-2

NAME _____ DATE _____ CLASS _____

Investigating Skin Sensitivity

Design Your Own Experiment

Lab Preview
1. What safety symbols are associated with this activity?
   sharp object and eye safety
2. Where are the receptors that allow you to sense touch located in the skin?
   in the dermis

Your body responds to touch, pressure, and temperature. Not all parts of your body are equally sensitive to stimuli. Some areas are more sensitive than others. For example, your lips are sensitive to heat. This protects you from burning your mouth. Now think about touch. How sensitive is the skin on various parts of your body to touch? Which areas can distinguish the smallest amount of distance between stimuli?

Possible Materials
- index cards (3-in. × 5-in.)
- toothpicks
- glue or tape
- metric ruler

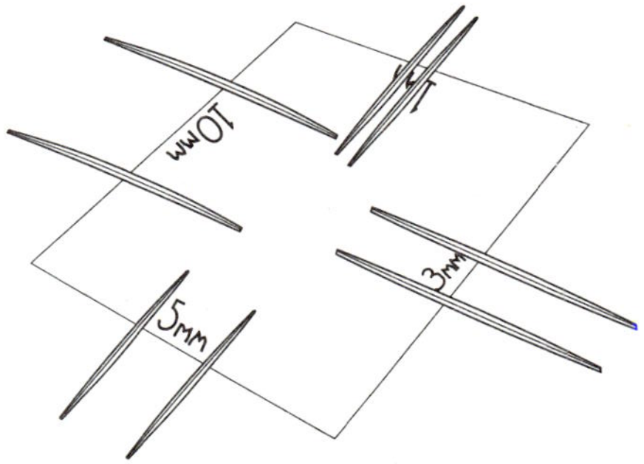

Recognize the Problem
What areas of the body are more sensitive to touch?

Form a Hypothesis
Based on your experiences, state a hypothesis about which five areas of the body you believe to be more sensitive than others. Rank the areas from 5 (the most sensitive) to 1 (the least sensitive).

Goals
- **Observe** the sensitivity to touch on various areas of the body.
- **Design an experiment** that tests the effects of a variable, such as the closeness of contact points, to determine which body areas can distinguish between the closest stimuli.

Safety Precautions
Do not apply heavy pressure when using the toothpicks.

226

NAME _____ DATE _____ CLASS _____

Activity (continued)

Test Your Hypothesis

Plan
1. As a group, agree upon and write out the hypothesis statement.
2. As a group, **list** the steps you need to take to test your hypothesis. Be very specific in describing exactly what you will do at each step. Consider the following factors as you list the steps. How will you know that sight is not a factor? How will you use the card shown on the preceding page to determine **sensitivity** to touch? How will you **determine** and **record** that one or both points of touch are felt? List your materials.
3. **Design** a data table in your Science Journal.
4. **Read** over your entire experiment to make sure that all steps are in order.
5. **Identify** any constants, variables, and controls of the experiment.

Do
1. Make sure your teacher approves the plan before you proceed.
2. **Carry out** the experiment as planned.
3. While the experiment is going on, **write down** any observations that you make and complete the data table in your Science Journal.

Analyze Your Data
1. **Compare** your results with those of other groups.
   Student results should be consistent with those of other groups.
2. **Identify** which part of the body tested can distinguish between the closest stimuli.
   fingertips and usually the palms
3. **Identify** which part of the body is least sensitive.
   back of hand, forearm
4. **Rank** body parts tested from most to least sensitive. How did your test results **compare** with your hypothesis?
   Answers will vary. Students should answer honestly if predictions do not match outcomes.

Draw Conclusions
1. Based on your answers to questions 2 and 3, what can you **infer** about the distribution of touch receptors in the skin?
   Touch receptors are closer together in the skin of the fingertips and farther apart on the back of the hand and forearm. Receptors in the palm and the back of the neck vary.
2. What other parts of your body would you predict to be less sensitive? Explain your predictions.
   Answers may include the back and the legs because they are unlikely to be used to gather new information about an object.

NAME _____ DATE _____ CLASS _____

Chapter 20
MINILAB 20-1

Observing Balance Control

Procedure
1. Place two narrow strips of paper on the wall to form two parallel vertical lines. Have a student stand between them, as still and straight as possible without leaning on the wall, for three minutes.
2. Observe how well balance is maintained.
3. Have the student close his or her eyes and repeat standing within the lines for three minutes.

Analysis
1. When was balance more difficult to maintain?

   When the eyes are closed; when the eyes are open, a person can focus on a point to help the

   body remain balanced.

2. What other factors might cause a person to lose the sense of balance?

   Answers will vary, but could include such conditions as an inner-ear infection or loud,

   continuous noise.

NAME _____ DATE _____ CLASS _____

Chapter 20
MINILAB 20-2

Comparing Sense of Smell

Procedure
1. Design an experiment to test your classmates' abilities to recognize the odors of different foods, colognes, or household products.
2. Record their responses in a data table according to the gender of the individuals tested.

Data and Observations

Male/Female	Substance	Responses	Responses will vary.

Analysis
1. Compare the numbers of correctly identified odors for both males and females.

   Answers may vary, but more females should correctly identify specific odors.

2. What can you conclude about the differences between males and females in their ability to recognize odors?

   Generally, females are more acutely aware of odors than are males.

NAME _____ DATE _____ CLASS _____

Chapter 21
ACTIVITY 21-1 • Interpreting Diagrams

Lab Preview
1. What happens during menstruation? _Tissue cells from the lining of the uterus and blood are discharged through the vagina._
2. At what age does menstruation usually begin? _For most females, the first menstrual cycle begins between ages 8 and 13._

Starting in adolescence, the hormone estrogen causes changes in the uterus. These changes prepare the uterus to accept a fertilized egg that may embed itself in the uterine wall.

What You'll Investigate
What happens to the uterus during a female's monthly cycle?

Materials
- paper and pencil

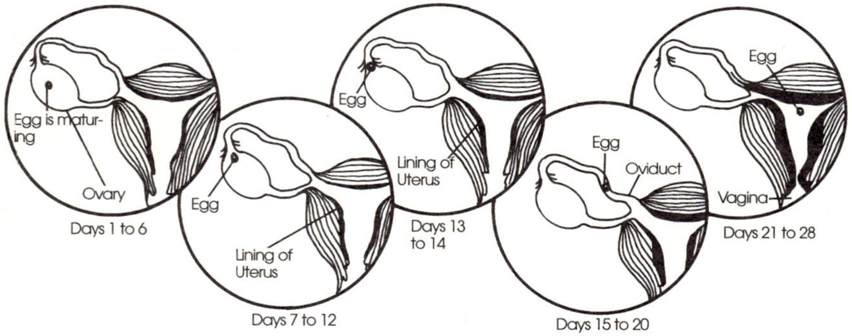

Goals
- Observe the stages in a diagram of the menstrual cycle.
- Relate the process of ovulation to the cycle.

Procedure
1. The diagrams above show what is explained in the previous section on the menstrual cycle.
2. Study the diagrams and their labels.
3. Use the information in the previous section and the diagrams above to complete a table like the one shown.
4. How are the diagrams different?
5. On approximately what day in a 28-day cycle is egg released from the ovary?

Days 1 to 6 — Egg is maturing, Ovary
Days 7 to 12 — Egg, Lining of Uterus
Days 13 to 14 — Egg, Lining of Uterus
Days 15 to 20 — Egg, Oviduct
Days 21 to 28 — Egg, Vagina

Menstruation Cycle

Days	Condition of uterus	What happens
1–6	breakdown of lining	menstruation
7–12	lining begins to thicken	egg matures in the ovary
13–14	lining is thicker	ovulation
15–28	lining thickens	egg moves to uterus

115

NAME _____ DATE _____ CLASS _____

Activity (continued)

Conclude and Apply
1. How long is the average menstrual cycle? _28 days_
2. How many days does menstruation usually last? _four to six days_
3. On what days does the lining of the uterus build up? _days 7 through 28_
4. Infer why this process is called a cycle. _If fertilization does not occur, menstruation takes place, another egg is released, and the process is repeated._
5. Calculate how many days before menstruation ovulation usually occurs. _about 14_
6. Interpret the diagram to explain the menstrual cycle. You can see what is happening to the lining of the uterus each day of the cycle. The labels show the sequence of events taking place.

116

228

Chapter 21
ACTIVITY 21-2
Average Growth Rate in Humans

Lab Preview
1. What are the five stages of growth described in Chapter 21?
   neonatal, infancy, childhood, adolescence, adulthood
2. What is puberty? **Puberty is the time of development when a person becomes physically able to reproduce.**

An individual's growth is dependent upon both the effects of hormones and his or her genetic makeup.

What You'll Investigate
Is average growth rate the same in males and females?

Goals
- Analyze the average growth rate of young males and females.
- Compare and contrast their growth rates.

Materials
- graph paper
- red and blue pencils

Procedure
1. **Construct** a graph similar to graph A. **Plot** mass on the vertical axis and age on the horizontal axis.
2. **Plot** the data given under Data and Observations for the average female growth in mass from ages eight to 18. **Connect** the points with a red line.
3. On the same graph, **plot** the data for the average male growth in mass from ages eight to 18. **Connect** the points with a blue line.
4. **Construct** a separate graph similar to graph B. **Plot** height on the vertical axis and age on the horizontal axis.
5. **Plot** the data for the average female growth in height from ages eight to 18. **Connect** the points with a red line. **Plot** the data for the average male growth in height from ages eight to 18. **Connect** the points with a blue line.

Data and Observations

Graph A

Averages for Growth in Humans		
Age	Mass (kg)	
	Female	Male
8	25	25
9	28	28
10	31	31
11	35	37
12	40	38
13	47	43
14	50	50
15	54	57
16	57	62
17	58	65
18	58	68

Graph B

Averages for Growth in Humans		
Age	Height (cm)	
	Female	Male
8	123	124
9	129	130
10	135	135
11	140	140
12	147	145
13	155	152
14	159	161
15	160	167
16	163	172
17	163	174
18	163	178

Conclude and Apply
1. Up to what age is average growth in mass similar in males and females? **up to about age 11**
2. Up to what age is average growth in height similar in males and females? **up to about age 12**
3. When does the mass of females generally change most? **Females increase the most in mass between the ages of 11 and 13.**
4. How can you explain the differences in growth between males and females? **Answers may vary slightly. Most students will say that girls enter adolescence at an earlier age than boys.**
5. Interpret the data to find whether the average growth rate is the same in males and females. **Average growth is the same until puberty. At puberty, girls have an earlier growth spurt than boys, but on the average boys grow taller than girls.**

Chapter 21
MINILAB 21-1

Interpreting Embryo Development

Procedure
1. Interpret the data in the table of embryo development below.
2. On a piece of paper, draw a line the length of the unborn baby at each date.
3. Using reference materials, find out what developmental events happen at each date.

Data and Observations

Age (mos.)	Developmental Events
3	Brain enlarging, epidermis and dermis obvious, liver secretes bile, most glands developed, bone marrow produces blood cells, arms and legs well developed, sex organs obvious
4	Cerebellum prominent, eyes and ears well developed, kidneys well developed, most bones distinct
5	Eyelashes and eyebrows present, fetus in fetal position, mother feels movement of fetus
6	Weight increases rapidly, finger and toe bones form, fingernails and toenails grow
7	Eyes open, skin wrinkled and red, body well proportioned
8	Fat forming under skin
9	Skin redness fades and wrinkles disappear

End of month	Length
3	8 cm
4	15 cm
5	25 cm
6	30 cm
7	35 cm
8	40 cm
9	51 cm

Analysis
1. During which month does the greatest increase in length occur?
   from the end of the eighth month to the end of the ninth month
2. What size is the unborn baby when movement can be felt by the mother?
   approximately 7-10 cm

Chapter 21
MINILAB 21-2

Investigating Immunizations

Procedure
1. Find out what immunizations are usually given to babies and young children.
2. Compare these to what vaccines are required for children to enter your school.

Analysis
1. What booster shots are given to school children?
   Answers will vary, but most likely will include having boosters for DTP, measles, and polio.
2. Investigate what immunizations are required to travel to foreign countries.
   Answers will vary according to local or state health regulations, but most likely will include DTP, polio, measles, mumps, and rubella.

Chapter 22
ACTIVITY 22-1 • Microorganisms and Disease

Lab Preview
1. Which safety symbols are associated with this activity? **disposal alert and chemical safety**
2. Read the procedure below. What is the source of microorganisms in this activity? **the rotting apple**

Microorganisms are all around us. They are on the surfaces of everything we touch. Try this experiment to see how microorganisms are involved in spreading infections.

What You'll Investigate
How do microorganisms cause infection?

Goals
- Observe the transmission of microorganisms.
- Relate microorganisms to infections.

Materials
- fresh apples (6)
- rotting apple
- alcohol (5 mL)
- self-sealing plastic bags (6)
- labels and pencil
- paper towels
- sandpaper
- cotton ball
- soap and water

Procedure
1. Label the plastic bags 1 through 6. **Put a fresh apple in bag 1 and seal it.**
2. **Rub** the rotting apple over the entire surface of the remaining five apples. This is your source of microorganisms. **CAUTION:** *Always wash your hands after handling microorganisms.* **Put one apple in bag 2.**
3. Hold one apple 1.5 m above the floor and drop it. **Put this apple into bag number 3.**
4. Rub one apple with sandpaper. **Place this apple in bag number 4.**
5. Wash one apple with soap and water. Dry it well. **Put this apple in bag number 5.**
6. Use a cotton ball to spread alcohol over the last apple. Let it air dry. Place it in bag number 6.
7. Place all of the apples in a dark place for three days. Then, wash your hands.
8. Write a **hypothesis** to explain what you think will happen to each apple.
9. At the end of three days and again on day 7, **compare** all of the apples. **Record** your observations in the following data table. **CAUTION:** *Give all apples to your teacher for proper disposal.*

Activity (continued)

Apple Data

Sample Data

Apple	Condition of the apple	Observations Day 3	Day 7
1	Fresh apple	No change	No change
2	Untreated apple	No change	Many brown spots, decay
3	Dropped apple	Brown spots	Decay at breaks
4	Apple rubbed with sandpaper	Some brown at soft areas	Decay at soft areas
5	Apple washed with soap and water	No change	Little or no change
6	Apple covered with alcohol	No change	No change

Conclude and Apply
1. Did you observe changes in apples number 5 and 6?
   Apples 5 and 6 did not decay. Their skins were not broken, so pathogens could not enter the apples. Alcohol could have killed some microbes.
2. Why is it important to clean a wound?
   Cleaning a wound removes pathogens, and infection is prevented.
3. Were your hypotheses supported?
   Answers will vary with the hypotheses.
4. Relate microorganisms to infections on your skin.
   Pathogens can cause infection by entering damaged or cut surfaces of an organism.

Chapter 22
ACTIVITY 22-2 • Microorganism Growth

Design Your Own Experiment

Lab Preview
1. What safety symbols are associated with this activity? **sharp object safety, disposal alert, clothing protection safety, eye safety, chemical safety**

2. What could you use as a source of microorganisms in this activity? **Answers will vary; possibly a student's fingertip.**

Infections are caused by microorganisms. Without cleanliness, the risk of getting an infection from a wound is high. Disinfectants are chemicals that kill or remove disease organisms from objects. Antiseptics are chemicals that kill or prevent growth of disease organisms on living tissues. You will test the effect of these chemicals on growing microorganisms in petri dishes filled with agar. Agar is a gel that provides the ideal nutrients for growing microorganisms.

Recognize the Problem
What conditions do microorganisms need to grow? How can they be prevented from growing?

Form a Hypothesis
Based on your knowledge of disinfectants and antiseptics, state a hypothesis about methods that will prevent the growth of microorganisms.

Goals
- **Observe** the effects of antiseptics and disinfectants on microorganism growth in petri dishes.
- **Design** an experiment that will test the effects of chemicals on microorganisms growing in contaminated petri dishes.

Safety Precautions
Handle the forceps carefully. When you complete the experiment, give your sealed petri dishes to your teacher for proper disposal.

Possible Materials
- sterile petri dishes with agar (5)
- filter paper (2-cm squares)
- test chemicals (disinfectant, hydrogen peroxide, mouthwash, alcohol)
- transparent tape
- pencil and labels
- scissors
- metric ruler
- forceps
- small jars for chemicals (4)
- cotton balls

123

Activity (continued)

Test Your Hypothesis
Plan
1. As a group, agree upon and write out a hypothesis statement.
2. To test disinfectants, first introduce microorganisms to the agar by rubbing your finger gently over each dish. Then, soak a different square of filter paper in each of the disinfectants. Place each square on the agar and seal the dishes with tape. Never break the seal. Look for bacteria growth under and around each square.
3. As a group, list the steps that you will need to take to test your hypothesis. Consider what you learned about how infections are stopped. **List your materials.**
4. **Design** a data table and record it in your Science Journal so that it is ready to use as your group collects data.
5. Read over your entire experiment to make sure that all steps are in logical order.
6. **Identify** any **constants, variables,** and the **control** of the experiment.

Do
1. Make sure your teacher approves your plan before you proceed.
2. Carry out the experiment as planned.
3. While the experiment is going on, write down any observations that you make and complete the data table in your Science Journal.

Analyze Your Data
1. Compare your results with those of other groups.
   Student results should be consistent with those of other groups.
2. How did you compare growth beneath and around each chemical-soaked square in the petri dishes?
   Answers will vary, but students should be able to observe that there are fewer colonies beneath and around the chemical-soaked squares.
3. Interpret the data to determine what substances appeared to be most effective in preventing microorganism growth. What substances appeared to be least effective?
   Answers will vary depending on the substances used. Household disinfectants and antiseptics (e.g., hydrogen peroxide) will have an effect. Some microorganisms are more susceptible to chemicals than others.

Draw Conclusions
1. What methods prevent the growth of microorganisms?
   Answers will vary, using antiseptics disinfecting regularly,
2. How does the growth of microorganisms on the control compare with their growth on the variables?
   Answers will vary.

Chapter 22
MINILAB 22-1
Detecting Bacteria

Procedure
1. Methylene blue is used to detect bacteria. The faster the color fades, the more bacteria are present.
2. Use the food samples provided by your teacher. Label four test tubes 1, 2, 3, and 4.
3. Fill three test tubes half full of the food samples.
4. Fill the fourth with water.
5. Add 20 drops of methylene blue and 2 drops of mineral oil to each tube.
6. Place the tubes into a warm-water bath for 20 minutes.
7. Record the time and your observations.

Data and Observations Data will vary.

Test Tube	Food Sample	Time	Observation
1			
2			
3			
4	water		

Analysis
1. Compare how long it takes each tube to lose its color.

Length of time will vary with the age of the product used.

2. What was the purpose of tube 4?

Tube 4 serves as a control.

3. Why is it important to eat and drink only the freshest food?

By eating and drinking fresh foods, the contact with potentially harmful bacteria will be reduced.

Chapter 22
MINILAB 22-2
Determining Reproduction Rates

Procedure
1. Make a chart like the one below.
2. Complete the chart up to the fifth hour. Assume that the bacteria divide every 20 minutes if conditions are favorable.
3. Graph your data.

Data and Observations

Time	Number of Bacteria	Time	Number of Bacteria
0 hours 0 minutes	1	3 hours 0 minutes	
20 minutes	2	20 minutes	
40 minutes	4	40 minutes	
1 hour 0 minutes	8	4 hours 0 minutes	
20 minutes	16	20 minutes	
40 minutes	32	40 minutes	
2 hours 0 minutes		5 hours 0 minutes	
20 minutes		20 minutes	
40 Minutes		40 minutes	

Analysis
1. How many bacteria are present after five hours?

At the five-hour point, there will be 32 768 bacteria. Students should label the vertical axis of the graph *thousands of bacteria* and the horizontal axis *time in hours*.

2. Why is it important to take antibiotics promptly if you have an infection?

It is important to take all of any antibiotic that is prescribed according to the directions. Failure to do so can leave a few bacteria that can begin dividing again and reinfect the body.

Chapter 23

ACTIVITY 23-1

Reflection from a Plane Mirror

Lab Preview

1. Do the properties of a reflecting surface change the way a light ray is reflected?
   No. The law of reflection states that the light is reflected in the same way, no matter what material a reflecting surface is made of.
2. What is a plane mirror? A plane mirror is a mirror with a flat reflecting surface.

A light ray strikes the surface of a plane mirror and is reflected. Is there a relationship between the direction of the incoming light ray and the direction of the reflected light ray?

What You'll Investigate

How does the angle of incidence compare with the angle of reflection for a plane mirror?

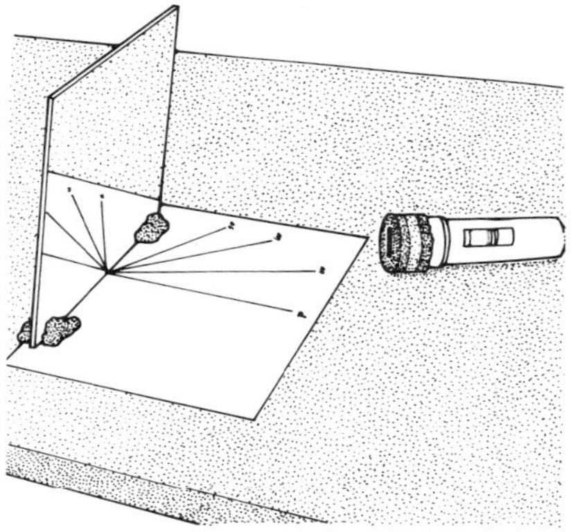

Goals

- **Measure** the angle of incidence and the angle of reflection for a light ray incident on a plane mirror.

Materials

- flashlight
- small plane mirror, at least 10 cm on a side
- protractor
- metric ruler
- scissors
- black construction paper
- tape
- modeling clay

Procedure

1. With the scissors, **cut** a slit in the construction paper and **tape** it over the flashlight lens. Make sure the slit is centered on the lens.
2. **Place** the mirror at one end of the unlined paper. Push the mirror into the lump of clay so it stands vertically, and tilt the mirror so it leans slightly toward the table.
3. **Measure** with the ruler to find the center of the bottom edge of the mirror and mark it. Then, use the protractor and the ruler to **draw** a line on the paper perpendicular to the mirror from the mark. Label this line P.
4. Using the protractor and the ruler, **draw** lines on the paper outward from the mark at the center of the mirror at angles of 30°, 45°, and 60° to line P.
5. Turn on the flashlight and place it so the beam is along the 60° line. This is the angle of incidence. **Locate** the reflected beam on the paper, and **measure** the angle the reflected beam makes with line P. **Record** this angle in your data table. This is the angle of reflection. If you cannot see the reflected beam, slightly increase the tilt of the mirror.

Activity (continued)

Data Table—Reflection in Plane Mirrors

Angle of incidence	Angle of reflection
0°	0°
30°	30°
45°	45°
60°	60°

6. Repeat step 5 for the 30° and 45° lines.

Conclude and Apply

1. What happened to the beam of light when it was shone along line P?
   It was reflected straight back along the same line.

2. What can you infer about the relationship between the angle of incidence and the angle of reflection?
   The angle of incidence equals the angle of reflection.

Chapter 23
ACTIVITY 23-2

Image Formation by a Convex Lens

Lab Preview

1. What is a convex (or converging) lens?
   A lens that is thicker in the center than at the edges is called a convex (or converging) lens.

2. If an object is closer than one focal length to a convex lens, how will the image's size compare to the size of the object? Will the image be upside-down or right-side-up?
   The image formed is right-side-up and larger than the object.

The type of image formed by a convex lens or a converging lens is related to the distance of the object from the lens. This distance is called the object distance. The location of the image is also related to the distance of the object from the lens. The distance from the lens to the image is called the image distance. What happens to the position of the image as the object gets nearer or farther from the lens?

What You'll Investigate
How are the image distance and object distance related for a convex lens?

Goals
- **Measure** the image distance as the object distance changes.
- **Observe** the type of image formed as the object distance changes.

Safety Precautions

Materials
- convex lens
- modeling clay
- meterstick
- flashlight
- masking tape
- cardboard with white surface, about 20-cm square

Procedure

1. **Design** a data table in which to record your data. You will need three columns in your table. One column will be for the object distance, another will be for the image distance, and the third will be for the type of image.

2. Use the modeling clay to make the lens stand vertically upright on the lab table.

3. **Form** the letter F on the glass surface of the flashlight with masking tape.

4. Turn on the flashlight and place it 1 m from the lens. **Position** the flashlight so the flashlight beam is shining through the lens.

5. **Record** the distance from the flashlight to the lens in the object distance column in your data table.

6. Hold the cardboard vertically upright on the other side of the lens, and move it back and forth until a sharp image of the letter F is obtained.

7. **Measure** the distance of the card from the lens using the meterstick, and **record** this distance in the image distance column in your data table.

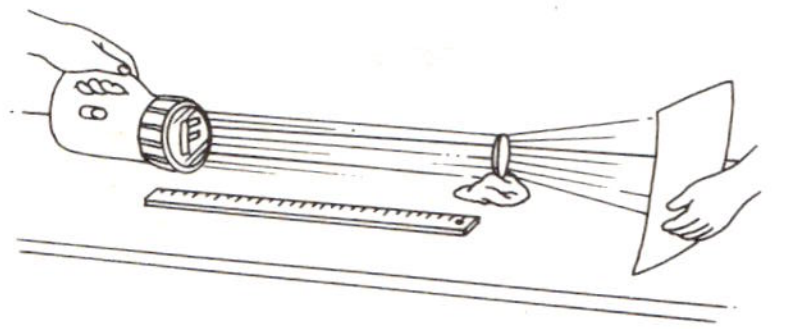

Activity (continued)

8. **Record** in the third column of your data table whether the image is upright or inverted, and smaller or larger.

9. Repeat steps 6–9 for an object distance of 50 cm and 25 cm.

Data and Observations

Conclude and Apply

1. How did the image distance change as the object distance decreased?
   The image distance increased as the object distance decreased.

2. How did the image change as the object distance decreased?
   The image size increased as the object distance decreased.

3. What would happen to the size of the image if the flashlight were much farther away than 1 m? **As the flashlight is moved outward, the rays become almost parallel, and the image appears as a bright spot at the focal point.**

NAME _____ DATE _____ CLASS _____

Chapter 23
MINILAB 23-1

Viewing Colors Through Color Filters

Procedure
1. Obtain sheets of red, green, and blue construction paper.
2. Obtain a piece of red cellophane and green cellophane.
3. Look at each sheet of paper through the red cellophane and record the color of each sheet.
4. Look at each sheet of colored paper through the green cellophane and observe the color of each sheet.
5. Hold both pieces of cellophane together and look at each sheet of colored paper. Record the color of each sheet.

Analysis
Explain why the sheets of paper changed color when you looked at them through the pieces of cellophane.
Certain colors of the light reflected from the construction paper do not pass through the filter.

_____
_____
_____

236

NAME _____ DATE _____ CLASS _____

Chapter 23
MINILAB 23-2

Forming an Image with a Lens

Procedure
1. Fill a glass test tube with water and seal it with a stopper.
2. Write your name on a 3 × 5 card. Lay the test tube on the card and observe the appearance of your name. Record your observations.
_____
3. Hold the test tube about 1 cm above the card and observe the appearance of your name. Record your observations.
_____
4. Now, observe what happens to your name as you slowly move the test tube away from the card. Record your observations.
_____

Analysis
1. Is the water-filled test tube a concave lens or a convex lens?
a convex lens
2. Compare the image formed when the test tube was close to the card with the image formed when the test tube was far from the card.
As the test tube gets closer to the card the image enlarges.
_____
_____

132

Chapter 24
ACTIVITY 24-1 • Time Trials

Lab Preview
1. Explain why making observations and predictions is an important part of scientific investigations. **The entire scientific method is based on observation and prediction. A scientist observes something, makes predictions based on the observation, and then tests those predictions.**

2. If a prediction is proven incorrect for an experiment, should the experiment be considered a failure? **No. Finding evidence which doesn't agree with predictions or hypotheses is often what leads to new discoveries or new levels of understanding. When something doesn't go as planned in a scientific procedure, there is an opportunity to learn new things about the object or material involved in the experiment.**

Before a big car race, all the contestants must pass the time trials. Time trials are races against the clock instead of against other cars.

What You'll Investigate
Can time trials be used to predict the winner of a race?

Goals
- Conduct time trials.
- Test speed and distance predictions from the results of time trials.

Materials
- metersticks (2)
- stopwatch or watch that measures in seconds
- toy cars
- masking tape

Procedure
1. Set up a straightaway using two metersticks as curbs. Use the tape to make a starting line at the beginning of the track.
2. Test the track with one car. If the car runs into the metersticks, move them farther apart or devise some other remedy.
3. Wind up or push the first car, starting with the front of the car on zero of the meterstick. Time its trip to the end of the metersticks.
4. Repeat this at least three times for each car, and **record** your distance and time measurements in a table on the next page.
5. Calculate the average time and distance.
6. Calculate the average speed using the averages for the time and distance.

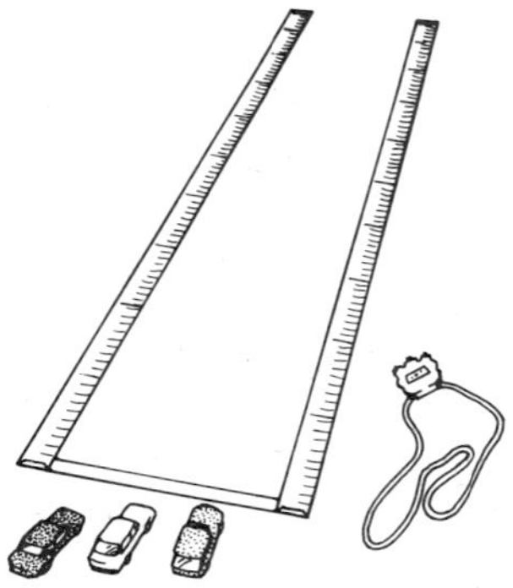

Activity (continued)

Time Trials Data

Sample data

Car	Time (s)	Distance (m)
Trial 1	2	1
Trial 2	2	1
Trial 3	3	1
Average	2.3	1

Conclude and Apply
1. Compare the average speed of your car with those of your classmates. **Check students' work.**

2. Predict which car should win a 1-m race based on the time trials. Test your prediction. **The car with the greatest average speed will win a short race.**

3. Predict which car will travel farthest based on your measurements and observations. Test your prediction. **The car able to run longest will win the distance race. Often this is a car that unwinds slowly but surely.**

4. Explain whether time trials accurately predict which car will win the race. Were you able to predict which car would travel the farthest? Explain why or why not. **Time trials can be used to accurately predict short races but are not effective in testing for endurance.**

NAME _____ DATE _____ CLASS _____

Chapter 24
MINILAB 24-1

Inferring Free Fall

Procedure
1. Attach a clothespin to either side of a rubber band. If the rubber band has bends, put the clothespins elsewhere on the band.
2. Hold one clothespin. Observe the shape of the band.
3. Drop the clothespin and observe the shape of the band as it falls.

Analysis
1. What did the rubber band look like as it fell? What does the shape mean?
   As the rubber band fell, it went from a stretched, oblong shape to a loose, circular shape, indicating that the clothespins were not stretching it.

2. Did the clothespins still have weight when they were falling? Why or why not?
   The clothespins still had weight. Weight is due to gravity, and gravity acted on the clothespins at all times.

135

NAME _____ DATE _____ CLASS _____

Chapter 24
MINILAB 24-2

Measuring Friction

Procedure
1. Use your ring binder or a book for a slope.
2. Place a metal washer on the cover. Slowly lift the cover and stop when the washer just starts to move. Measure this angle with a protractor.
3. Repeat step 2 with a rubber washer.
4. Change the surface of your binder by taping a piece of plain, waxed, or sandpaper to it. Repeat steps 2 and 3.

Analysis
1. Which surface required the smallest angle to get the washer to move? What makes this combination different from the others?
   The smoothest surface (waxed paper) with the smoothest washer (metal) requires the smallest angle. Both surfaces reduce friction.

2. What could you do to make the angle even smaller?
   Using even smoother surfaces, such as a greased surface, would reduce friction and therefore the angle.

3. Compare and contrast the friction of the metal and rubber washers.
   The metal washer started sliding at a smaller angle on each surface.

136

Chapter 25
ACTIVITY 25-1 • Building the Pyramids

Lab Preview

1. In a scientific sense, what is positive work? Give an example. **Positive work occurs when a force produces motion in the same direction as a force. Pushing, lifting, or pulling an object is an example of positive work.**

2. How is work measured? What units are used? **Work is mathematically defined as the measure of force × distance. So you must calculate the force (only along the direction of motion) and the distance. Work is measured in joules, abbreviated J.**

The workers who built the Great Pyramid at Giza needed to move 2.3 million blocks of limestone. Each block weighed more than 1 metric ton. The designers knew how to use ramps to reduce the force needed to lift the blocks into place.

What You'll Investigate
How does the force needed to lift a block a certain height depend on the distance traveled?

Goals
- **Model** the method that was probably used to build the pyramids.
- **Compare** the force needed to lift a block straight up with the force needed to pull it up a ramp.

Materials
- wood block
- tape
- spring scale
- ruler
- 3-ring binder
- books
- meterstick

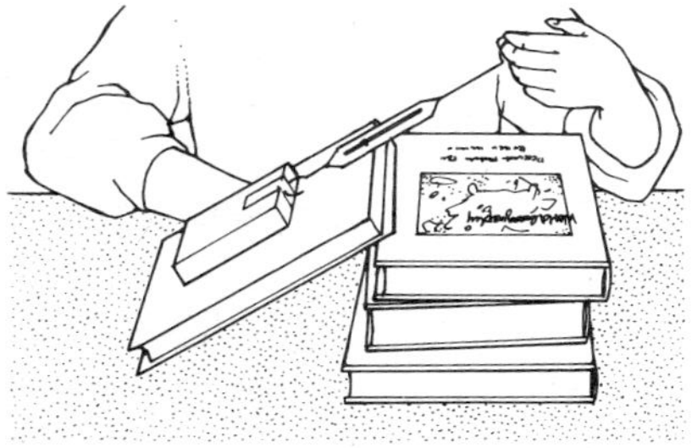

Procedure

1. Use a pile of books to **model** a half-completed pyramid. **Measure** the height.

2. The wooden block **models** a block of stone. Attach it to the spring scale and **measure** the force needed to lift it straight up the side of the books.

3. Use a binder to **model** a ramp. **Measure** the force needed to pull the block up the ramp. Be sure to pull parallel to the ramp. Repeat the experiment with at least two other ramp lengths. Fill in the table.

Ramp Data   Sample data

Distance (cm)	Force (N)	Work (J)
40	0.04	0.016
30	0.05	0.015

Activity (continued)

Conclude and Apply

1. What happens to the force needed as the distance increases? **It decreases.**

2. Compare and contrast your results for each case. **In each case, the effort force is less than the amount necessary to lift it straight up and, as the ramp length is increased, the effort force decreases.**

3. Calculate the work in each case. **Check students' work; the work should be similar in each case, but because of losses to friction, not exact.**

4. How could you modify your setup to use less force? **Sample responses: make the ramp longer; make it slipperier; add wheels to reduce friction.**

Chapter 25
ACTIVITY 25-2 • Pulley Power
Design Your Own Experiment

Lab Preview
1. What is a pulley?
   A pulley is a surface, such as a wheel, that redirects force using a rope. It allows you to pull down to lift a weight rather than having to lift directly upward.

2. Why is it important to use safety goggles and to be careful when using a pulley?
   A pulley can break or the object can fall. It is important to protect yourself from any possible mishap. Using safety goggles is a good precaution for protecting your eyes.

It would have taken decades to build the Sears Tower without the aid of a pulley system attached to a crane. Hoisting the 1-ton I beams to a maximum height of 110 stories required tremendous lifting forces and precise control of the beam's movement.

Recognize the Problem
How can you use a pulley system to reduce the force needed to lift a load?

Form a Hypothesis
Write a hypothesis about how pulleys can be combined to make a system of pulleys to lift a heavy load, such as a building block. Consider the efficiency of your system.

Goals
- **Design** a pulley system.
- **Measure** the mechanical advantage and efficiency of the pulley system.

Safety Precautions
The brick could be dangerous if it falls. Don't stand under it.

Possible Materials
- single- and multiple-pulley systems
- nylon rope
- steel bar to support the pulley system
- meterstick
- *metric tape measure*
- variety of weights to test pulleys
- force spring scale
- a brick
- balance or scale
- *alternate materials*

Activity (continued)

Test Your Hypothesis
Plan
1. Decide how you are going to support your pulley system.
2. How will you measure the effort force and the resistance force? How will you determine the mechanical advantage? How will you measure efficiency?
3. Experiment by lifting small weights with a single pulley, double pulley, and so on. How efficient are the pulleys?
4. Use the results of step 3 to **design** a pulley system to lift the building block.

Do
1. Make sure your teacher has approved your plan before you proceed.
2. Assemble the pulley system you designed. You may want to **test** it with a smaller weight before attaching the brick.
3. **Measure** the force needed to lift the brick. How much rope must you pull to raise the brick 10 cm?

Analyze Your Data
1. Calculate the theoretical mechanical advantage of your pulley system. (You can refer to the *Field Guild to Machines* at the end of this chapter.)
   Use (length of rope pulled)/(distance load raised).

2. Calculate the actual mechanical advantage of your pulley system.
   Use (weight of load)/(effort force).

3. Calculate the efficiency of your pulley system.
   Use $(W_{out}/W_{in})100$, where W_{out} = (weight)(distance raised) and
   W_{in} = (effort force)(length rope pulled).

Draw Conclusions
1. Explain how increasing the number of pulleys increases the mechanical advantage.
   When a pulley is added, the mechanical advantage is increased by 1, as a rule.

2. How could you modify the pulley system to lift a weight twice as heavy with the same effort force used here?
   Double the number of pulleys in the system (plus some for friction losses).

3. Compare this real machine with an ideal machine.
   An ideal pulley system would have an efficiency of 100 percent. The real system has losses due to friction.

Chapter 25
MINILAB 25-1

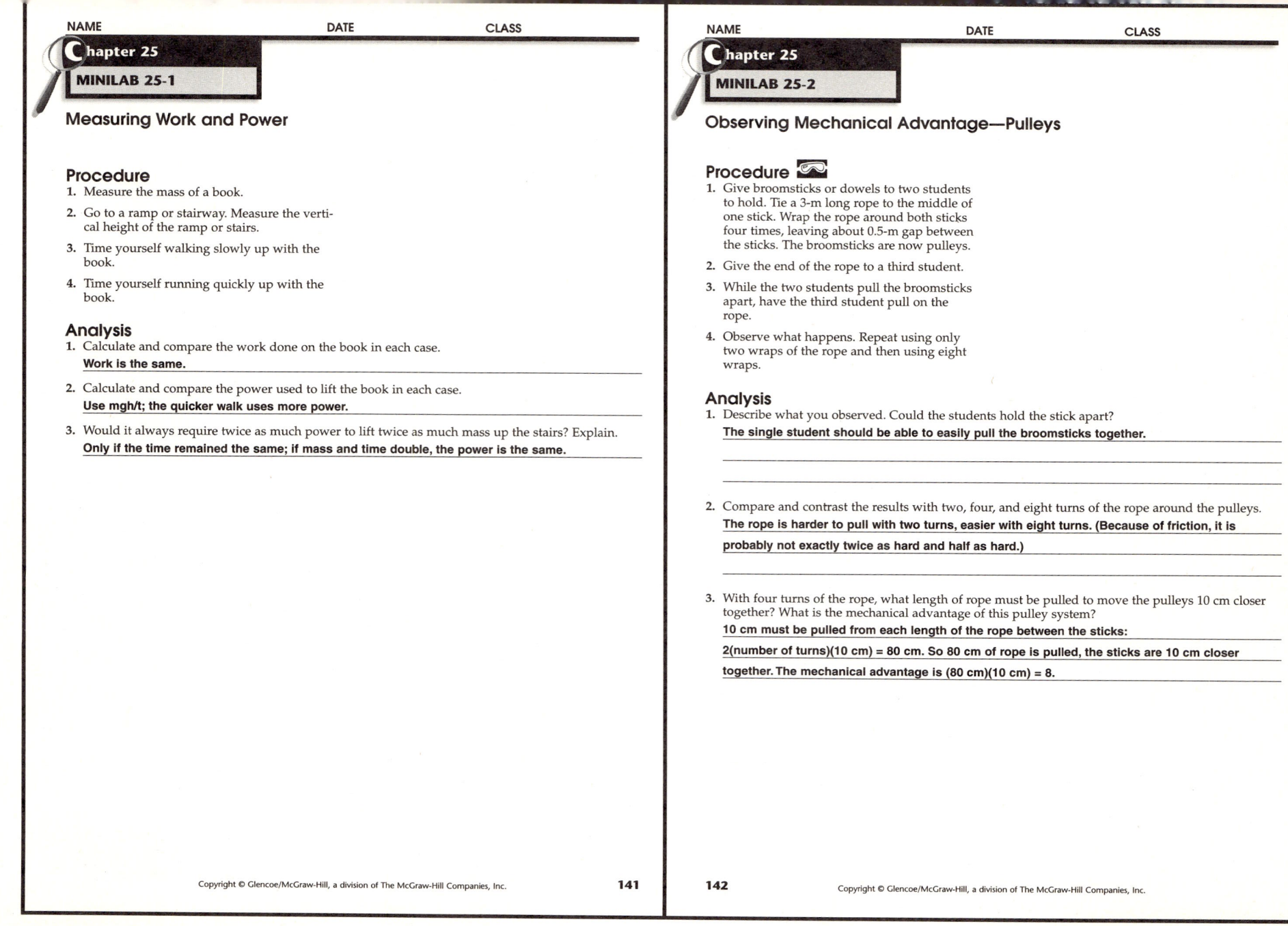

Measuring Work and Power

Procedure

1. Measure the mass of a book.
2. Go to a ramp or stairway. Measure the vertical height of the ramp or stairs.
3. Time yourself walking slowly up with the book.
4. Time yourself running quickly up with the book.

Analysis

1. Calculate and compare the work done on the book in each case.
   Work is the same.
2. Calculate and compare the power used to lift the book in each case.
   Use mgh/t; the quicker walk uses more power.
3. Would it always require twice as much power to lift twice as much mass up the stairs? Explain.
   Only if the time remained the same; if mass and time double, the power is the same.

Chapter 25
MINILAB 25-2

Observing Mechanical Advantage—Pulleys

Procedure

1. Give broomsticks or dowels to two students to hold. Tie a 3-m long rope to the middle of one stick. Wrap the rope around both sticks four times, leaving about 0.5-m gap between the sticks. The broomsticks are now pulleys.
2. Give the end of the rope to a third student.
3. While the two students pull the broomsticks apart, have the third student pull on the rope.
4. Observe what happens. Repeat using only two wraps of the rope and then using eight wraps.

Analysis

1. Describe what you observed. Could the students hold the stick apart?
   The single student should be able to easily pull the broomsticks together.

2. Compare and contrast the results with two, four, and eight turns of the rope around the pulleys.
   The rope is harder to pull with two turns, easier with eight turns. (Because of friction, it is probably not exactly twice as hard and half as hard.)

3. With four turns of the rope, what length of rope must be pulled to move the pulleys 10 cm closer together? What is the mechanical advantage of this pulley system?
   **10 cm must be pulled from each length of the rope between the sticks:
   2(number of turns)(10 cm) = 80 cm. So 80 cm of rope is pulled, the sticks are 10 cm closer together. The mechanical advantage is (80 cm)(10 cm) = 8.**

Chapter 26
ACTIVITY 26-1
A Model for Voltage and Current

Lab Preview
1. What safety symbols are associated with this activity?
   eye safety, clothing protection
2. What is the unit of measure of electric potential energy?
   volts (V)

The flow of electrons in an electric circuit is something like the flow of water. By raising or lowering the height of a water tank, you can increase or decrease the potential energy of the water. In this activity, you will use a water system to investigate how the flow of water in a tube depends on the height of the water and the diameter of the tube the water flows through.

What You'll Investigate
How is the flow of water through a tube affected by changing the height of a container of water and the diameter of the tube?

Goals
- **Make a model** for the flow of current in a simple circuit.

Materials
- plastic funnel
- rubber or plastic tubing of different diameters (1 m each)
- meterstick
- ring stand with ring
- stop watch
- *clock displaying seconds
- hose clamp
- *clothespin
- beakers (500-mL) (2)
- *alternate materials

Procedure
1. **Design** a data table similar to the example on the next page in which to record your data.
2. **Connect** the tubing to the bottom of the funnel and place the funnel in the ring of the ring stand.
3. **Measure** the diameter of the rubber tubing. **Record** your data.
4. **Place** a 500-mL beaker at the bottom of the ring stand, and lower the ring so the open end of the tubing is in the beaker.
5. **Use** the meterstick to **measure** the height from the top of the funnel to the bottom of the ring stand. **Record** your data.
6. **Pour** water into the funnel fast enough to keep the funnel full but not overflowing. **Measure** the time needed for 100-mL of water to flow into the beaker. Use the hose clamp to start and stop the flow of water. **Record** your data.
7. **Connect** tubing with a different diameter to the funnel and repeat steps 2–6.
8. **Reconnect** the original piece of tubing and repeat steps 4–6 for several lower positions of the funnel, lowering the height by 10 cm each time.
9. **Calculate** the rate of flow for each trial by dividing 100-mL by the measured time.

143

Activity (continued)

Flow Rate Data
Sample data

Trial number	Height (cm)	Diameter of tubing (cm)	Time (s)	Rate of flow (mL/s)
1	40	0.50	4	25.0
2	40	0.25	15	6.7
3	30	0.50	5	20.0
4	20	0.50	6	16.7

Conclude and Apply
1. Make a graph to show how the rate of flow depends on the funnel height.
   Student graphs should indicate that flow rate increases as height increases.
2. How does the rate of flow depend on the diameter of the tubing?
   As the diameter of the tube decreases, the rate of flow of the water decreases.
3. Which of the variables that you changed in your trials corresponds to the voltage in a circuit? Which variable corresponds to the resistance in a circuit? What part of a circuit would the hose clamp correspond to?
   Height of the funnel corresponds to voltage. Width of tube corresponds to resistance. Hose clamp corresponds to a switch.
4. Based on your results, how would the current in a circuit depend on the voltage? How would the current depend on the resistance?
   As voltage increases, the current increases. As resistance increases, the current decreases.

144

Chapter 26
ACTIVITY 26-2 • Current in a Parallel Circuit

Lab Preview
1. Describe a series circuit.
   A series circuit has only one path for the electric current to follow. If this path is broken, the current will no longer flow.

2. Describe a parallel circuit.
   A parallel circuit has more than one path for the electric current to follow. The current branches so that electrons flow through each of the paths. If one path is broken, current continues to flow through the other path(s).

In this activity you will investigate how the current in a circuit changes when two or more lightbulbs are connected in parallel. Because the brightness of a lightbulb increases or decreases as more or less current flows through it, the brightness of the bulbs in the circuits can be used to determine which circuit has more current.

What You'll Investigate
How does connecting devices in series or parallel affect the electric current in a circuit?

Goals
- **Observe** how the current in a parallel circuit changes as more devices are added.

Safety Precautions

Materials
- lightbulbs (1.5V) (4)
- batteries (1.5V) (2)
- pieces of insulated wire, each about 10 cm long (8)
- battery holders (2)
- minibulb sockets (4)

Procedure
1. Connect one lightbulb to the battery in a complete circuit. After you've made the bulb light, disconnect the bulb from the battery to keep the battery from running down. This series circuit will be the brightness tester.

2. Make a parallel circuit by connecting two bulbs together as shown in the diagram. Reconnect the bulb in the brightness tester and compare its brightness with the brightness of the two bulbs in the parallel circuit. Record your observations.

   The bulb in the tester should be brighter than the bulbs in the circuit.

3. Add another bulb to the parallel circuit as shown in the figure. How does the brightness of the bulbs change? Record your observations.

   Students should observe the bulbs grow dimmer

Activity (continued)

4. Disconnect one bulb in the parallel circuit. What happens to the brightness of the remaining bulbs?
   They grow brighter.

Conclude and Apply

1. Compared to the brightness tester, is the current in the parallel circuit more or less?
   The current is less in the brightness tester.

2. How does adding additional devices affect the current in a parallel circuit.
   There is more current in the parallel circuit.

3. Are the electric circuits in your house wired in series or parallel? How do you know? The devices in a house are wired in parallel. When devices are removed from a parallel circuit, the remaining devices are unaffected. In a house, turning off one light in a circuit does not turn off the other lights.

NAME _____ DATE _____ CLASS _____

Chapter 26
MINILAB 26-1

Analyzing Electric Forces

Procedure
1. Rub a glass rod with a piece of silk.
2. Quickly separate the glass rod and the silk, and then slowly bring them close together.
3. Charge two pieces of silk by rubbing each on a glass rod.
4. Bring the two charged pieces of silk together slowly.

Analysis
Which materials have the same charge? Which have different charges? How do you know? **The two pieces of silk have the same charge; they repel one another. The glass rod and the silk have opposite charges; they attract one another. The force between objects with the same charge is repulsive. The force between objects with different charges is attractive.**

147

NAME _____ DATE _____ CLASS _____

Chapter 26
MINILAB 26-2

Lighting a Bulb with One Wire

Procedure
1. The filament in a lightbulb is a piece of wire. For the bulb to light, an electric current must flow through the filament in a complete circuit. Examine the base of the flashlight lightbulb carefully. Where are the ends of the filament connected to the base?
2. Connect a piece of wire, a battery, and a flashlight bulb to make the bulb light. (There are four possible ways to do this.)

Analysis
Draw and label a diagram showing the path followed by electrons in your circuit. Explain your diagram.

Drawings and answers will vary.

148

Chapter 27

ACTIVITY 27-1 • Igneous Rocks

Lab Preview

1. Why does the safety symbol for goggles appear in this activity?
   The goggles symbol indicates that safety goggles should be worn while examining the materials in this activity to avoid getting grains or dust in your eyes.

2. What does the use of a hand lens tell you about this activity? It tells you that the information you gather will be based on close observation.

One way that rocks can form is from melted rock material, called magma. Some rocks formed in this way cool quickly from lava at or near Earth's surface. Others cool slowly from magma deep inside Earth. How igneous rocks form affects their mineral content and the size of the mineral grains.

What You'll Investigate

How can you determine how igneous rocks were formed?

Goals

- Observe and classify igneous rocks based on texture and color.
- Recognize that the texture of igneous rocks is determined by how fast they cool.
- Recognize that the color of igneous rocks is an indication of mineral content and chemical composition.

Materials

- igneous rock samples (5)
- hand lens
- table (Common Igneous Rocks) in the textbook
- Appendices F and G

Procedure

1. Observe your samples using the hand lens.
2. Determine the texture of each rock sample. If the grains or crystals are large and easy to see, the texture is coarse, and the rocks formed slowly. If the grains or crystals are small and are not easy to see, the texture is described as fine, and the rocks formed quickly.
3. Separate your samples into two groups based on texture (coarse or fine grained) of the rocks. **Record** which rocks were in which group in your Science Journal.
4. Determine whether any of your samples has both coarse and fine crystals in it.
5. Classify your rocks based on chemical composition. Igneous rocks that are dark colored generally have a higher percentage of iron and magnesium in them. Igneous rocks that are light colored generally have a higher percentage of the compound silica (SiO_2) in them. Rocks that are intermediate in color are also intermediate in composition. Record your data in your Science Journal.
6. Can you **infer** what minerals have formed in the light-colored rocks? What about the dark-colored or intermediate-colored rocks? Record your inferences in the data table on the next page.
7. Using the table, Appendices F and G, and the information you have entered in your Science Journal, fill in the data table on the next page.

Activity (continued)

Igneous Rock Data

Sample Data

Texture*	Color	Minerals present	Rock name
glassy	usually black	none visible	obsidian
coarse	light colored	feldspar hornblende quartz mica	granite
fine	dark colored	feldspar augite olivine	basalt
glassy, with abundant holes	usually light colored	none visible	pumice
fine, with abundant holes	dark colored	none visible	scoria

*Glassy and fine-textured rocks may not have visible minerals.

Conclude and Apply

1. Dark-colored igneous rocks are classified as basaltic, light-colored ones as granitic, and intermediate-colored ones as andesitic composition. Based on this, how would yours be classified?
   Answers will vary depending on the igneous rock. Examples include: scoria-basaltic; granite-granitic; pumice-granitic; basalt-basaltic

2. What minerals might be causing the varying colors found in your rocks?
   Dark minerals include biotite mica, hornblende, pyroxene, olivine. Light-colored minerals include quartz and feldspar.

3. Place your pumice sample in a container of water. What happens? Explain the cause of what you observe.
   The pumice will float. It is very porous.

4. What process could form a rock that has large crystals surrounded by small crystals?
   The large crystals form first, slowly beneath Earth's surface. Then the magma with crystals erupts on the surface and forms small crystals around the large ones.

NAME _____ DATE _____ CLASS _____

Chapter 27
ACTIVITY 27-2 • Sedimentary Rocks

Lab Preview

1. What warning does the eye safety symbol in this activity give you? **It warns you to wear goggles to protect your eyes when handling a substance such as hydrochloric acid.**

2. How do the materials for classifying sedimentary rocks differ from the materials you used for classifying igneous rocks? **Classifying Igneous rocks relies on the use of a hand lens and a reaction test. requires using a hand lens and a reaction test.**

Sedimentary rocks are formed by the compaction and cementation of sediment. Because sediment is found in all shapes and sizes, do you think these characteristics could be used to classify detrital sedimentary rocks? Sedimentary rocks also can be classified as chemical or organic.

What You'll Investigate
You will observe how rock characteristics are used to classify rocks as detrital, chemical, or organic.

Goals
- **Observe** sedimentary rock characteristics.
- **Compare and contrast** clastic and nonclastic textures.
- **Classify** sedimentary rocks as detrital, chemical, or organic.

Safety Precautions

Materials
- unknown sedimentary rock samples
- marking pen
- 5 percent hydrochloric acid (HCl) or vinegar
- dropper
- goggles
- hand lens
- paper towels
- water

Procedure

1. In your Science Journal, make a Data and Observations chart similar to the one on the next page.

2. **Determine** the types of sediments in each sample. Using the table in this section, classify the sediments in the detrital rocks as gravel, sand, silt, or clay.

3. Put a few drops of HCl or vinegar on each rock sample. Bubbling on a rock indicates the presence of calcite. **CAUTION:** *HCl is an acid and can cause burns. Wear goggles. Rinse spills with water. Wash hands afterward.*

4. Look for fossils and **describe** them if any are present.

5. **Determine** whether each sample has a clastic or nonclastic texture.

6. **Classify** your samples as detrital, chemical, or organic. Identify each rock sample.

151

NAME _____ DATE _____ CLASS _____

Activity (continued)

Data and Observations

Sample data

Sample	Observations	Minerals or fossils present	Sediment size	Detrital, chemical, or organic	Rock name
A	fizzes in HCl	calcite, fossils	usually silt	organic	limestone
B	gritty	quartz, feldspar, mica	sand	detrital	sandstone
C	layers	quartz, kaolinite, feldspar	clay	detrital	shale
D	large particles	pebbles composed of quartz, rocks	sand and pebbles	detrital	conglomerate
E	tastes salty	halite	varies	chemical	rock salt

Conclude and Apply

1. Why did you test the rocks with acid? What minerals react with acid? **The acid test identifies calcite if effervescence occurs on a rock sample.**

2. The mineral halite forms by evaporation. Would you classify halite as a detrital, a chemical, or an organic rock? **chemical**

3. Compare and contrast sedimentary rocks with a clastic texture with sedimentary rocks with a nonclastic texture. **Detrital sedimentary rocks with a clastic texture are grainy; nonclastic rocks have a crystalline, interlocking texture.**

4. Explain how you can classify sedimentary rocks. **Sedimentary rocks are classified according to texture, mineral content, and the presence or absence of organic material.**

152

Chapter 27
MINILAB 27-1

Changing Rocks

Procedure
1. Obtain samples of fine-grained sand and glitter from your teacher.
2. Place the sand and glitter into a flat pan.
3. Mix a solution of water and white glue.
4. Pour the solution into the pan and mix thoroughly with the sand and glitter.
5. Place a layer of waxed paper over the mixture, then place a heavy weight on top of the waxed paper.

Analysis
1. After several days, remove the weight and examine the mixture. **Sand and glitter form a framework of grains, and glue fills the interstices.**
2. How is the process used to make the model mixture similar to one part of the rock cycle? **Sand and glitter are held together by the glue solution and compacted by the heavy weight, just as sediment in nature is glued together by mineral cements and compacted by overlying sediment.**
3. Describe other processes that might be used to model mixture other parts of the rock cycle. **Answers will vary. Deposit several layers of crayon shavings onto a sheet of paper. Place a sheet of paper over the shavings and press down. The pressure rearranges the crayon shavings, producing a model of metamorphism.**

Chapter 27
MINILAB 27-2

Classifying Sediments

Procedure
1. CAUTION: *Use care when handling sharp objects.* Spread different samples of sediment on a sheet of paper.
2. Use the table on the same page as the minilab to determine the size-range of gravel-sized sediment.
3. Use tweezers or a dissecting probe and magnifying lens to separate the gravel-sized sediments.
4. Separate each of these three piles into two more piles based on shape—rounded or angular.

Analysis
1. Compare the different piles of sediments. **Answers will vary.**
2. Describe each pile. **Students should describe their sediments by size and angularity.**
3. Use the table on the same page as the minilab to determine what rock is probably made from each type of sediment that you have. **conglomerate from rounded gravel, breccia from angular gravel**

Chapter 28

ACTIVITY 28-1 • Is it biodegradable?

Lab Preview

1. Name two types of organisms that act as decomposers. **monerans (bacteria), fungi (molds) and earthworms**

2. What are solid wastes? **Solid waste is unwanted solid material that must be disposed of (often in landfills).**

As you probably know, all trash is not the same. One important way in which one waste material may differ from another is whether or not the material is biodegradable. A biodegradable substance is anything that can be broken down by organisms in the environment. After it is broken down, the substance can become part of the environment. Whether a material is biodegradable or not can make a big difference in how it affects the environment.

What You'll Investigate
What kinds of materials are biodegradable?

Goals
- Distinguish between biodegradable and nonbiodegradable substances.
- Observe the decomposition of biodegradable materials.

Materials
- soft-drink bottles (2-L) (2)
- plastic wrap
- potting soil
- gravel or sand
- labels
- biodegradable and nonbiodegradable waste materials
- hand lens
- plastic teaspoon
- transparent tape
- scissors

Safety Precautions
Wash hands after handling soil or waste materials.

Procedure

1. Cut a square about 6 cm × 6 cm in the straight sides of the soft-drink bottles as near the top as possible.
2. Label the bottles 1 and 2.
3. Add 1 cm of sand or gravel to each bottle and then fill with 4 cm of potting soil.
4. Your teacher will give you ten substances. Hypothesize which substances are biodegradable and which ones are not. Record your hypotheses in your Science Journal. **Make a table in your Science Journal to record your observations.**
5. Place the substances you think are biodegradable in bottle 1 and the others in bottle 2.
6. Cover each substance with 1 cm to 2 cm of potting soil.
7. Sprinkle water on the top of the soil. Cover the hole in the bottle with plastic wrap and secure it with transparent tape.

155

Activity (continued)

8. Observe each bottle at the end of five days. Note any change in the level of the layers. Use the teaspoon to carefully remove the soil from each substance. Use your hand lens to observe the substance and record your observations in the table below. Carefully replace each substance and cover with soil.
9. Observe the contents of the bottles after five more days and record your results.

Sample Data Table

Time	Biodegradable substances					Nonbiodegradable substances				
	1	2	3	4	5	1	2	3	4	5
5 days	Substances begin to decompose. (Specific observations will vary.)					Substances have not changed.				
10 days	Most substances are highly decomposed. (Specific observations will vary.)					Substances have not changed.				

Conclude and Apply

1. Which substances decomposed?
   leaves, vegetables, fruit peelings, newspaper (organic substances)

2. Which substances decomposed partially?
   Answers will vary depending on the amount of time the experiment is observed.

3. Was your hypothesis supported? Why or why not?
   Answers will vary.

4. Describe any organisms you observed.
   fungi (molds) and the action of bacteria

5. Explain how substances that are biodegradable affect the environment.
   Biodegradable substances are recycled and used again by organisms that make food.

6. Explain how substances that are not biodegradable affect the environment.
   Substances that are not biodegradable remain in the environment and cause pollution.

156

Chapter 28
ACTIVITY 28-2
Modeling the Greenhouse Effect

Lab Preview

1. Why is it important to place the lamp exactly ½ inch from each container? **The two setups must be identical except for the factor being tested—the effect of the plastic wrap.**

2. What is the greenhouse effect? **the ability of Earth's atmosphere to trap heat**

You can create models of Earth with and without heat-reflecting greenhouse gases, then experiment with the models to observe the greenhouse effect.

What You'll Investigate
How does the greenhouse effect influence temperatures on Earth?

Goals
- **Observe** the greenhouse effect.
- **Describe** the effect that a heat source has on an environment.

Materials
- clear, plastic, 2-L soda bottles with tops cut off and labels removed (2)
- thermometers (2)
- potting soil (4 cups)
- masking tape
- plastic wrap
- rubber band
- lamp with 100-watt lightbulb
- chronometer or watch with a second hand

Procedure

1. Put an equal volume of potting soil in the bottom of each container.

2. Use masking tape to affix a thermometer to the inside of each container. Place the thermometers at the same height relative to the soil. Shield each thermometer bulb by putting a double layer of masking tape over it.

3. Seal the top of one container with plastic wrap held in place with the rubber band.

4. Place the lamp with exposed 100-watt bulb between the two containers and exactly ½ inch from each, as shown in the diagram. Do not turn on the light.

5. Let the apparatus sit undisturbed for five minutes, then record the temperature in each container.

6. Turn on the light. Record the temperature in each container every two minutes for the next 15 to 20 minutes. **Record** your temperature measurements in the data table on the next page.

7. **Plot** the results for each container on a graph.

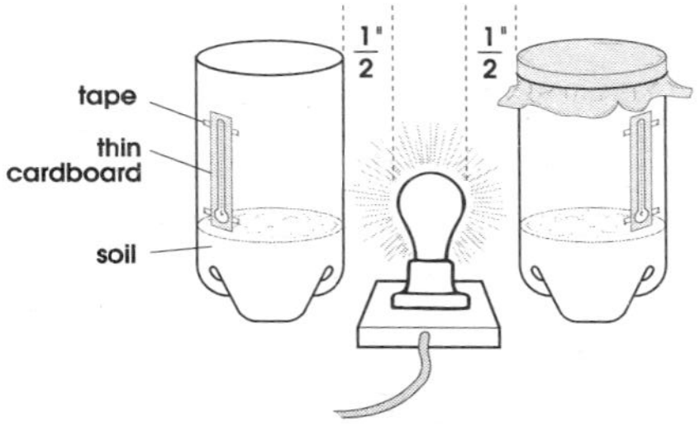

tape
thin cardboard
soil

Activity (continued)

Data and Observations

Time	Open container temperature	Sealed container temperature
0 minutes	22°C	22°C
2 minutes	22°C	22°C
4 minutes	22°C	22.5°C
6 minutes	22°C	23°C

Conclude and Apply

1. How did the temperature of each container change during the experiment? **In most cases, students observe that the temperature increased, then leveled off; at the end of the experiment the open bottle was cooler than the closed bottle.**

2. What was the temperature difference between the two containers at the end of the experiment? **Answers will vary.**

3. What does the plastic wrap represent in this experimental model? What does the plastic wrap represent? **sunlight; greenhouse gases**

4. Describe the ways in which this experimental setup is similar to and different from Earth and its atmosphere. **Both sun and lightbulb represent a constant source of light and heat. The open container is unlike Earth because there is nothing to model heat-reflecting gases. The plastic wrap is similar to heat-reflecting greenhouse gases, but not quite the same because it is a solid, not a gas.**

NAME _____ DATE _____ CLASS _____

Chapter 28
MINILAB 28-1

Observing Mineral Mining Effects

Procedure
1. Place a chocolate chip cookie or nut-filled brownie on a paper plate. Pretend the cookie is Earth's crust and the nuts or chips are mineral deposits. **CAUTION:** *Never eat food or put anything in your mouth from an experiment.*
2. Use a toothpick to locate and dig up mineral deposits. Try to disturb the "land" as little as possible.
3. When mining is completed, do your best to restore the land to its original condition.

Analysis
1. Were you able to restore the land to its original condition? Describe the kinds of changes in an ecosystem that might result from a mining operation.

   Students will experience difficulty in the restoration process. This compares with how some

   forms of mining disrupt Earth's surface. An ecosystem could be permanently damaged from

   mining.

2. How do mining deposits found close to the surface compare with mining deposits found deeper within Earth's crust?

   The ones closer to the surface are easier to remove than those found deeper within Earth's

   crust.

159

Copyright © Glencoe/McGraw-Hill, a division of The McGraw-Hill Companies, Inc.

NAME _____ DATE _____ CLASS _____

Chapter 28
MINILAB 28-2

Measuring Acid Rain

Procedure
1. Use a container to collect samples of rain.
2. Dip a piece of pH indicator paper into the sample.
3. Compare the color of the paper with the pH chart provided. Record the pH of the rainwater.
4. Use separate pieces of pH paper to test the pH of tap water and distilled water. Record these values.

Data and Observations
Data will vary.

Sample	pH
Rainwater	
Tap water	
Distilled water	

Analysis
1. Is the rainwater acidic, basic, or neutral?

   pH will be either acid or neutral. The pH of normal rain is 5.6. Students' results may range from

   pH 4 to pH 7.

2. How does the pH of the rainwater compare with the pH of tap water? Distilled water?

   Tap water is about pH 6; distilled water is pH 7.

160

Copyright © Glencoe/McGraw-Hill, a division of The McGraw-Hill Companies, Inc.

250

Chapter 29
ACTIVITY 29-1 • Relative Age Dating

Lab Preview

1. To find out the relative ages of rocks, do you need to know their exact ages? Explain. **No—a relative age only indicates whether one rock is older than another.**

2. State the principle of superposition. **In an undisturbed layer of rock, the oldest rocks are on the bottom and the rocks become progressively younger toward the top.**

Can you tell which of two rock layers is older? You don't need to know the exact ages of the layers to tell. Geologists can learn a lot about rock layers simply by studying their arrangement.

What You'll Investigate
Can the relative ages of rocks be determined by studying the rock layers and structures?

Goals
- **Determine** the relative order of events by interpreting illustrations of rock layers.

Materials
- paper
- pencil

Procedure
1. Study Figures A and B. The legend will help you interpret the figures.
2. Determine the relative ages of the rock layers, unconformities, igneous dikes, and faults in each figure.

FIGURE A

FIGURE B

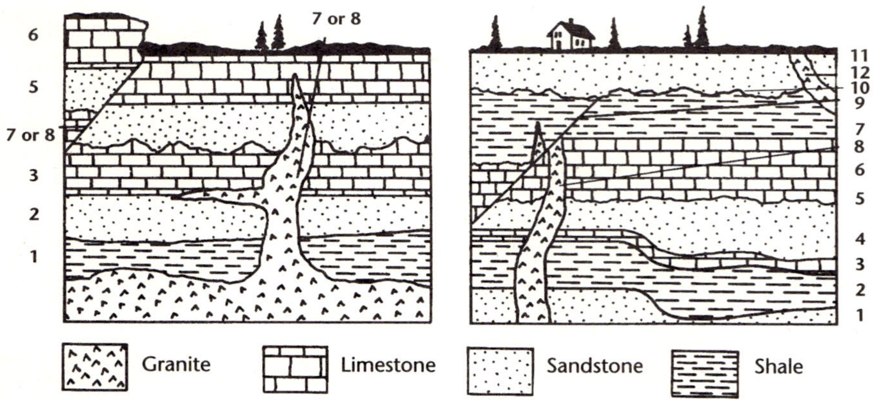

Granite | Limestone | Sandstone | Shale

Activity (continued)

Conclude and Apply

Figure A

1. Were any layers of rock deposited after the igneous dike formed? Explain. **No, since the dike intrudes into every layer, it must be the youngest feature.**

2. What type of unconformity is shown? Is it possible that there were originally more layers of rock than are shown here? Explain. **A disconformity; yes, other rock could have existed and been eroded.**

3. What type of fault is shown? **a reverse fault**

4. Explain how to determine whether the igneous dike formed before or after the fault occurred. **The fault and the igneous dike cut across the youngest limestone but do not cut across each other. It is uncertain which of the two is younger.**

Figure B

5. What type of fault is shown? **a normal fault**

6. Is the igneous dike on the left older or younger than the unconformity near the top? Explain. **Because the dike is offset by the fault but the unconformity is not, the dike is older.**

7. Are the two igneous dikes shown the same age? How do you know? **Because the dike on the right intrudes the sandstone and the dike that has been offset by the fault is older than the sandstone, the two dikes formed at different times.**

8. Which two layers of rock may have been much thicker at one time than they are now? **The sandstone and shale exhibit disconformities at their upper surfaces. These may indicate erosion.**

Interpreting Scientific Illustrations

1. Make a sketch of Figure A. On it, identify the relative age of each rock layer, igneous dike, fault, and unconformity. For example, the shale layer is the oldest, so mark it with a 1. Mark the next-oldest feature with a 2, and so on.

1. shale, 2. sandstone, 3. limestone, 4. disconformity, 5. sandstone, 6. limestone, 7. fault, 8. igneous intrusion; note that another possible solution is 7. igneous intrusion, 8. fault

2. Repeat the procedure in question 1 for Figure B.

1. sandstone, 2. shale, 3. limestone, 4. sandstone, 5. disconformity, 6. limestone, 7. shale, 8. igneous intrusion (left), 9. fault, 10. disconformity, 11. sandstone, 12. igneous intrusion (right)

Chapter 29
ACTIVITY 29-2 • Radioactive Decay

Lab Preview
1. What do *absolute* and *relative* mean when they refer to the age of a rock?
   The relative age of a rock is its age in relation to rocks above it or below it. Its absolute age is the time since its formation.

2. What is the half-life of an isotope?
   the time it takes for half of the atoms in the isotope to decay

Radioactive isotopes decay into their daughter elements in a certain amount of time. The rate of decay varies for each individual isotope. This rate can be used to determine the age of rocks that contain the isotopes under study. In this activity, you will develop a model that demonstrates how the half-life of certain radioactive isotopes can be used to determine absolute ages.

What You'll Investigate
What materials can be used to model age determination using radioactive half-lives?

Goals
- **Model** radioactive half-lives using listed materials.
- **Model** absolute age determination using the half-lives of radioactive isotopes.

Materials
- shoe box with lid
- brass fasteners (100)
- paper clips (100)
- graph paper
- pennies (100)
- colored pencils (2)

Procedures
1. Place 100 pennies into the shoe box with all heads up.
2. Place the lid on the box and shake it one time.
3. Remove the lid. Replace the pennies that are now tails up with paper clips. Record the number of pennies remaining in the box in a data table similar to the one shown on the next page.
4. Repeat steps 2 and 3 until all the pennies have been removed.
5. Remove the paper clips from the box. Put an "X" on one of the shorter sides of the box. Place 100 fasteners in the box.
6. Repeat step 2.
7. Remove the lid. Replace the fasteners that point toward the "X" with paper clips. Record the number of fasteners remaining in the box in a data table similar to the one shown on page 114.
8. Repeat steps 2 and 7 until all the fasteners have been removed.
9. **Plot** both sets of data on the same graph. Graph the "shake number" on the horizontal axis and the "number of pennies or fasteners remaining" on the vertical axis. Be sure to use a different colored pencil for each set of data.

Activity (continued)

Data and Observations

Shake number	Number remaining	
	Pennies	Fasteners
0	100	100
1	49	81
2	27	67
⋮		
12	0	5
13	0	2
14	0	2
15	0	0

Conclude and Apply
1. In this model of radioactive decay, what do the coins and fasteners represent? The box? Each shake?
   The coins and fasteners represent radioactive parent isotopes; paper clips represent the stable daughter products; the box represents the rock in which decay occurs; and each shake represents a time interval.

2. What was the half-life of the pennies? The fasteners?
   Answers will vary. The number of shakes it takes to have half of each set of object replaced is one half-life.

3. How does the difference between the two objects affect the half-life? Compare the objects to the differences among radioactive elements.
   Answers will vary. The two types of objects have different probabilities of landing either heads down or pointing toward the X. Different elements have different half-lives because their atomic structures differ.

4. Suppose you could make only one shake in 100 years. How many years would it take to have 25 coins and 75 paper clips remaining? To have 25 fasteners and 75 paper clips remaining?
   It would take two half-lives. Assuming the sample data shown, it would take two shakes (200 years) for the pennies and seven shakes (700 years) for the fasteners.

5. How can the absolute age of rocks be determined?
   First, determine the percentage of original radioactive material remaining in the rock as compared to the daughter material into which it decays. Then multiply the number of half-lives that have occurred by the length of time required for each half-life.

Chapter 29
MINILAB 29-1

Predicting Fossil Preservation

Procedure

1. Take a brief walk outside and observe the area near your school or home.
2. Look around and notice what type of litter has been discarded on the school grounds. Note whether there is a paved road near your school. Note anything else that was made by humans.

List of Observations

Analysis

1. Predict what human-made or natural objects from our time might be preserved far into the future. **This kind of group activity is designed to make students think about conditions necessary for fossils to form. There are no right or wrong answers.**

2. Explain what conditions would need to exist for these objects to be preserved as fossils. **To be preserved, it is best if the object has hard parts and is buried quickly.**

Chapter 29
MINILAB 29-2

Sequencing Earth's History

Procedure

1. Sequence these events in Earth's history in relative order: Earth forms, first many-celled organisms, first land plants, first mammals, dinosaurs become extinct, first amphibians, first human ancestors, oldest known fossils, first many-celled animals.
2. Make a time line, using these dates: 4.6 billion years, 3.5 billion years, 1.25 billion years, 600 million years, 439 million years, 408 million years, 225 million years, 65 million years, and 4.4 million years ago.
3. Match each event with the absolute date on your time line.

Event	Years before present
Earth forms	4.6 B
oldest known fossils	3.5 B
1st many-celled organisms	1.25 B
1st many-celled animals	600 M
1st plants on land	439 M
1st amphibians	408 M
1st mammals	225 M
dinosaurs extinct	65 M
1st human ancestors	4.4 M

Analysis

1. Check your time line with your teacher.
2. Did you correctly list the events in relative order? **opportunity for self-assessment**
3. How does the age of Earth compare with the presence of humans on the time line? **Presence of humans amounts to about 1% of Earth's age.**

Chapter 30
ACTIVITY 30-1 • Changing Species

Lab Preview

Name three traits that would help identify a type of animal. **Answers may include height, length, habitat, body covering, teeth, and ways of bearing young.**

In this activity, you will observe how adaptation within a species might cause the evolution of a particular trait, leading to the development of a new species.

What You'll Investigate

How might adaptation within a species cause the evolution of a particular trait?

Goals

- Model adaptation within a species.

Materials

- deck of playing cards

Procedure

1. **Remove** all of the kings, queens, jacks, and aces from a deck of playing cards.
2. Each remaining card represents an individual in a population of animals called "varimals." The number on each card represents the height of the individual. For example, the 5 of diamonds is a varimal that's 5 units tall.
3. **Calculate** the average height of the population of varimals represented by your cards.
4. Suppose varimals eat grass, shrubs, and leaves from trees. A drought causes many of these plants to die. All that's left are a few tall trees. Only varimals at least 6 units tall can reach the leaves on these trees.
5. All the varimals under 6 units leave the area to seek food elsewhere or die from starvation. **Discard** all of the cards with a number value less than 6. **Calculate** the new average height of the population of varimals.
6. **Shuffle** the deck of remaining cards.
7. **Draw** two cards at a time. Each pair represents a pair of varimals that will mate and produce offspring.
8. The offspring of each pair reaches a height equal to the average height of his or her parents. **Calculate** and **record** the height of each offspring.
9. Repeat by discarding all parents and offspring under 8 units tall. Now **calculate** the new average height of varimals. Include both the parents and offspring in your calculation.

Conclude and Apply

1. How did the average height of the population change over time? **The average height increased over time.**

2. If you hadn't discarded the shortest varimals, would the average height of the population have changed as much? Explain. **No. The average would remain at about 6.**

3. What trait was selected for? **height; specifically, the ability to reach food above the ground**

167

Activity (continued)

4. Why didn't every member of the original population reproduce? **Some of the original varimals weren't able to obtain enough food to survive and, therefore, weren't able to reproduce.**

5. If there had been no varimals over 6 units tall in step 5, what would have happened to the population? **This particular population of varimals would have become extinct.**

6. If there had been no variation in height in the population before the droughts occurred, would the species have been able to evolve into a taller species? Explain. **Probably not. If all of the individuals would have been the same height, no group of individuals would have had an advantage in reaching the high food. In that case, any evolution of the varimal population would have likely occurred from some variation of a trait other than height.**

7. How does this activity demonstrate that traits evolve in species? **By creating the variation of a trait within the varimal population, in this case height, the model demonstrates how the species was able to evolve into one capable of reaching food high above the ground. This process, by which individuals with more favorable traits are able to survive and produce offspring with these same traits, is known as natural selection.**

168

Chapter 30
MINILAB 30-1

Interpreting Rock Layers

Procedure

1. Draw a sequence of three sedimentary rock layers.
2. Number the rock layers 1 through 3, bottom to top.
3. Identify the fossils in each layer as follows: Layer 1 contains fossils B and A; layer 2 contains fossils A, B, and C; layer 3 contains only fossil C.
4. Assign each of the fossils to one or more geologic periods. For example, fossil A lived from the Cambrian period through the Devonian periods. Fossil C lived from the Devonian through the Permian periods, and so on.
5. Analyze the fossils' occurrence in each layer to help you determine the ages of each rock layer.

Data and Observations

Period	Fossil A	Fossil B	Fossil C
Permian			
Pennsylvanian			
Mississippian			
Devonian			←
Silurian			
Ordovician		←	
Cambrian	←		

3			C
2	A	B	C
1	A	B	

Analysis

1. Which layer or layers were you able to date to a specific period? **For this example, layer 2, because it contains fossils from A and C, from the Devonian period.**
2. Why isn't it possible to determine during which specific period the other layers formed? **Absence of a specific fossil does not necessarily mean that it did not exist; it may not have been found.**
3. What is the age or possible age of each layer? **For this example, layer 1 could be Ordovician, Silurian, or Devonian. Layer 2 is Devonian. Layer 3 could have formed anytime from the Devonian through the Permian.**

Chapter 30
MINILAB 30-2

Measuring Seafloor Spreading

Procedure

1. On a globe or world map, measure the distance in kilometers between a point near the east coast of South America and a corresponding point on the west coast of Africa.
2. Assuming that the rate of spreading has been about 3.5–4.0 cm per year, calculate how many years it took to create the present Atlantic Ocean if the continents were once joined.
3. Measure the distance across the Atlantic Ocean in several other locations and calculate the average of your results.
4. Check your calculations with the information provided in the geological time scale at the beginning of the chapter.

Data and Observations

Points selected			
in South America	in Africa	Distance (cms)	Time (years)
1			
2			
3			

Analysis

1. Did the values used to obtain your average value vary much? **Values used to obtain the average value for the age of the Atlantic Ocean will vary. Expect answers in the range of 160 to 210 million years.**
2. How close did your average value come to the accepted estimate for the beginning of the breakup of Pangaea? **Student answers will vary, depending on the points on each continent they choose for their measurements. Separations of 6000 to 7000 kilometers would take from 160 to 200 million years to achieve. As an example, at a 3.5 cm/year rate of spread, 700 000 000 cm ÷ 3.5 cm/year = 200 000 000 years.**